**Companion Volumes**

The companion volumes in this series are: *Curriculum in Context* edited by Bob Moon and Patricia Murphy, *Learners, Learning and Assessment* edited by Patricia Murphy and *Learning and Knowledge* edited by Robert McCormick and Carrie Paechter.

All of these Readers are part of a course, Learning, Curriculum and Assessment, that is itself part of the Open University MA Programme.

## The Open University MA in Education

The Open University MA in Education is now firmly established as the most popular postgraduate degree for education professionals in Europe, with over 3,500 students registering each year. The MA in Education is designed particularly for those with experience of teaching, the advisory service, educational administration or allied fields.

### Structure of the MA

The MA is a modular degree, and students are therefore free to select from a range of options the programme which best fits in with their interests and professional goals. Specialist lines in management and primary education are also available. Study in the Open University's Advanced Diploma and Certificate Programmes can also be counted towards the MA, and successful study in the MA programme entitles students to apply for entry into the Open University Doctorate in Education programme.

COURSES CURRENTLY AVAILABLE:
- Management
- Child Development
- Primary Education
- Learning, Curriculum and Assessment
- Inclusive Education
- Language and Literacy
- Mentoring
- Education, Training and Employment
- Gender in Education
- Educational Research
- Science Education
- Adult Learners
- Maths Education

### OU supported open learning

The MA in Education programme provides great flexibility. Students study at their own pace, in their own time, anywhere in the European Union. They receive specially pre-pared study materials, supported by tutorials, thus offering the chance to work with other students.

## The Doctorate in Education

The Doctorate in Education is a new part-time doctoral degree, combining taught courses, research methods and a dissertation designed to meet the needs of professionals in education and related areas who are seeking to extend and deepen their knowledge and understanding of contemporary educational issues. It should help them to:

- develop appropriate skills in educational research and enquiry

- carry out research in order to contribute to professional knowledge and practice.

The Doctorate in Education builds upon successful study within the Open University MA in Education programme.

### How to apply

If you would like to register for this programme, or simply to find out more information, please write for the *Professional Development in Education* prospectus to the Course Reservations Centre, PO Box 724, The Open University, Walton Hall, Milton Keynes, MK7 6ZS, UK (Telephone 0[044] 1908 653231).

# LEARNERS AND PEDAGOGY

*edited by*
Jenny Leach and Bob Moon
at The Open University

Paul Chapman
Publishing Ltd

Paul Chapman Publishing

in association with

The Open University

Paul Chapman Publishing Ltd
A SAGE Publications Company
6 Bonhill Street
London EC2A 4PU

SAGE Publications Inc.
2455 Teller Road
Thousand Oaks, California 91320

SAGE Publications India Pvt Ltd
32, M-Block Market
Greater Kailash - I
New Delhi 110 048


**British Library Cataloguing in Publication data**
A catalogue record for this book is available from the British Library

ISBN 1 85396 428 X
ISBN 1 85396 429 8 (pbk)

**Library of Congress catalog card number available**

Typeset by Dorwyn Ltd, Rowlands Castle
Printed in Great Britain by The Cromwell Press, Trowbridge

A   B   C   D   E   F   G   H      4   3   2   1   0   9

# Contents

# Series Introduction

Learning, curriculum and assessment are at the core of the educational process. In the politically charged and value-laden context of curriculum reform, an understanding of well grounded evidence about learning theories, knowledge and teaching and assessment practice is essential. Policy development and educational practice in a number of countries are being built around new understandings about the nature of mind, an acknowledgement that knowledge has long outgrown the traditional discipline categorizations of schools and universities and a realization that learning and assessment are an essentially social process.

This book is one of a series of four readers that gather together recent research and writing around a number of key issues and themes in curriculum. The books, therefore, act as sources from which a number of narratives can be deduced. The broader contexts of curriculum are considered in the first volume of the series; the remaining three books focus us on learning and assessment, knowledge and pedagogy. The selection is a resource for anyone seeking a deeper understanding of the way any curriculum, formal and informal, is constructed, enacted and experienced. The accompanying Open University course (E836 *Learning, Curriculum and Assessment*) sets out to show one interpretation of the relevance of these ideas to practice in schools, colleges and other educational settings.

*Jenny Leach*
*Robert McCormick*
*Bob Moon*
*Patricia Murphy*

The Open University, Milton Keynes

# Acknowledgements

The editors and publishers wish to thank the following for permission to use copyright material:

Beverly Caswell for Beverly Caswell and Mary Lamon, 'Development of Scientific Literacy: the Evolution of Ideas in a Knowledge Building Classroom', lecture delivered to AERA Conference, San Diego, April 1998;

Cambridge University Press for material from J Lave and E Wenger, *Situated Learning: Legitimate Peripheral Participation* (1991) pp. 91–117;

Harvard Educational Review for material from Lee S Shulman, 'Knowledge and Teaching: Foundations of the New Reform', *Harvard Educational Review*, 57:1 (1987) pp. 1–22. Copyright © 1987 by the President and Fellows of Harvard College; and Paulo Freire and Donaldo P Macedo, 'A Dialogue: Culture, Language, and Race', *Harvard Educational Review*, 65:3 (1995) pp. 377–402. Copyright © 1995 by the President and Fellows of Harvard College;

Harvard University Press for Jerome Bruner, *The Culture of Education* (1996) pp. 44–65. Copyright © 1996 by the President and Fellows of Harvard College;

Jossey-Bass Inc., Publishers for material from Martha Stone Wiske, 'What is Teaching for Understanding?' in M S Wiske, ed., *Teaching for Understanding* (1998) pp. 61–86. Copyright © 1998 Jossey-Bass Inc., Publishers;

Kluwer Academic Publishers for material from S E Pirie and L Martin, 'The Equation, The Whole Equation and Nothing But the Equation! One approach to the teaching of linear equations', *Educational Studies in Mathematics*, 34:2 (1997) pp. 159–181;

Kogan Page Ltd for material from C Engel, 'Not Just a Method But a Way of Learning' from D Boud and G Feletti, eds. *The Challenge of Problem Based Learning* (1991) pp. 23–31.

Routledge for material from P Woods, 'Chances of a Lifetime: Exceptional Educational Events' in J Bourne, ed., *Thinking Through Primary Practice* (1993) pp. 168–76; and W Morgan, *Critical Literacy in the Classroom* (1997) pp. 167–203;

Brian Simon for 'Why no Pedagogy in England?' from Brian Simon, *Issues for the 80's*, Batsford;

Taylor & Francis Ltd for material from P Menck, 'Didactics as construction of content', *Journal of Curriculum Studies*, 27:4 (1995) pp. 353–363;

Teachers College Record for Howard Gardner and Veronica Boix-Mansilla, 'Teaching for Understanding in the Disciplines and Beyond', *Teachers College Record*, 96:2 (1994) pp. 198–208, 216–17;

UNESCO for material from A-M Kruse, 'Single Sex Settings: Pedagogies for Girls and Boys in Danish Schools' from P F Murphy and C V Gipps, eds., *Equity in the Classroom: Towards Effective Pedagogy for Girls and Boys* (1996) Falmer Press/ UNESCO Publishing, pp. 173–90. Copyright © UNESCO 1996;

John Wiley & Sons, Inc for material from Wanda T May, 'Constructing History in a Graduate Curriculum Class', *Curriculum Inquiry* 21:2 (1991) pp. 163–83, 188–9;

Every effort has been made to trace the copyright holders but if any have been inadvertently overlooked the publishers will be pleased to make the necessary arrangements at the first opportunity.

# SECTION 1
# PERSPECTIVES ON PEDAGOGY

# Introduction

## Jenny Leach and Bob Moon

This fourth book in the series *Learning, Curriculum and Assessment* explores some contemporary and significant thinking about the nature and meaning of pedagogy. Together with the other volumes, *Learners and Pedagogy* looks at the relationship between pedagogy, curriculum and assessment; the different theories of mind and of learning that underpin these practices; and examples of the way aspects of these theories are interpreted in practice across a wide range of educational contexts. This volume, in particular, provides readers with critical frameworks for examining views of pedagogy and analysing and developing pedagogic practice.

In the last decade there has been a rapid development of new theoretical frameworks for understanding the nature of the learning process. Such views of learning are, however, strongly contested. Indeed, Murphy (1998) argues that the field is in a state of upheaval. At the same time the nature of educational practice itself has become the focus of conflicting pressures at the turn of a century that is witnessing radical change in the nature of public, community and economic life. In many parts of the world education is being subjected to a succession of policy initiatives and political interventions. Such developments have shown the practice of teaching itself to be a highly contested area. Questions about what should be taught, and how, are subjects of constant public debate, infrequently based on research findings or theoretical principles. In this atmosphere of controversy and contention many educational practitioners – regardless of their approach to teaching – feel dissatisfied with the level on which these discussions occur. The chapters in this volume have been chosen to show ways in which theories can provide frameworks for analysing pedagogy, creating a dialogue about new possibilities for the advancement of practice.

Jerome Bruner, in the first chapter of this book, argues that a choice of pedagogy inevitably communicates a conception of the learning process and the learner. Pedagogy is never innocent. It is a medium that carries its own message.

All the contributors to the first part of *Learners and Pedagogy* present contrasting perspectives on the taken-for-granted assumptions we bring to the teaching and learning process. The chapters illustrate contemporary debates about pedagogy and the role of the teacher in the learning process. Bruner's chapter highlights the way in which folk myths about how the mind works can assume a status and legitimacy that go unchallenged and that deeply influence both the practice of teaching and interactions between teachers and learners. From Bruner's perspective, it is essential that teachers and learners are equipped with a 'good theory of mind'. He illustrates how key dimensions of pedagogy – educational goals, curriculum and assessment, learning activities and the roles of teachers and learners – are transformed by different views of mind and the learning process. Bruner emphasizes the importance of the cultural context in which teaching and learning take place, and is unequivocal that learning should fundamentally be 'a participatory, proactive, collaborative process'.

Chapter 2 is an extract from Lave and Wenger's influential work *Situated Learning* which introduces the concept of 'community of practice'. Their analysis presents a radical critique of contemporary views of pedagogy. They argue that pedagogic practice reflects too narrowly rationalistic a perspective on learners' experiences and their motivation. In particular they distinguish between a 'teaching curriculum' which is limiting and fragmented, mediated by an external view of knowing, and a 'learning curriculum' which is viewed from the perspective of learners. If learning is achieved through *participation*, absorbing and being absorbed in the 'culture of practice' as Lave and Wenger argue, the implications for pedagogy are significant.

Brian Simon's 'Why no pedagogy in England?' (Chapter 3) was first published in the early 1980s. This essay also explores the link between views of learners and the teaching and learning process, whilst analysing pedagogic practice in a specific social and political context. In order to develop effective pedagogy, Simon suggests, we must start 'from what individuals have in common as members of the human species'. This common feature, the human capacity to learn, makes it possible to envisage a body of general principles, a 'science of teaching' relevant for most individuals.

Reflecting on this article 12 years later in his lecture 'Some problems of pedagogy revisited' (1994), Simon has argued that the introduction of a National Curriculum in the English education system has created the first necessary condition for identifying effective pedagogic means. Despite this opportunity, he contends, pedagogy continues to be marginalized. Drawing on a variety of educational reports and government policy documents he suggests that the main focus of effective teaching has become twofold:

1) *Classroom organization*, such as choice of groups, individual and whole-class teaching and fitness for purpose of such strategies.
2) *Teaching skills*, for example teachers' use of explanation, questioning and so forth.

The pedagogic 'means' underlying these teaching strategies continues to be ignored. Questions remain, he argues, about how the cognitive development of all children can be developed and what learning tasks should be provided that will provide challenge and move their understanding forward.

A dialogue involving one of the twentieth century's most resolute critiques of prevailing pedagogic orthodoxies, Paulo Freire provides the concluding chapter of this section. This is an extract from a continuing debate Freire conducted with Donaldo Macedo between 1983 and Freire's death in 1997. It is of particular interest in addressing some of the contemporary criticisms of Freire's work. He refutes the caricatures of his ideas advanced by some conservative critics that imply the playing down of the significance of the teacher in the learning process. All educational practice presupposes an objective to be reached, there is no real education without direction, he argues. Teachers need to assume this given authority in working with learners to plan education, helping them create the critical capacity to participate in the dreams of education. The radical educator must actively create 'pedagogical spaces' in which learners become apprentices in the 'rigors of exploration and epistemological curiosity'. To avoid merely reproducing the values of the power structure the educator must always combat a *laissez-faire* pedagogy, no matter how progressive it may be. For Freire, therefore, pedagogy is a social process which extends to the political arena. Not a comfortable message for those who seek to depoliticize teaching and learning, but an important perspective in the debates about the purpose and function of education systems that has characterized the final years of the twentieth century.

# References

Murphy, M. (1998) *Learners and Learning*, London, Paul Chapman.
Simon, B. (1994) 'Some problems of pedagogy revisited.' Lecture delivered to the Eighth Annual Conference of the Educational Research Network of Northern Ireland, 13 November.

# 1

# Folk Pedagogies

## Jerome Bruner

Thoughtful people have been forever troubled by the enigma of applying theoretical knowledge to practical problems. Applying psychological theory to educational practice is no exception to the rule, not much less puzzling than applying science to medicine. Aristotle comments (rather touchingly) in the *Nichomachean Ethics* (Book V, 1137a): 'It is an easy matter to know the effects of honey, wine, hellebore, cautery, and cutting. But to know how, for whom, and when we should apply these as remedies is no less an undertaking than being a physician.' Even with scientific advances, the physician's problem is not much easier today than it was in the times of hellebore and cautery: 'how, for whom, and when' still loom as problems. The challenge is always to *situate* our knowledge in the living context that poses the 'presenting problem', to borrow a bit of medical jargon. And that living context, where education is concerned, is the schoolroom – the schoolroom situated in a broader culture.

That is where, at least in advanced cultures, teachers and pupils come together to effect that crucial but mysterious interchange that we so glibly call 'education'. Obvious though it may seem, we would do better to concentrate in what follows on 'learning and teaching in the setting of school' rather than, as psychologists sometimes do, generalizing from learning in a rat maze, from the nonsense-syllable learning of sophomores incarcerated in a laboratory cubicle, or from the performance of an AI computer simulation at Carnegie–Mellon. Keep before you a busy classroom of nine-year-olds, say, with a hard-working teacher, and ask what kind of theoretical knowledge would help them. A genetic theory that assures them that people differ? Well, perhaps, but not much. Do you work harder with the not-so-bright or ignore them? What about an associationist theory that tells you that nonsense syllables are associated with each other through frequency, recency, contiguity, and similarity effects? Would you want to design a curriculum on knowledge about how nonsense syllables are learned? Well, perhaps a little – where things are a little nonsense-like anyway, such as the names of elements in the periodic table: cerium, lithium, gold, lead . . .

There is one 'presenting problem' that is always with us in dealing with teaching and learning, one that is so pervasive, so constant, so much part of the fabric of living, that we often fail to notice it, fail even to discover it – much as in the proverb 'the fish will be the last to discover water'. It is the issue of how human beings achieve a meeting of minds, expressed by teachers usually as 'how do I reach the children?' or by children as 'what's she trying to get at?' This is the classic problem of Other Minds, as it was originally called in philosophy, and its relevance to education has mostly been overlooked until very recently. In the last decade it has become a topic of passionate interest and intense research among psychologists, particularly those interested in development. It is what this chapter is about – the application of this new work to the process of education.

To a degree almost entirely overlooked by anti-subjective behaviourists in the past, our interactions with others are deeply affected by our everyday intuitive theories about how other minds work. These theories, rarely made explicit, are omnipresent but have only recently been subjected to intense study. Such lay theories are now referred to professionally by the rather condescending name of 'folk psychology'. Folk psychologies reflect certain 'wired-in' human tendencies (like seeing people normally as operating under their own control), but they also reflect some deeply ingrained cultural beliefs about 'the mind'. Not only is folk psychology preoccupied with how the mind works here and now, it is also equipped with notions about how the child's mind learns and even what makes it grow. Just as we are steered in ordinary interaction by our folk psychology, so we are steered in the activity of helping children learn about the world by notions of *folk pedagogy*. Watch any mother, any teacher, even any babysitter with a child and you'll be struck by how much of what they do is steered by notions of 'what children's minds are like and how to help them learn', even though they may not be able to verbalize their pedagogical principles.

From this work on folk psychology and folk pedagogy has grown a new, perhaps even a revolutionary insight. It is this: in theorizing about the practice of education in the classroom (or any other setting, for that matter), you had better take into account the folk theories that those engaged in teaching and learning already have. For any innovations that you, as a 'proper' pedagogical theorist, may wish to introduce will have to compete with, replace, or otherwise modify the folk theories that already guide both teachers and pupils. For example, if you as a pedagogical theorist are convinced that the best learning occurs when the teacher helps lead the pupil to discover generalizations on her own, you are likely to run into an established cultural belief that a teacher is an authority who is supposed to *tell* the child what the general case is, while the child should be occupying herself with memorizing the particulars. And if you study how most classrooms are conducted, you will often find that most of the teacher's questions to pupils are about particulars that can be answered in a few words or even by 'yes' or 'no'. So your introduction of an innovation in teaching will necessarily involve changing the folk psychological and folk pedagogical theories of teachers – and, to a surprising extent, of pupils as well.

Teaching, in a word, is inevitably based on notions about the nature of the learner's mind. Beliefs and assumptions about teaching whether in a school or in any other context, are a direct reflection of the beliefs and assumptions the teacher holds about the learner. (Later, we will consider the other side of this coin: how learning is affected by the child's notion of the teacher's mind-set, as when girls come to believe that teachers expect them not to come up with unconventional answers.) Of course, like most deep truths, this one is already well known. Teachers have always tried to adjust their teaching to the backgrounds, abilities, styles and interests of the children they teach. This is important, but it is not quite what we are after. Our purpose, rather, is to explore more general ways in which learners' minds are conventionally thought about, and the pedagogic practices that follow from these ways of thinking about mind. Nor will we stop there, for we also want to offer some reflections on 'consciousness raising' in this setting: what can be accomplished by getting teachers (and students) to think *explicitly* about their folk psychological assumptions, in order to bring them out of the shadows of tacit knowledge.

One way of presenting the general matter of folk psychology and folk pedagogy most starkly is by contrasting our own human species with non-human primates. In our species, children show an astonishingly strong 'predisposition to culture'; they are sensitive to and eager to adopt the folkways they see around them. They show a striking interest in the activity of their parents and peers and with no prompting at all try to imitate what they observe. As for adults, as Kruger and Tomasello insist,[1] there is a uniquely human 'pedagogic disposition' to exploit this tendency, for adults to demonstrate correct performance for the benefit of the learner. One finds these matching tendencies in different forms in all human societies. But note that these imitative and demonstrational dispositions seem scarcely to exist at all in our nearest primate kin, the chimpanzees. Not only do adult chimpanzees not 'teach' their young by demonstrating correct performance, the young for their part seem not to imitate the actions of adults either, at least if we use a sufficiently stringent definition of imitation. If by imitation one means the ability to observe not just the goal achieved but also the means to that achievement, there is little evidence of imitation in chimpanzees raised in the wild[2] and, even more conspicuously, little attempt at teaching. It is very revealing, however, that when a young chimpanzee is raised 'as if' he were a human child, and exposed to the ways of humans, he begins to show more imitative dispositions.[3] The evidence on 'demonstrational' dispositions in adult chimpanzees is much less clear, but such dispositions may also be there in a rudimentary form.[4]

Tomasello, Ratner, and Kruger have suggested that because non-human primates do not naturally attribute beliefs and knowledge to others, they probably do not recognize their presence in themselves.[5] We humans show, tell, or teach someone something only because we first recognize that they don't know, or that what they believe is false. The failure of non-human primates to ascribe ignorance or false beliefs to their young may, therefore, explain the absence of pedagogic efforts, for it is only when these states are recognized that we try to correct the deficiency by demonstration, explanation, or discussion. Even the most humanly 'enculturated' chimpanzees show little, if any, of the attribution that leads to instructional activity.

Research on lesser primates shows the same picture. On the basis of their observations of the behavior of vervet monkeys in the wild,[6] Cheney and Seyfarth were led to conclude: 'While monkeys may use abstract concepts and have motives, beliefs, and desires, they . . . seem unable to attribute mental states to others: they lack a "theory of mind".' Work on other species of monkeys reveals similar findings.[7] The general point is clear: assumptions about the mind of the learner underlie attempts at teaching. No ascription of ignorance, no effort to teach.

But to say only that human beings understand other minds and try to teach the incompetent is to overlook the varied ways in which teaching occurs in different cultures. The variety is stunning.[8] We need to know much more about this diversity if we are to appreciate the relation between folk psychology and folk pedagogy in different cultural settings.

Understanding this relationship becomes particularly urgent in addressing issues of educational reform. For once we recognize that a teacher's conception of a learner shapes the instruction he or she employs, then equipping teachers (or parents) with the best available theory of the child's mind becomes crucial. And in the process of doing that, we also need to provide teachers with some insight about their own folk theories that guide their teaching.

Folk pedagogies, for example, reflect a variety of assumptions about children: they may be seen as willful and needing correction; as innocent and to be protected from a vulgar society; as needing skills to be developed only through practice; as empty vessels to be filled with knowledge that only adults can provide; as egocentric and in need of socialization. Folk beliefs of this kind, whether expressed by laypeople or by 'experts', badly want some 'deconstructing' if their implications are to be appreciated. For whether these views are 'right' or not, their impact on teaching activities can be enormous.

A culturally oriented cognitive psychology does not dismiss folk psychology as mere superstition, something only for the anthropological connoisseur of quaint folkways. I have long argued that explaining what children *do* is not enough;[9] the new agenda is to determine what they *think* they are doing and what their reasons are for doing it. Like new work on children's theories of mind,[10] a cultural approach emphasizes that the child only gradually comes to appreciate that she is acting not directly *on* 'the world' but on beliefs she holds *about* that world. This crucial shift from naive realism to an understanding of the role of beliefs, occurring in the early school years, is probably never complete. But once it starts, there is often a corresponding shift in what teachers can do to help children. With the shift, for example, children can take on more responsibilities for their own learning and thinking.[11] They can begin to 'think about their thinking' as well as about 'the world'. It is not surprising, then, that achievement testers have become increasingly concerned not just with what children *know* but with how they think they came by their knowledge.[12] It is as Howard Gardner puts it in *The Unschooled Mind*: 'We must place ourselves inside the heads of our students and try to understand as far as possible the sources and strengths of their conceptions.'[13]

Stated boldly, the emerging thesis is that educational practices in classrooms are premised on a set of folk beliefs about learners' minds, some of which may have worked advertently toward or inadvertently against the child's own welfare. They need to be made explicit and to be reexamined. Different approaches to learning and different forms of instruction – from imitation, to instruction, to discovery, to collaboration – reflect differing beliefs and assumptions about the learner – from actor, to knower, to private experiencer, to collaborative thinker.[14] What higher primates lack and humans continue to evolve is a set of beliefs about the mind. These beliefs, in turn, alter beliefs about the sources and communicability of thought and action. Advances in how we go about understanding children's minds are, then, a prerequisite to any improvement in pedagogy.

Obviously, all this involves much more than learners' minds. Young learners are people in families and communities, struggling to reconcile their desires, beliefs, and goals with the world around them. Our concern may be principally cognitive, relating to the acquisition and uses of knowledge, but we do not mean to restrict our focus to the so-called 'rational' mind. Egan reminds us that 'Apollo without Dionysus may indeed be a well-informed, good citizen, but he's a dull fellow. He may even be "cultured", in the sense one often gets from traditionalist writings in education . . . But without Dionysus he will never make and remake a culture'.[15] Although our discussion of folk psychology and folk pedagogy has emphasized 'teaching and learning' in the conventional sense, we could as easily have emphasized other aspects of the human spirit, ones equally important for educational practice, like folk conceptions of desire, intention, meaning, or even 'mastery'. But even the notion of 'knowledge' is not as peacefully Apollonian as all that.

Consider for example the issue of what knowledge is, where it comes from, how we come by it. These are also matters that have deep cultural roots. To begin with, take the distinction between knowing something concretely and in particular and knowing it as an examplar of some general rule. Arithmetic addition and multiplication provide a stunning example. Somebody, say, has just learned a concrete arithmetic fact. What does it mean to grasp a 'fact' of multiplication, and how does that differ from the idea that multiplication is simply repeated addition, something you already 'know'? Well, for one thing, it means that you can *derive* the unknown from the known. That is a pretty heady notion about knowledge, one that might even delight the action-minded Dionysus.

In some much deeper sense, grasping something abstractly is a start toward appreciating that seemingly complicated knowledge can often be derivationally reduced to simpler forms of knowledge that you already possess. The Ellery Queen mystery stories used to include a note inserted on a crucial page in the text telling the reader that he or she now had all the knowledge necessary to solve the crime. Suppose one announced in class after the children had learned multiplication that they now had enough knowledge to understand something called 'logarithms', special kinds of numbers that simply bore the names '1', '2', '3', '4', and '5', and that they ought to be able to figure out what these logarithm names 'mean' from three examples, each example being a series that bore those names. The first series is 2, 4, 8, 16, 32; the second series 3, 9, 27, 81, 243, and the third series 1, 10, 100, 1,000, 10,000, 100,000. The numbers in each series correspond to the logarithmic names 1, 2, 3, 4, and 5. But how can 8 be called '3', and so too 27 and 1,000? Not only do children 'discover' (or invent) the idea of an *exponent* or *power*, but they also discover/invent the idea of exponents to some *base*: that 2 to the third power is 8, that 3 to the third power is 27, and that 10 to the third power is 1,000. Once children (say around age ten) have gone through that experience, their conception of mathematical knowledge as 'derivational' will be forever altered: they will grasp that once you know addition and know that addition can be repeated different numbers of times to make multiplication, you already know what logarithms are. All you need to determine is the 'base'.

Or if that is too 'mathematical', you can try getting children to act out Little Red Riding Hood, first as a class drama with everybody having a part, then by actors chosen to represent the main characters to an audience, and finally as a story to be told or read by a storyteller to a group. How do they differ? The moment some child informs you that in the first instance there are only actors and no audience, but in the second there are both, the class will be off and running into a discussion of 'drama' to match Victor Turner for excitement.[16] As with the previous example, you will have led children to recognize that they know far more than they thought they ever knew, but that they have to 'think about it' to know what they know. And that, after all, was what the Renaissance and the Age of Reason were all about! But to teach and learn that way means that you have adopted a new theory of mind.

Or take the issue of where you get knowledge, an equally profound matter. Children usually begin by assuming that the teacher has the knowledge and passes it on to the class. Under appropriate conditions, they soon learn that others in the class might have knowledge too, and that it can be shared. (Of course they know this from the start, but only about such matters as where things are to be found.) In this second phase, knowledge exists in the group – but inertly in the group. What about group discussion as a way of *creating* knowledge rather than merely finding who has what knowledge.[17] And there is even one step beyond that, one of the most profound aspects of human knowledge. If nobody in the group 'knows' the answer, where do you go to 'find things out'? This is the leap into culture as a warehouse, a toolhouse, or whatever. There are things known by each individual (more than each realizes); more still is known by the group or is discoverable by discussion within the group; and much more still is stored somewhere else – in the 'culture', say, in the heads of more knowledgeable people, in directories, books, maps, and so forth. Virtually by definition, nobody in a culture knows all there is to know about it. So what do we do when we get stuck? And what are the problems we run into in getting the knowledge we need? Start answering that question and you are on the high road toward understanding what a culture is. In no time at all, some kid will begin to recognize that knowledge is power, or that it is a form of wealth, or that it is a safety net.

So let us consider more closely, then, some alternative conceptions about the minds of learners commonly held by educational theorists, teachers, and ultimately by children themselves. For these are what may determine the educational practices that take place in classrooms in different cultural contexts.

## Models of Mind and Models of Pedagogy

There are four dominant models of learners' minds that have held sway in our times. Each emphasizes different educational goals. These models are not only conceptions of mind that determine how we teach and 'educate', but are also conceptions about the relations between minds and cultures. Rethinking educational psychology requires that we examine each of these alternative conceptions of human development and reevaluate their implications for learning and teaching.

*1. Seeing children as imitative learners: The acquisition of 'know-how'.* When an adult demonstrates or models a successful or skilled action to a child, that demonstration is implicitly based on the adult's belief that (a) the child does not know how to do *x*, and (b) the child can learn how to do *x* by being *shown*. The act of modeling also presupposes that (c) the child wants to do *x*, and (d) that she may, in fact, be trying to do *x*. To learn by imitation the child must recognize the goals pursued by the adult, the means used to achieve those goals, and the fact that the demonstrated action will successfully get her to the goal. By the time children are two years of age, they are capable, unlike chimpanzees raised in the wild, of imitating the act in question. Adults, recognizing children's proclivity for imitation, usually turn their own demonstrative actions into *performances*, acting in a way to demonstrate more vividly just what is involved in 'doing it right'. In effect, they provide 'noiseless exemplars',[18] of the act, preter-naturally clear examples of the desired action.[19]

Such modeling is the basis of apprenticeship, leading the novice into the skilled ways of the expert. The expert seeks to transmit a skill he has acquired through repeated practice to a novice who, in his turn, must then practice the modeled act in order to succeed. There is little distinction in such an exchange between procedural knowledge (knowing how) and propositional knowledge (knowing that). An underlying assumption is that the less skilled can be taught by showing, and that they have the ability to learn through imitation. Another assumption in this process is that modeling and imitating make possible the accumulation of culturally relevant knowledge, even the transmission of culture[20] from one generation to the next.

But using imitation as the vehicle for teaching entails an additional assumption about human competence as well: that it consists of talents, skills, and abilities, rather than knowledge and understanding. Competence on the imitative view comes only through practice. It is a view that precludes teaching about logarithms or drama in the way described earlier. Knowledge 'just grows as habits' and is linked neither to theory nor to negotiation or argument. Indeed, we even label cultures that rely heavily upon an imitative folk psychology and folk pedagogy as 'traditional'. But more technically advanced cultures also rely heavily upon such implicit imitative theories – for example, on apprenticeships for transmitting sophisticated skills. Becoming a scientist or a poet requires more than 'knowing the theory'[21] or knowing the rules of iambic pentameter. It is Aristotle and the physician all over again.

So what do we know about demonstration and apprenticeship? Not much, but more than one might suspect. For example, simply demonstrating, 'how to' and providing practice at doing so is known not to be enough. Studies of expertise demonstrate that just learning how to perform skillfully does not get one to the same level of flexible skill as when one learns by a combination of practice and conceptual explanation – much as a really skillful pianist needs more than clever hands, but needs as well to know something about the theory of harmony, about solfège, about melodic structure. So if a simple theory of imitative learning suits a 'traditional' society (and it usually turns out on close inspection that there is more to it than that),[22] it certainly does not suit a more advanced one. Which leads us to the next set of assumptions about human minds.

*2. Seeing children as learning from didactic exposure: The acquisition of propositional knowledge.* Didactic teaching usually is based on the notion that pupils should be presented with facts, principles, and rules of action which are to be learned, remembered, and then applied. To teach this way is to assume that the learner 'does not know that *p*' that he or she is ignorant or innocent of certain facts, rules, or principles that can be conveyed by telling. What is to be learned by the pupil is conceived as 'in' the minds of teachers as well as in books, maps, art, computer databases, or wherever. Knowledge is simply to be 'looked up' or 'listened to'. It is an explicit canon or corpus – a representation of the what-is-known. Procedural knowledge, knowing how to, is assumed to follow automatically from knowing certain propositions about facts, theories, and the like: 'the square of the hypotenuse of a right-angled triangle is equal to the squares of the other two sides.'

In this teaching scenario, abilities are no longer conceived as knowing how to *do* something skillfully, but rather as the ability to acquire new knowledge by the aid of certain 'mental abilities': verbal, spatial, numerical, interpersonal, or whatever. This is probably the most widely adhered to line of folk pedagogy in practice today – whether in history, social studies, literature, geography, or even science and mathematics. Its principal appeal is that it purports to offer a clear specification of just what it is that is to be learned and, equally questionable, that it suggests standards for assessing its achievement. More than any other theory of folk pedagogy, it has spawned objective testing in all its myriad guises. To detemine whether a student has 'learned' the capital of Albania, all one need do is offer him a multiple choice of Tirana, Milano, Smyrna, and Samarkand.

But damning the didactic assumption is too much like beating a dead horse. For plainly there are contexts where knowledge can usefully be treated as 'objective' and given – like knowing the different writs under which a case can be brought under English common law, or knowing that the Fugitive Slave Law became an American statute in 1793, or that the Lisbon earthquake destroyed that city in 1755. The world is indeed full of facts. But facts are not of much use when offered by the hatful – either by teacher to student in class, or in the reverse direction as name dropping in an 'objective' exam. We shall return to this point later in considering our fourth perspective.

What we must concentrate upon here is the conception of the child's mind that the didactic view imposes on teaching – its folk pedagogy. In effect, this view presumes that the learner's mind is a tabula rasa, a blank slate. Knowledge put into the mind is taken as cumulative, with later knowledge building upon priorly existing knowledge. More important is this view's assumption that the child's mind is passive, a receptacle waiting to be filled. Active interpretation or construal does not enter the picture. The didactic bias views the child from the outside, from a third-person perspective, rather than trying to 'enter her thoughts'. It is blankly one-way: teaching is not a mutual dialogue, but a telling by one to the other. In such a regimen, if the child fails to perform adequately, her shortcomings can be explained by her lack of 'mental abilities' or her low IQ and the educational establishment goes scot-free.

It is precisely the effort to achieve a first-person perspective, to reconstruct the child's point of view, that marks the third folk pedagogy, to which we turn now.

*3. Seeing children as thinkers: The development of intersubjective interchange.* The new wave of research on 'other minds' described earlier is the latest manifestation of a more general modern effort to recognize the child's perspective in the process of learning. The teacher, on this view, is concerned with understanding what the child thinks and how she arrives at what she believes. Children, like adults, are seen as constructing a *model* of the world to aid them in construing their experience. Pedagogy is to help the child understand better, more powerfully, less one-sidedly. Understanding is fostered through discussion and collaboration, with the child encouraged to express her own views better to achieve some meeting of minds with others who may have other views.

Such a pedagogy of mutuality presumes that all human minds are capable of holding beliefs and ideas which, through discussion and interaction, can be moved toward some shared frame of reference. Both child and adult have points of view, and each is encouraged to recognize the other's, though they may not agree. They must come to recognize that differing views may be based on recognizable reasons and that these reasons provide the basis for adjudicating rival beliefs. Sometimes you are 'wrong', sometimes others are – that depends on how well reasoned the views are. Sometimes opposing views are both right – or both wrong. The child is *not* merely ignorant or an empty vessel, but somebody able to reason, to make sense, both on her own and through discourse with others. The child no less than the adult is seen as capable of thinking about her own thinking, and of correcting her ideas and notions through reflection – by 'going meta', as it is sometimes called. The child, in a word, is seen as an epistemologist as well as a learner.

No less than the adult, the child is thought of as holding more or less coherent 'theories' not only about the world but about her own mind and how it works. These naive theories are brought into congruence with those of parents and teachers not through imitation, not through didactic instruction, but by discourse, collaboration, and negotiation. Knowledge is what is shared within discourse,[23] within a 'textual' community.[24] Truths are the product of evidence, argument, and construction rather than of authority, textual or pedagogic. This model of education is mutualist and dialectical, more concerned with interpretation and understanding than with the achievement of factual knowledge or skilled performance.

It is not simply that this mutualist view is 'child-centered' (a not very meaningful term at best), but it is much less patronizing toward the child's mind. It attempts to build an exchange of understanding between the teacher and the child: to find in the intuitions of the child the roots of systematic knowledge, as Dewey urged.

Four lines of recent research have enriched this perspective on teaching and learning. While they are all closely related, they are worth distinguishing. The first has to do with how children develop their ability to 'read other minds', to get to know what others are thinking or feeling. It usually gets labeled as research on *intersubjectivity*. Intersubjectivity begins with infant's and mother's pleasure in eye-to-eye contact in the opening weeks of life, moves quickly into the two of them sharing joint attention on common objects, and culminates a first preschool phase with the child and a caretaker achieving a meeting of minds by an early exchange of words – an achievement that is never finished.[25]

The second line of research involves the child's grasp of another's 'intentional states' – his beliefs, promises, intentions, desires, in a word his *theories of mind*, as this research is often referred to. It is a program of inquiry into how children acquire their notions about how others come to hold or relinquish various mental states. It is particularly concerned, as well, with the child's sorting of people's beliefs and opinions as being true or right versus being false and wrong, and in the process, this research has found out many intriguing things about the young child's ideas about 'false beliefs'.[26]

The third line is the study of *metacognition* – what children think about learning and remembering and thinking (especially their own), and how 'thinking about' one's own cognitive operations affects one's own mental procedures. The first important contribution to this work, a study by Ann Brown, illustrated how remembering strategies were profoundly changed by the child turning her inner eye on how she herself proceeded in attempting to commit something to memory.[27]

Studies in *collaborative learning* and problem solving constitute the fourth line of new research, which focuses on how children explicate and revise their beliefs in discourse.[28] It has flourished not only in America but also in Sweden, where much recent pedagogical research has been given over to studying how children understand and how they manage their own learning.[29]

What all this research has in common is an effort to understand how children themselves organize their own learning, remembering, guessing, and thinking. Unlike older psychological theories, bent on imposing 'scientific' models on children's cognitive activities, this work explores the child's own framework to understand better how he comes to the views that finally prove most useful to him. The child's *own* folk psychology (and its growth) becomes the object of study. And, of course, such research provides the teacher with a far deeper and less condescending sense of what she will encounter in the teaching–learning situation.

Some say that the weakness of this approach is that it tolerates an unacceptable degree of relativity in what is taken as 'knowledge'. Surely more is required to justify beliefs than merely sharing them with others. That 'more' is the machinery of justification for one's beliefs, the canons of scientific and philosophical reasoning. Knowledge, after all, is *justifed* belief. One must be pragmatist enough in one's views about the nature of knowledge to recognize the importance of such criticism. It is a foolish 'postmodernism' that accepts that all knowledge can be justified simply by finding or forming an 'interpretive community' that agrees. Nor need we be so old guard as to insist that knowledge is only knowledge when it is 'true' in a way that precludes all competing claims. 'True history', without regard to the perspective from which it was written, is at best a mischievous joke and at worst a bid for political hegemony. Claims about 'truth' must always be justified.

They must be justified by appeal to reasons that, in the logician's stricter sense, resist disproof and disbelief. Reasons of this kind obviously include appeals to evidence that defy falsifiability. But falsifiability is rarely a 'yes-no' matter, for there are often variant interpretations that are compatible with available evidence – if not all of the evidence, then enough of it to be convincing.

There is no reason a priori why the third approach to teaching and learning should not be compatible with this more pragmatic epistemology.

It is a very different conception of knowledge from the second perspective, where knowledge was taken to be fixed and independent of the knower's perspective. For the very nature of the knowledge enterprise has changed in our times. Hacking points out, for example, that prior to the seventeenth century an unbridgeable gap was thought to exist between knowledge and opinion, the former objective, the latter subjective.[30] What modernism sponsors is a healthy skepticism about the absoluteness of that gap. We are considering here not 'analytic' knowledge – as in logic and mathematics – where the rule of contradiction has a privileged position (that something cannot be both A and not-A). But even at the analytic level the view we are discussing casts a skeptical eye at the premature imposition of formal, logical forms on bodies of empirical knowledge outside the 'hard' natural sciences.

In the light of all this, it is surely possible to take one step further in conceiving folk pedagogy – a step that, like the others we have considered, rests on epistemological considerations. At issue is how subjectively held beliefs are turned into viable theories about the world and its facts. How are beliefs turned into hypotheses that hold not because of the faith we place in them but because they stand up in the public marketplace of evidence, interpretation, and agreement with extant knowledge? Hypotheses cannot simply be 'sponsored'. They must be openly tested. 'Today is Tuesday' turns into a conventional fact not by virtue of its being 'true' but through conformity with conventions for naming the days of the week. It achieves intersubjectivity by virtue of convention and thereby becomes a 'fact' independent of individual beliefs. This is the basis of Popper's well-known defense of 'objective knowledge'[31] and of Nagel's view of what he calls 'the view from nowhere'.[32]

Issues of this order are precisely the ones that this third perspective most admirably and directly deals with. We now turn to the fourth and last of the perspectives on folk pedagogy.

*4. Children as knowledgeable: The management of 'objective' knowledge.* Too exclusive a focus on beliefs and 'intentional states' and on their negotiation in discourse risks overestimating the importance of social exchange in constructing knowledge. That emphasis can lead us to underestimate the importance of knowledge accumulated in the past. For cultures preserve past reliable knowledge much as the common law preserves a record of how past communal conflicts were adjudicated. In both instances there is an effort to achieve a workable consistency, to shun arbitrariness, to find 'general principles'. Neither culture nor law is open to abrupt reconstrual. Reconstrual is typically undertaken (to use the legal expression) with 're-straint'. Past knowledge and reliable practice are not taken lightly. Science is no different: it too resists being stampeded into 'scientific revolutions', profligately throwing out old paradigms.[33]

Now to pedagogy. Early on, children encounter the hoary distinction between what is known by 'us' (friends, parents, teachers, and so on) and what in some larger sense is simply 'known'. In these post-positivist, perhaps 'post-modern' times, we recognize all too well that the 'known' is neither God-given truth nor, as it were, written irrevocably in the Book of Nature. Knowledge in this dispensation is always putatively revisable. But revisability is not to be confused with free-for-all relativism, the view that since *no* theory is the ultimate truth, *all* theories, like all people, are equal; We surely recognize the distinction between Popper's 'World Two' of personally held beliefs, hunches, and opinions and his 'World Three' of justified knowledge. But what makes the latter 'objective' is not that it constitutes some positivist's free-standing, aboriginal reality, but rather that it has stood up to sustained scrutiny and been tested by the best available evidence. All knowledge has a history.

The fourth perspective holds that teaching should help children grasp the distinction between personal knowledge, on the one side, and 'what is taken to be known' by the culture, on the other. But they must not only grasp this distinction, but also understand its basis, as it were, in the history of knowledge. How can we incorporate such a perspective in our pedagogy? Stated another way, what have children gained when they begin to distinguish what is known canonically from what they know personally and idiosyncratically?

Janet Astington offers an interesting twist on this classic problem.[34] She finds that when children begin to understand how evidence is used to check beliefs, they often see the process as akin to forming a belief about a belief: 'I now have reason to believe that this belief is true (or false, as the case may be)'. 'Reasons for believing' a hypothesis are not the same order of thing as the belief embodied in the hypothesis itself, and if the former work out well, then the latter graduates from being a belief (or hypothesis) to becoming something more robust – a proved theory or even a body of fact.

And by the same intuition, one can as easily come to see one's personal ideas or beliefs as relating (or not relating) to 'what is known' or what is generally believed to have stood the test of time. In this way, we come to view personal conjecture against the background of what has come to be shared with the historical past. Those presently engaged in the pursuit of knowledge become sharers of conjectures with those long dead. But one can go a step further and ask how past conjecture settled into something more solid over the years. You can share Archimedes with seesaw partners on the playground, and know how he came to hold his view. But what about your interpretation of Kate in *Taming of the Shrew* as being like the class tomboy? That couldn't be what Shakespeare had in mind: he didn't 'know about' her in that sense. So was there something else like that in his day? There is something appealing and, indeed, enspiriting about facing off one's own version of 'knowledge' with the foibles of the archivally famous in our past. Imagine an inner-city high school class – it was a real one, mostly San Antonio Latinos – staging *Oedipus Rex*. They 'knew' things about incest that Sophocles may never have dreamt of. It was plain to their gifted teacher/director that they were not in the least intimidated by the DWEM (Dead White European Male) who had written the play some two millennia ago. Yet they were true to the play's spirit.

So the fourth perspective holds that there is something special about 'talking' to authors, now dead but still alive in their ancient texts – so long as the objective of the encounter is not worship but discourse and inter-pretation, 'going meta' on thoughts about the past. Try several trios of teenagers, each staging a play about the astonishingly brief account in Genesis where Abraham at God's instruction takes Isaac, his only son, to sacrifice him to God on Mount Moriah. There is a famous set of 'versions' of the Abraham story in Kierkegaard's *Fear and Trembling*; try that on them too. Or try out some teenagers on a dozen different reproductions of Annunciation paintings in which the Angel announces to the Virgin that she is to be Queen of Heaven. Ask them what they judge, from the various pictures, might be going through Mary's mind – in a painting where Mary looks like a haughty Renaissance princess, in another where she resembles a humble Martha, in yet another where she looks quite a brazen young lady. It is striking how quickly teenagers leap across the gulf that separates Popper's subjective World Two from his 'objective' World Three. The teacher, with class exercises like these, helps the child reach beyond his own impressions to join a past world that would otherwise be remote and beyond him as a knower.[35]

## Real Schooling

Real schooling, of course, is never confined to one model of the learner or one model of teaching. Most day-to-day education in schools is designed to cultivate skills and abilities, to impart a knowledge of facts and theories, and to cultivate understanding of the beliefs and intentions of those nearby and far away. Any choice of pedagogical practice implies a conception of the learner and may, in time, be adopted by him or her as the appropriate way of thinking about the learning process. For a choice of pedagogy inevitably communicates a conception of the learning process and the learner. Pedagogy is never innocent. It is a medium that carries its own message.

## Summary: Rethinking Minds, Cultures, and Education

We can conceive of the four views of teaching-and-learning just set forth as being ordered on two dimensions. The first is an 'inside-outside' dimension: call it the *internalist-externalist* dimension. Externalist theories emphasize what adults can do for children from outside to foster learning – the bulk of traditional educational psychology. Internalist theories focus on what the child can do, what the child thinks he or she is doing, and how learning can be premised on those intentional states.

The second dimension describes the degree of intersubjectivity or 'common understanding' assumed to be required between the pedagogical theorist and the subjects to whom his theories relate. Let us call this the *intersubjective-objectivist* dimension. Objectivist theories regard children as an entomologist might regard a colony of ants or an elephant-trainer an elephant; there is no presumption that the subjects should see themselves in the same terms that the theorist does. Intersubjective theorists, on the other hand, apply the same theories to themselves as they do to their clients. Hence, they seek to create psychological theories that are as useful for the children in organizing their learning and managing their lives as they are for the adults that work with them.

Internalist theories tend to be intersubjective in emphasis. That is to say, if one is concerned with what the child is up to mentally, one is likely to be concerned with formulating a theory of teaching-and-learning that one can share with him or her in order to facilitate the child's efforts. But this is not necessarily so. Much Western cultural anthropology, for example, is internalist and very concerned with 'how natives think'. But anthropologists' theories are, as it were, not for the 'natives' but for their colleagues back home.[36] It is usually assumed, however tacitly, that the natives are 'different' or that they simply would not understand. And, indeed, some psychoanalytically oriented theories of early childhood pedagogy are of this same order – not to be shared with the child. Such theories are much occupied with the child's internal states, but like the native, the child is 'different'. The adult – theorist or teacher – becomes like an omniscient narrator in nineteenth-century novels: he knows perfectly what is going on in the minds of the novel's protagonist, even though the protagonist herself may not know.

Modern pedagogy is moving increasingly to the view that the child should be aware of her own thought processes, and that it is crucial for the pedagogical theorist and teacher alike to help her to become more metacognitive – to be as aware of how she goes about her learning and thinking as she is about the subject matter she is studying. Achieving skill and accumulating knowledge are not enough. The learner can be helped to achieve full mastery by reflecting as well upon how she is going about her job and how her approach can be improved. Equipping her with a good theory of mind – or a theory of mental functioning – is one part of helping her to do so.

In the end, then, the four perspectives on pedagogy are best thought of as parts of a broader continent, their significance to be understood in the light of their partialness. Nobody can sensibly propose that skills and cultivated abilities are unimportant. Nor can they argue that the accumulation of factual knowledge is trivial. No sensible critic would ever claim that children should not become aware that knowledge is dependent upon perspective and that we share and negotiate our perspectives in the knowledge-seeking process. And it would take a bigot to deny that we become the richer for recognizing the link between reliable knowledge from the past and what we learn in the present. What is needed is that the four perspectives be fused into some congruent unity, recognized as parts of a common continent. Older views of mind and how mind can be cultivated need to be shorn of their narrow exclusionism, and newer views need to be modulated to recognize that while skills and facts never exist *out* of context, they are no less important *in* context.

Modern advances in the study of human development have begun providing us with a new and steadier base upon which a more integrated theory of teaching-and-learning can be erected. And it was with these advances that this chapter was principally concerned – with the child as an active, intentional being; with knowledge as 'man-made' rather than simply there; with how our knowledge about the world and about each other gets constructed and negotiated with others, both contemporaries and those long departed.

# Notes

1. A. C. Kruger and M. Tomasello, 'Cultural Learning and Learning Culture', in *Handbook of Education and Human Development* (Oxford: Blackwell, 1996).

2. M. Tomasello, A. C. Kruger, and H. Ratner, 'Cultural Learning', *Behavioral and Brain Sciences*, 16(3) (1993): 495–511.

3. E. S. Savage-Rumbaugh, J. Murphy, R. A. Sevcik, K. E. Brakke, S. L. Williams, and D. L. Rumbaugh, 'Language Comprehension in Ape and Child', *Monographs of the Society for Research in Child Development*, 58 (3–4, Serial No. 233) (1993).

4. R. S. Fouts, D. H. Fouts, and D. Schoenfeld, 'Sign Language Conversational Interaction between Chimpanzees', *Sign Language Studies*, 42 (1984): 1–12; J. Goodall, *The Chimpanzees of Gombe: Patterns of Behavior* (Cambridge, Mass.: Harvard University Press, 1986).

5. Tomasello, Kruger, and Ratner, 'Cultural Learning'.

6. D. L. Cheney and R. M. Seyfarth, *How Monkeys See the World* (Chicago: University of Chicago Press, 1990).

7. E. Visalberghi and D. M. Fragaszy, 'Do Monkeys Ape?' in S. Parker and K. Gibson, eds., *'Language' and Intelligence in Monkeys and Apes: Comparative Developmental Perspectives* (Cambridge: Cambridge University Press, 1991).

8. B. Rogoff, J. Mistry, A. Goncu, and C. Mosier, 'Guided Participation in Cultural Activity by Toddlers and Caregivers', *Monographs of the Society for Research in Child Development*, 58 (8, Serial No. 236) (1993).

9. J. Bruner, *Acts of Meaning* (Cambridge, Mass.: Harvard University Press, 1990).

10. J. Astington, P. Harris, and D. Olson, eds., *Developing Theories of Mind* (Cambridge: Cambridge University Press, 1988).

11. C. Bereiter and M. Scardarnaglia, *Surpassing Ourselves: An Inquiry into the Nature and Implications of Expertise* (Chicago: Open Court, 1993).

12. A. L. Brown and J. C. Campione, 'Communities of Learning and Thinking, Or a Context by Any Other Name', in Deanna Kuhn, ed., *Developmental Perspectives on Teaching and Learning Thinking Skills, Contributions in Human Development*, 21 (Baser: Krager, 1990): 108–126.

13. H. Gardner, *The Unschooled Mind* (New York: Basic Books, 1991): 253.

14. Tomasello, Kruger, and Ramer, 'Cultural Learning'.

15. K. Egan, *Primary Understanding* (New York: Routledge, 1988): 45.

16. V. Turner, *From Ritual to Theater: The Human Seriousness of Play* (New York: Performing Arts Journal Publications, 1982).

17. Brown and Campione, 'Communities of Learning and Thinking'.

18. See J. S. Bruner, J. J. Goodnow, and G. A. Austin, *A Study of Thinking* (New York: Wiley, 1956).

19. See also J. S. Bruner and D. R. Olson, 'Learning through Experience and Learning through Media', G. Gerbner, L. P. Gross, and W. Melody, eds., *Communications Technology and Social Policy: Understanding the New Cultural Revolution* (New York: Wiley, 1973).

20. Tomasello, Kruger, and Ratner, 'Cultural Learning'.

21. B. Latour and S. Woolgar, *Laboratory Life: The Social Construction of Scientific Facts* (Princeton, NJ.: Princeton University Press, 1986).

22. See T. Gladwin, *East Is a Big Bird* (Cambridge, Mass.: Harvard University Press, 1970).

23. C. F. Feldman, 'Oral Metalanguage', in D. R. Olson and N. Torrance, eds., *Literacy and Orality* (Cambridge: Cambridge University Press, 1991): 47–65.

24. B. Stock, *The Implications of Literacy* (Princeton, N.J.: Princeton University Press, 1983).

25. See J. Bruner, 'From Joint Attention to the Meeting of Minds', in C. Moore and F. Dunham, eds., *Joint Attention* (New York: Academic Press).

26. See J. Astington, *The Child's Discovery of the Mind* (Cambridge, Mass.: Harvard University Press, 1993) for a summary of this work.

27. A. Brown, 'The Development of Memory: Knowing, Knowing about Knowing, and Knowing How to Know', in H. W. Reese, ed., *Advances in Child Development and Behavior*, vol. 10 (New York: Academic Press, 1975).

28. C. Bereiter and M. Scardamaglia, *Surpassing Ourselves: An Inquiry into the Nature and Implications of Expertise* (Chicago: Open Court, 1993); M. Scardamaglia, C. Bereiter, C. Brett, P. J. Burtis, C. Calhoun, and N. Smith Lea, 'Educational Applications of a Networked Communal Database', *Interactive Learning Environments*, 2(1) (1992): 45–71; Ann L. Brown and Joseph C. Campione, 'Communities of Learning and Thinking, Or a Context by any Other Name', in Deanna Kuhn, ed., *Developmental Perspectives on Teaching and Learning Thinking Skills*, Contributions in Human Development, 21 (Basel: Krager, 1990): 108–126; Roy D. Pea, 'Seeing What We Build Together: Distributed Multimedia Learning Environments for Transformative Communications', *The Journal of the Learning Sciences*, 3(3) (1994): 219–225.

29. See, for example, Ingrid Pramling, *Learning to Learn: A Study of Swedish Preschool Children* (New York: Springer-Verlag, 1990).

30. I. Hacking, *The Emergence of Probability: A Philosophical Study of Early Ideas about Probability, Induction, and Statistical Inference* (Cambridge: Cambridge University Press, 1975).

31. K. Popper, *Objective Knowledge: An Evolutionary Approach* (Oxford: Oxford University Press, 1972).

32. T. Nagel, *The View from Nowhere* (New York: Oxford University Press, 1986).

33. T. Kuhn, *The Structure of Scientific Revolutions* (Chicago: University of Chicago Press, 1962).

34. Personal communication.

35. M. Donaldson, *Human Minds: An Exploration* (London: Allen Lane, Penguin Press, 1992).

36. For a particularly thoughtful account of the Western orientation of anthropological writing, see Clifford Geertz, *Works and Lives: The Anthropologist as Author* (Stanford, Calif: Stanford University Press, 1988).

# 2

# Learning and Pedagogy in Communities of Practice

## Jean Lave and Etienne Wenger

[ . . . ] In [this chapter] we recast the central characteristics of [ . . . ] apprenticeship in terms of legitimate peripheral participation. First, we discuss the structuring resources that shape the process and content of learning possibilities and apprentices' changing perspectives on what is known and done. Then we argue that 'transparency' of the sociopolitical organization of practice, of its content and of the artifacts engaged in practice, is a crucial resource for increasing participation. We next examine the relation of newcomers to the discourse of practice. [ . . . ] Finally, we explore contradictions inherent in learning, and the relations of the resulting conflicts to the development of identity and the transformation of practice.

## Structuring Resources for Learning in Practice

One of the first things people think of when apprenticeship is mentioned is the master–apprentice relation. But in practice the roles of masters are surprisingly variable across time and place. A specific master–apprentice relation is not even ubiquitously characteristic of apprenticeship learning. Indeed, neither Yucatec midwives nor quartermasters learn in specific master–apprentice relations. Newcomers to AA [Alcoholics Anonymous] do have special relations with specific old-timers who act as their sponsors, but these relations are not what defines them as newcomers. In contrast, tailors' apprentices most certainly have specific relations with their masters, without whom they wouldn't be apprentices. Master tailors must sponsor apprentices before the latter can have legitimate access to participation in the community's productive activities. In short, the form in which such legitimate access is secured for apprentices depends on the characteristics of the division of labor in the social milieu in which the community of practice is located. Thus, the midwife is learning a specialism within her own family of orientation, a form of labor different, but not separated in marked ways, from the widely distributed 'ordinary' activities of everyday

---

This chapter has been edited

life; legitimate participation comes diffusely through membership in family and community. Where apprentices learn a specialized occupation, sponsorship into a community of practice – within a community in the more general sense – becomes an issue. Intentional relations, and even contractual relations with a specific master, are common. It should be clear that, in shaping the relation of masters to apprentices, the issue of conferring legitimacy is more important than the issue of providing teaching.

Even in the case of the tailors, where the relation of apprentice to master is specific and explicit, it is not this relationship, but rather the apprentice's relations to other apprentices and even to other masters that organize opportunities to learn; an apprentice's own master is too distant, an object of too much respect, to engage with in awkward attempts at a new activity. In AA, old-timers who act as 'sponsors' reportedly withhold advice and instruction appropriate to later stages; they hold back and wait until the newcomer becomes 'ready' for a next step through increasing participation in the community (Alibrandi 1977). In all five cases [ . . . ] researchers insist that there is very little observable teaching; the more basic phenomenon is learning. The practice of the community creates the potential 'curriculum' in the broadest sense – that which may be learned by newcomers with legitimate peripheral access. Learning activity appears to have a characteristic pattern. There are strong goals for learning because learners, as peripheral participants, can develop a view of what the whole enterprise is about, and what there is to be learned. Learning itself is an improvised practice: A learning curriculum unfolds in opportunities for engagement in practice. It is not specified as a set of dictates for proper practice.

In apprenticeship opportunities for learning are, more often than not, given structure by work practices instead of by strongly asymmetrical master–apprentice relations. Under these circumstances learners may have a space of 'benign community neglect' in which to configure their own learning relations with other apprentices. There may be a looser coupling between relations among learners on the one hand and the often hierarchical relations between learners and old-timers on the other hand, than where directive pedagogy is the central motive of institutional organization. It seems typical of apprenticeship that apprentices learn mostly in relation with other apprentices There is anecdotal evidence (Butler personal communication; Hass n.d.) that where the circulation of knowledge among peers and near-peers is possible, it spreads exceedingly rapidly and effectively. [ . . . ] The effectiveness of the circulation of information among peers suggests [ . . . ] that engaging in practice, rather than being its object, may well be a *condition* for the effectiveness of learning.

So far, we have observed that the authority of masters and their involvement in apprenticeship varies dramatically across communities of practice. We have also pointed out that structuring resources for learning come from a variety of sources, not only from pedagogical activity. We argue that a coherent explanation of these observations depends upon *decentering* common notions of mastery and pedagogy. This decentering strategy is, in fact, deeply embedded in our situated approach – for to shift as we have from the notion of an individual learner to the concept of legitimate peripheral participation in communities of practice is precisely to decenter analysis of learning. To take a decentered view of master–apprentice relations leads to an understanding that mastery resides not in the master but in the organization of the community of practice of which the master is part. The master as the locus of authority (in several senses) is, after all, as much a product of the conventional, centered theory of learning as is the individual learner. Similarly, a decentered view of the master as pedagogue moves the focus of analysis away from teaching and onto the intricate structuring of a community's learning resources.

## The Place of Knowledge: Participation, Learning Curricula, Communities of Practice

The social relations of apprentices within a community change through their direct involvement in activities; in the process, the apprentices' understanding and knowledgeable skills develop. In the recent past, the only means we have had for understanding the processes by which these changes occur have come from conventional speculations about the nature of 'informal' learning: That is, apprentices are supposed to acquire the 'specifics' of practice through 'observation and imitation'. But this view is in all probability wrong in every particular, or right in particular circumstances, but for the wrong reasons. We argue instead that the effects of peripheral participation on knowledge-in-practice are not properly understood; and that studies of apprenticeship have presumed too literal a coupling of work processes and learning processes.

To begin with, newcomers' legitimate peripherality provides them with more than an 'observational' lookout post: It crucially involves *participation* as a way of learning – of both absorbing and being absorbed in – the 'culture of practice'. An extended period of legitimate peripherality provides learners with opportunities to make the culture of practice theirs. From a broadly peripheral perspective, apprentices gradually assemble a general idea of what constitutes the practice of the community. This uneven sketch of the enterprise (available if there is legitimate access) might include who is involved; what they do; what everyday life is like; how masters talk, walk, work, and generally conduct their lives; how people who are not part of the community of practice interact with it; what other learners are doing; and what learners need to learn to become full practitioners. It includes an increasing understanding of how, when, and about what old-timers collaborate, collude, and collide, and what they enjoy, dislike, respect, and admire. In particular, it offers exemplars (which are grounds and motivation for learning activity), including masters, finished products, and more advanced apprentices in the process of becoming full practitioners.

Such a general view, however, is not likely to be frozen in initial impressions. Viewpoints from which to understand the practice evolve through changing participation in the division of labor, changing relations to ongoing community practices, and changing social relations in the community. This is as true, in different ways, of reformed alcoholics as they socialize with other AA members as it is of quartermasters as they move through different aspects of navigation work. And learners have multiply structured relations with ongoing practice in other ways. Apprenticeship learning is not 'work-driven' in the way stereotypes of informal learning have suggested; the ordering of learning and of everyday practice do not coincide. Production activity-segments must be learned in different sequences than those in which a production process commonly unfolds, if peripheral, less intense, less complex, less vital tasks are learned before more central aspects of practice.

Consider, for instance, the tailors' apprentices, whose involvement starts with both initial preparations for the tailors' daily labor and finishing details on completed garments. The apprentices progressively move backward through the production process to cutting jobs. (This kind of progression is quite common across cultures and historical periods.) Under these circumstances, the initial 'circumferential' perspective absorbed in partial, peripheral, apparently trivial activities – running errands, delivering messages, or accompanying others – takes on new significance. It provides a first approximation to an armature of the structure of the community of practice. Things learned, and various and changing viewpoints, can be arranged and interrelated in ways that gradually transform that skeletal understanding.

When directive teaching in the form of prescriptions about proper practice generates one circumscribed form of participation (in school), pre-empting participation in ongoing practice as the legitimate source of learning opportunities, the goal of complying with the requirements specified by teaching engenders a practice different from that intended (Bourdieu 1977). In such cases, even though the pedagogical structure of the circumstances of learning has moved away from the principle of legitimate peripheral participation with respect to the target practice, legitimate peripheral participation is still the core of the learning that takes place. This leads us to distinguish between a *learning curriculum* and a *teaching curriculum*. A learning curriculum consists of situated opportunities (thus including exemplars of various sorts often thought of as 'goals') for the improvisational development of new practice (Lave 1989). A learning curriculum is a field of learning resources in everyday practice *viewed from the perspective of learners*. A teaching curriculum, by contrast, is constructed for the instruction of newcomers. When a teaching curriculum supplies – and thereby limits – structuring resources for learning, the meaning of what is learned (and control of access to it, both in its peripheral forms and its subsequently more complex and intensified, though possibly more fragmented, forms) is mediated through an instructor's participation, by an external view of what knowing is about. The learning curriculum in didactic situations, then, evolves out of participation in a specific community of practice engendered by pedagogical relations and by a prescriptive view of the target practice as a subject matter, as well as out of the many and various relations that tie participants to their own and to other institutions.

A learning curriculum is essentially situated. It is not something that can be considered in isolation, manipulated in arbitrary didactic terms, or analyzed apart from the social relations that shape legitimate peripheral participation. A learning curriculum is thus characteristic of a community. In using the term community, we do not imply some primordial culture-sharing entity. We assume that members have different interests, make diverse contributions to activity and hold varied viewpoints. In our view, participation at multiple levels is entailed in membership in a *community of practice*. Nor does the term community imply necessarily co-presence, a well-defined, identifiable group, or socially visible boundaries. It does imply participation in an activity system about which participants share understandings concerning what they are doing and what that means in their lives and for their communities.

The concept of community underlying the notion of legitimate peripheral participation, and hence of 'knowledge' and its 'location' in the lived-in world, is both crucial and subtle. The community of practice of midwifery or tailoring involves much more than the technical knowledgeable skill involved in delivering babies or producing clothes. A community of practice is a set of relations among persons, activity, and world, over time and in relation with other tangential and overlapping communities of practice. A community of practice is an intrinsic condition for the existence of knowledge, not least because it provides the interpretive support necessary for making sense of its heritage. Thus, participation in the cultural practice in which any knowledge exists is an epistemological principle of learning. The social structure of this practice, its power relations, and its conditions for legitimacy define possibilities for learning (i.e., for legitimate peripheral participation).

[ . . . ]

Claims *about* the definition of a community of practice and the community of practice actually in process of reproduction in that location may not coincide – a point worth careful consideration.

For example, in most high schools there is a group of students engaged over a substantial period of time in learning physics. What community of practice is in the process of reproduction? Possibly the students participate only in the reproduction of the high school itself. But assuming that the practice of physics is also being reproduced in some form, there are vast differences between the ways high school physics students participate in and give meaning to their activity and the way professional physicists do. The actual reproducing community of practice, within which school-children learn about physics, is not the community of physicists but the community of schooled adults. Children are introduced into the latter community (and its humble relation with the former community) during their school years. The reproduction cycles of the physicists' community start much later, possibly only in graduate school (Traweek 1988).

In this view, problems of schooling are not, at their most fundamental level, pedagogical. Above all, they have to do with the ways in which the community of adults reproduces itself, with the places that newcomers can or cannot find in such communities, and with, relations that can or cannot be established between these newcomers and the cultural and political life of the community.

In summary, rather than learning by replicating the performances of others or by acquiring knowledge transmitted in instruction, we suggest that learning occurs through centripetal participation in the learning curriculum of the ambient community. Because the place of knowledge is within a community of practice, questions of learning must be addressed within the developmental cycles of that community, a recommendation which creates a diagnostic tool for distinguishing among communities of practice.

## The Problem of Access: Transparency and Sequestration

The key to legitimate peripherality is access by newcomers to the community of practice and all that membership entails. But though this is essential to the reproduction of any community, it is always problematic at the same time. To become a full member of a community of practice requires access to a wide range of ongoing activity, old-timers, and other members of the community; and to information, resources, and opportunities for participation. The issue is so central to membership in communities of practice that, in a sense, all that we have said so far is about access. Here we discuss the problem more specifically in connection with issues of understanding and control, which along with involvement in productive activity are related aspects of the legitimate peripherality of participants in a practice.

The artifacts employed in ongoing practice, the technology of practice, provide a good arena in which to discuss the problem of access to understanding. In general, social scientists who concern themselves with learning treat technology as a given and are not analytic about its interrelations with other aspects of a community of practice. Becoming a full participant certainly includes engaging with the technologies of everyday practice, as well as participating in the social relations production processes, and other activities of communities of practice. But the understanding to be gained from engagement with technology can be extremely varied depending on the form of participation enabled by its use. Participation involving technology is especially significant because the artifacts used within a cultural practice carry a substantial portion of that practice's heritage. For example, the alidade used by the quartermasters for taking bearings has developed as a navigational instrument over hundreds of years, and embodies calculations invented long ago (Hutchins, 1993). Thus, understanding the technology of practice is more than learning to use tools; it is a way to connect with the history of the practice and to participate more directly in its cultural life.

The significance of artifacts in the full complexity of their relations with the practice can he more or less *transparent* to learners. Transparency in its simplest form may just imply that the inner workings of an artifact are available for the learner's inspection: The black box can be opened, it can become a 'glass box'. But there is more to understanding the use and significance of an artifact: Knowledge within a community of practice and ways of perceiving and manipulating objects characteristic of community practices are encoded in artifacts in ways that can be more or less revealing. Moreover, the activity system and the social world of which an artifact is part are reflected in multiple ways in its design and use and can become further 'fields of transparency', just as they can remain opaque. Obviously, the transparency of any technology always exists with respect to some purpose and is intricately tied to the cultural practice and social organization within which the technology is meant to function: It cannot he viewed as a feature of an artifact in itself but as a process that involves specific forms of participation, in which the technology fulfils a mediating function. Apprentice quartermasters not only have access to the physical activities going on around them and to the tools of the trade; they participate in information flows and conversations, in a context in which they can make sense of what they observe and hear. In focusing on the epistemological role of artifacts in the context of the social organization of knowledge, this notion of transparency constitutes, as it were, the cultural organization of access. As such, it does not apply to technology only, but to all forms of access to practice.

Productive activity and understanding are not separate, or even separable, but dialectically related. Thus, the term *transparency* when used here in connection with technology refers to the way in which using artifacts and understanding their significance interact to become one learning process. Mirroring the intricate relation between using and understanding artifacts, there is an interesting duality inherent in the concept of transparency. It combines the two characteristics of *invisibility* and *visibility*: invisibility in the form of unproblematic interpretation and integration into activity, and visibility in the form of extended access to information. This is not a simple dichotomous distinction, since these two crucial characteristics are in a complex interplay, their relation being one of both conflict and synergy.

[ . . . ]

Control and selection, as well as the need for access, are inherent in communities of practice. Thus access is liable to manipulation, giving legitimate peripherality an ambivalent status: Depending on the organization of access, legitimate peripherality can either promote or prevent legitimate participation. In the study of the butchers' apprentices, Marshall (1972) provides examples of how access can be denied. The trade school and its shop exercises did not simulate the central practices of meat cutting in supermarkets, much less make them accessible to apprentices; on-the-job training was not much of an improvement. Worse, the master butchers confined their apprentices to jobs that were removed from activities rather than peripheral to them. To the extent that the community of practice routinely sequesters newcomers, either very directly as in the example of apprenticeship for the butchers, or in more subtle and pervasive ways as in schools, these newcomers are prevented from peripheral participation. In either case legitimacy is not in question. Schoolchildren are legitimately peripheral, but kept from participation in the social world more generally. The butchers' apprentices participate legitimately, but not peripherally, in that they are not given productive access to activity in the community of practitioners.

An important point about such sequestering when it is institutionalized is that it encourages a folk epistemology of dichotomies, for instance, between 'abstract' and 'concrete' knowledge. These categories do not reside in the world as distinct forms of *knowledge*, nor do they reflect some putative hierarchy of forms of knowledge among practitioners. Rather, they derive from the nature of the new practice generated by sequestration. *Abstraction* in this sense stems from the disconnectedness of a particular cultural practice. Participation in that practice is neither more nor less abstract or concrete, experiential or cerebral, than in any other. Thus, legitimate peripheral participation as the core concept of relations of learning places the explanatory burden for issues such as 'understanding' and 'levels' of abstraction or conceptualization not on one type of learning as opposed to another, but on the cultural practice in which the learning is taking place, on issues of access, and on the transparency of the cultural environment with respect to the meaning of what is being learned. Insofar as the notion of transparency, taken very broadly, is a way of organizing activities that makes their meaning visible, it opens an alternative approach to the traditional dichotomy between learning experientially and learning at a distance, between learning by doing and learning by abstraction.

## Discourse and Practice

The characterization of language in learning has, in discussions of conventional contrasts between formal and informal learning, been treated as highly significant in classifying ways of transmitting knowledge. Verbal instruction has been assumed to have special, and especially effective properties with respect to the generality and scope of the understanding that learners come away with, while instruction by demonstration – learning by 'observation and imitation' – is supposed to produce the opposite, a literal and narrow effect.

Close analysis of both instructional discourse and cases of apprentice-ship raise a different point: Issues about language, like those about the role of masters, may well have more to do with legitimacy of participation and with access to peripherality than they do with knowledge transmission. Indeed, as Jordan (1989) argues, learning to become a legitimate participant in a community involves learning how to talk (and be silent) in the manner of full participants. In AA telling the story of the life of the nondrinking alcoholic is clearly a major vehicle for the display of membership. Models for constructing AA life stories are widely available in published accounts of alcoholics' lives and in the storytelling performances of old-timers. Early on, newcomers learn to preface their contributions to AA meetings with the simple identifying statement 'I'm a recovering alcoholic', and, shortly, to introduce themselves and sketch the problems that brought them to AA. They begin by describing these events in non-AA terms. Their accounts meet with counterexemplary stories by more-experienced members who do not criticize or correct newcomers accounts directly. They gradually generate a view that matches more closely the AA model, eventually producing skilled testimony in public meetings and gaining validation from others as they demonstrate the appropriate understanding.

[ . . . ]

In the *Psychology of Literacy*, Scribner and Cole (1981) speculate that asking questions – learning how to 'do' school appropriately may be a major part of what school teaches. This is also Jordan's conclusion about Yucatec midwives' participation in biomedical, state-sponsored training courses. She argues that the verbal instruction provided by health officials has the effect of teaching midwives how to talk in biomedical terms when required. Such talk only serves to give them 'face validity' in the eyes of others who believe in the authoritative character of biomedicine. But Jordan argues that it has no effect on their existing practice.

This point about language use is consonant with the earlier argument that didactic instruction creates unintended practices. The conflict stems from the fact that there is a difference between talking *about* a practice from outside and talking *within* it. Thus the didactic use of language, not itself the discourse of practice, creates a new linguistic practice, which has an existence of its own. Legitimate peripheral participation in such linguistic practice is a form of learning, but does not imply that newcomers learn the actual practice the language is supposed to be about.

In a community or practice, there are no special forms of discourse aimed at apprentices or crucial to their centripetal movement toward full participation that correspond to the marked genres of the question–answer–evaluation format of classroom teaching, or the lecturing of college professors or midwife-training course instructors. But Jordan makes a further, acute, observation about language, this time about the role of *stories* in apprenticeship: She points out that stories play a major role in decision making (1989). This has implications for what and how newcomers learn.

For apprenticeship learning is supported by conversations and stories about problematic and especially difficult cases.

> What happens is that as difficulties of one kind or another develop, stories of similar cases are offered up by the attendants (at a birth), all of whom, it should be remembered, are experts, having themselves given birth. In the ways in which these stories are treated, elaborated, ignored, taken up, characterized as typical and so on, the collaborative work of deciding on the present case is done . . . These stories, then, are packages of situated knowledge . . . To acquire a store of appropriate stories and, even more importantly, to know what are appropriate occasions for telling them, is then part of what it means to become a midwife (1989: 935).

[ . . . ] Telling the personal story is a tool of diagnosis and reinterpretation. [ . . . ] It becomes a display of membership by virtue of fulfilling a crucial function in the shared practice.

It is thus necessary to refine our distinction between *talking about* and *talking within* a practice. Talking within itself includes both talking within (e.g., exchanging information necessary to the progress of ongoing activities) and talking about (e.g., stories, community lore). Inside the shared practice, both forms of talk fulfill specific functions: engaging, focusing, and shifting attention, bringing about coordination, etc., on the one hand; and supporting communal forms of memory and reflection, as well as signaling membership, on the other. (And, similarly, talking about includes both forms of talk once it becomes part of a practice of its own, usually sequestered in some respects.) For newcomers then the purpose is not to learn *from* talk as a substitute for legitimate peripheral participation; it is to learn *to* talk as a key to legitimate peripheral participation.


## Contradictions and Change: Continuity and Displacement


To account for the complexity of participation in social practice, it is essential to give learning and teaching independent status as analytic concepts. Primary reliance on the concept of pedagogical structuring in learning research may well prevent speculation about what teaching consists of, how it is perceived, and how – as perceived – it affects learning. Most analyses of schooling assume, whether intentionally or not, the uniform motivation of teacher and pupils, because they assume, sometimes quite explicitly, that teacher and pupils share a goal of the main activity (e.g., Davydov and Markova 1983). In our view, this assumption has several consequences. First, it ignores the conflicting viewpoints associated with teaching and learning, respectively, and obscures the distortions that ensue (Fajans and Turner, 1988). Furthermore, it reflects too narrowly rationalistic a perspective on the person and motivation. The multiple viewpoints that are characteristic of participation in a community of practice, and thus of legitimate peripheral participation, are to be found in more complex theories of the person-in-society, such as those proposed by critical psychologists. Finally, assumptions of uniformity make it difficult to explore the mechanisms by which processes of change and transformation in communities practice and processes of learning are intricately implicated in each other.

In considering learning as part of social practice, we have focused our attention on the structure of social practice rather than privileging the structure of pedagogy as the source of learning. Learning understood as legitimate peripheral participation is not necessarily or directly dependent on pedagogical goals or official agenda, even in situations in which these goals appear to be a central factor (e.g., classroom instruction, tutoring). We have insisted that exposure to resources for learning is not restricted to a teaching curriculum and that instructional assistance is not construed as a purely interpersonal phenomenon; rather we have argued that learning must be understood with respect to a practice as a whole, with its multiplicity of relations – both within the community and with the world at large. Dissociating learning from pedagogical intentions opens the possibility of mismatch or conflict among practitioners' viewpoints in situations where learning is going on. These differences often must become constitutive of the content of learning.

[ ... ]

We have claimed that the development of identity is central to the careers of newcomers in communities of practice, and thus fundamental to the concept of legitimate peripheral participation. [ ... ] In fact, we have argued that, from the perspective we have developed here, learning and a sense of identity are inseparable: They are aspects of the same phenomenon.

Insofar as the conflicts in which the continuity–displacement contradiction is manifested involve power – as they do to a large extent – the way the contradiction is played out changes as power relations change. Conflicts between masters and apprentices (or, less individualistically, between generations) take place in the course of everyday participation. Shared participation is the stage on which the old and the new, the known and the unknown, the established and the hopeful, act out their differences and discover their commonalities, manifest their fear of one another, and come to terms with their need for one another. Each threatens the fulfillment of the other's destiny, just as it is essential to it. Conflict is experienced and worked out through a shared everyday practice in which differing viewpoints and common stakes are in interplay. Learners can be overwhelmed, overawed, and overworked. Yet even when submissive imitation is the result, learning is never simply a matter of the 'transmission' of knowledge or the 'acquisition' of skill; identity in relation with practice, and hence knowledge and skill and their significance to the subject and the community, are never unproblematic. This helps to account for the common observation that knowers come in a range of types, from clones to heretics.

Granting legitimate participation to newcomers with their own viewpoints introduces into any community of practice all the tensions of the continuity–displacement contradiction. These may be muted, though not extinguished, by the differences of power between old-timers and new-comers. As a way in which the related conflicts are played out in practice, legitimate peripheral participation is far more than just a process of learning on the part of newcomers. It is a reciprocal relation between persons and practice. This means that the move of learners toward full participation in a community of practice does not take place in a static context. The practice itself is in motion. Since activity and the participation of individuals involved in it, their knowledge, and their perspectives are mutually constitutive, change is a fundamental property of communities of practice and their activities. Goody (1989) argues that the introduction of strangers into what was previously strictly domestic production (a change that occurred within an expanding market in West Africa in the recent past) led masters to think more comprehensively about the organization of their production activities. She points out that the resulting division of work processes into segments to be learned has been mirrored in subsequent generations in new, increasingly specialized occupations. Legitimate peripherality is important for developing 'constructively naive' perspectives or questions. From this point of view, inexperience is an asset to be exploited. It is of use, however, only in the context of participation, when supported by experienced practitioners who both understand its limitations and value its role. Legitimacy of participation is crucial both for this naive involvement to invite reflection on ongoing activity and for the newcomer's occasional contributions to be taken into account. Insofar as this continual interaction of new perspectives is sanctioned, everyone's participation is legitimately peripheral in some respect. In other words, everyone can to some degree be considered a 'newcomer' to the future of a changing community.

# References

Alibrandi, L. A. (1977) The recovery process in Alcoholics Anonymous: The sponsor as folk therapist. Social Sciences Working Paper 130. University of California, Irvine.

Bourdieu, P. (1977) *Outline of a theory of practice*, Cambridge: Cambridge University Press.

Davydov, V. and A. Markova. (1983) A concept of educational activity for school children. *Soviet Psychology* 11(2): 50–76.

Fajans, J. and T. Turner. (In preparation.) Where the action is: An anthropological perspective on 'activity theory', with ethnographic applications. Paper presented at the annual meeting of the American Anthropolitical Association, 1988.

Goody, E. (1989) Learning and the division of labor, in M. Coy (ed.), *Anthropological perspectives on apprenticeship*. New York: SUNY Press.

Hass, M. (n.d.) Cognition-in-context: The social nature of the transformation of mathematical knowledge in a third-grade classroom. Program in Social Relations, University of California, Irvine.

Hutchins, E. (1993) Learning to navigate, in S. Chaiklin and J. Lave (eds.), *Understanding practice*, New York: Cambridge University Press.

Jordan, B. (1989) Cosmopolitical obstetrics: Some insights from the training of traditional midwives. *Social Science and Medicine* 28(9): 925–44.

Lave, J. (1989) The acquisition of culture and the practice of understanding, in J. Stigler, R. Shweder, and G. Herdt (eds.), *The Chicago symposia on human development*, Cambridge, Cambridge University Press.

Marshall, H. (1972) Structural constrains on learning, in B. Geer (ed.), *Learning to work*. Beverly Hills, CA: Sage Publications.

Scribner, S. and Cole, M. (1981) *The psychology of literacy*, Cambridge, MA: Harvard University Press.

Traweek, S. (1988) Discovering machines: Nature in the age of its mechanical reproduction, in F. Dubinskas (ed) *Making time: Ethnographies of high technology organisations*, Philadelphia: Temple University Press.

# 3

# Why No Pedagogy in England?

## Brian Simon

The term 'pedagogy' is used here in the sense of the 'science of teaching' (OED). The title of the chapter is meant to imply that no such science exists in England; the fact that the term is generally shunned implies that such a science is either undesirable or impossible to achieve. And such, it is argued, is the situation in England.

The contrast here with other European countries, both west and east, is striking. In the educational tradition of the Continent, the term 'pedagogy' has an honoured place, stemming perhaps particularly from the work and thinking of Comenius in the seventeenth century, but developed and elaborated in the nineteenth century through the work of Pestalozzi, Herbart and others. The concept of teaching as a science has strong roots in this tradition.

Not so in England. It is now one hundred years since Alexander Bain published *Education as a Science* (1879). Since then, less and less has been heard of this claim. The most striking aspect of current thinking and discussion about education is its eclectic character, reflecting deep confusion of thought, and of aims and purposes, relating to learning and teaching – to pedagogy.

It may be useful to advance an interpretation as to why the concept of 'pedagogy' has been shunned in England, and why instead our approach to educational theory and practice has tended to be amateurish, and highly pragmatic in character.[1] Relevant here is the practice and approach of our most prestigious educational institutions (historically speaking), the ancient universities and leading public schools. Until recently, and even perhaps today, these have been dominant, both socially and in terms of the formation of the climate of opinion. It is symptomatic that the public schools, in general, have until recently contemptuously rejected the idea that a professional training is in any sense relevant to the job of a public schoolmaster. Although toying with the idea in the late nineteenth century, the Headmasters Conference has never adopted a positive attitude to such training, which traditionally has been seen as perhaps relevant and important for an elementary school teacher, but certainly not to someone taking up the gentlemanly profession of teaching in a public school. This was seen, perhaps, not so much as a job anyone from the middle or upper middle class could do, but as something those who wished to teach, having the appropriate social origins including a degree at Oxford or Cambridge, could learn, through experience, on the job. Certainly no special training was necessary.[2]

The reasons for this are clear. The public schools developed as a cohesive system from the mid- to late 1860s serving the new Victorian upper middle class; indeed they played a major role in the symbiosis of aristocracy and bourgeoisie which characterised the late nineteenth century. As Honey makes clear, these schools were centrally concerned with the socialisation of these classes which could not be effectively undertaken in the home. This, he argues, is why, in spite of the epidemics, outrageous bullying, sexual dangers and insanitary conditions to which their pupils were exposed (and all of which took their toll), the popularity of these schools mounted irresistibly at this time (Honey, 1977).

The result has been that education, as a subject of enquiry and study, still less as a 'science', has, historically, had little prestige in this country, having been to all intents and purposes ignored in the most prestigious educational institutions. As Matthew Arnold tirelessly pointed out over one hundred years ago, in France, Prussia and elsewhere the problems of education for the middle class were taken really seriously. In Britain, on the other hand, everything was neglected; a laissez-faire pragmatism predominated.[3] This situation has, to some extent, been perpetuated. The dominant educational institutions of this country have had no concern with theory, its relation to practice, with pedagogy. This is the first point to establish.

But this, of course, is only part of the picture, if an important one. For while the public schools expressed, at least in their practice, a total disregard for pedagogy, in fact a systematic, rational approach was being developed elsewhere – as an indigenous growth within the system of elementary education, and specifically in the last decade of the nineteenth century, just as this system 'became of age', as it were, after its establishment in 1870. This is an interesting and relevant phenomenon, and worth serious attention for its lessons today.

The context of what was, in fact, a serious attempt to integrate theoretical knowledge with the practice of education is to be found in the work of the advanced School Boards in the main industrial cities at this time. Described as 'citadels of radicalism' by Elie Halévy, the French historian, these, with their higher grade schools, pupil-teacher centres, and technical institutions of various kinds (some of which supported, or merged with local universities) were now, in cooperation with the Technical Education Boards established after 1888, deliberately developing cohesive systems of education with an organic relation between the various stages, having the perspective of covering the whole field from infant school to university. This potential development was sharply cut off and circumscribed by a series of administrative and legislative measures brought in by a deeply Conservative government in the period 1899–1904.[4] But through the 1890s, such a perspective appeared realisable. Now at last the mass of the children had been brought into the schools; buildings erected (some of them massive), teaching developing as a profession. The so-called 'extravagance' of the School Boards, as seen by such as Sir John Gorst (and the Tories generally), had some basis in fact. The outlook was optimistic. This was the context of the quite sudden, and apparently rapid, development of educational theory and practice – of positive, all-embracing, pedagogical means.

The social context of this development has been outlined; its theoretical context is equally important. This is personified – or crystallised – in Alexander Bain's *Education as a Science*, published in 1879, reprinted six times in the 1880s, and a further ten times before 1900. Examination of a number of student-teacher manuals, which proliferated in the 1890s, indicates their indebtedness to Bain's approach – or the extent to which they shared common interpretations both of theoretical issues relating to education, and of the practice of teaching.

Of course the theories, and the practices, advocated by Bain and the authors of these manuals, had their limitations as well as theoretical weaknesses. That goes without saying. But, in the 1890s, the approach was serious, systematic, all-embracing. The pedagogy of this specific decade pointed the way to universal education, and was seen as such by its progenitors. What happened? Why was this embryo pedagogy not systematically developed? What went wrong?

First, the social and political context underwent an abrupt change, as indicated earlier. The development referred to took place within the *elementary* system, but one having for a short period a realistic perspective of organic growth. This was the backcloth, the crucial feature, of this movement as a whole. The administrative and legislative events of 1899 to 1904, almost traumatic in their effects, put a stopper on this, and apart from abolishing the School Boards, confined elementary education within precise limits, setting up a system of 'secondary' schooling parallel to, but quite separate from, the elementary system.

This created a new situation. A positive pedagogy based on scientific procedures and understanding and relevant for *all* was no longer seen as appropriate, or required. Intellectual development in the elementary schools was now at a discount (in parallel with the public schools, but for different reasons). The social-disciplinary ('containment') function of elementary education was now especially emphasised. The soil required to nurture a science of education no longer existed.

However, with the demise of the elementary school as the ground of pedagogy, there now emerged the new local authority-controlled systems of secondary education; it seems to have been into these new systems that the most advanced local authorities put their main efforts. These new systems, although strictly contained in their development by the central authority (the Board of Education), and designed specifically for what can best be described as the lower middle class (all such schools had to charge fees), were the only growth points permitted in the new dispensation. The more advanced local authorities, determined to extend educational provision, approached this new field with energy and developed a considerable pride in the school systems so created.[5]

It was the establishment, and rapid development of this new system of secondary schools which underlay new developments in the theory and practice of education. This system insistently required a pedagogy – the development of effective pedagogical means. Thus we find, in the period 1900–1914, a renewed concern to develop a relevant pedagogy and it is this that lies behind the great interest in, almost the discovers of, the work of Herbart, and of the Prussian educators who had developed Herbartianism into a system – itself a phenomenon of some interest.

Until now, the rational foundation for pedagogical theories – for the concept of education as a science – had lain in associationist psychological theories concerning learning. These were espoused by Bain, as we have seen, and underlay his whole approach; as also by Herbart and his protagonists (or elaborators). So it was theory and practice based on these ideas which gave rise both to the positive, or optimistic, pedagogics of the 1890s relating to elementary education, and to those of the period 1900–1920 relating to the new system of secondary education. But it was just at this period that new approaches came to predominate in the field of psychology which either relegated associationism to the background, or denied its significance altogether.

The two major influences leading to the demise of associationism as a major determinant of pedagogy were, on the one hand, the rise of philosophic idealism which denied the material basis of mind and decisively rejected the model of human formation of the strict materialists of the late eighteenth century (with its emphasis on man as the passive product of external stimuli); and, on the other hand, the triumph of Darwinism with its emphasis on heredity (Murphy, 1938, pp. 109–113). With the latter is linked Galton's work (*Hereditary Genius* was published as early as 1869), the rise of the eugenics movement with its associated theories (the Eugenics Education Society was founded in 1908), and the work of the Galton Laboratory at University College, London, associated with the names of Pearson, Spearman, and later Cyril Burt. 'No request is more frequently made to the psychologist', wrote Burt in 1921, when he was educational psychologist to the London County Council, 'than the demand for a simple mental foot-rule' (Burt, 1921, p. 1). It was precisely this that the psychologists were now ready to supply.

The demands of the system and the movement of ideas now coincided. In the field of educational theory psychometry (or mental testing) now established its hegemony which lasted over forty years from the 1920s. The triumph of psychometry tied in with a new stress on individualism after World War I and a kind of reductionist biologism, both of which are central to the thinking of Sir Percy Nunn whose *Education, its Data and First Principles* was the central student manual of the interwar years.[6] For reasons which will be discussed later, this spelt the end of pedagogy – its actual death. If education cannot promote cognitive growth, as the psychometrists seemed to aver, its whole purpose or direction was lost. 'Othello's occupation gone', as Hayward, an LCC Inspector, once put it.

This, I suggest, is the background to our present discontents. For a combination of social, political and ideological reasons pedagogy – a scientific basis to the theory and practice of education – has never taken root and flourished in Britain. For a single decade in the late nineteenth century in the field of elementary education; for a similar short period early this century in secondary education, pedagogic approaches and analyses flowered – though never in the most socially prestigious system of the public schools and ancient universities. Each 'system', largely self-contained, developed its own specific educational approach, each within its narrowly defined field, and each 'appropriate' to its specific social function. In these circumstances the conditions did not, and could not, exist for the development of an all-embracing, universalised, scientific theory of education relating to the practice of teaching. Nor is it an accident that, in these circumstances, fatalistic ideas preaching the limitation of human powers were in the ascendant.

## Education and the Technological Revolution

The main objective of this [chapter] is to argue first, that we can no longer afford to go on in the old way, muddling through on a largely pragmatic, or historically institutionalised basis, tinkering with this and that, but that a really serious effort can and should now be made to clear up current confusions and dichotomies. Second, in spite of what must surely be temporary setbacks in the provision of educational facilities, the conditions now exist for a major breakthrough in terms of pedagogy. This statement is made on the basis of two contemporary developments, the one structural, the other theoretical. Of major importance here is the insistent tendency towards unification of the historically determined separate systems of schooling through the transition to comprehensive secondary education. This has been accompanied, in the realm of ideas or theory, by a shift in the concern of educators and psychologists from static concepts of the child (derived from intelligence testing) towards dynamic and complex theories of child development. Both open new perspectives relating to the grounding of educational theory and practice on science (or on scientific procedures).

## A Revitalised Pedagogy?

What, then, are the requirements for a renewal of scientific approaches to the practice of teaching – for a revitalised pedagogy?

First, we can identify two essential conditions without which there can be no pedagogy having a generalised significance or application. The first is recognition of the human capacity for learning. It may seem unnecessary, even ridiculous, to single this out in this connection, but in practice this is not the case. Fundamentally, psychometric theory, as elaborated in the 1930s to 1950s, denied the ability of learning capacity, seeing each individual as endowed, as it were, with an engine of a given horse-power which is fixed, unchangeable and measurable in each particular case, irrevocably setting precise and definable limits to achievement (or learning).[7] It was not until this view had been discredited in the eyes of psychologists that serious attention could be given to the analysis and interpretation of the *process* of human learning.

The second condition has been effectively defined by Professor Stones in his helpful and relevant book *Psychopedagogy*, sub-titled 'Psychological Theory and the Practice of Teaching' (1979). It is the recognition that in general terms, the process of learning among human beings is similar across the human species as a whole. The view on which Stones's book is based is that 'except in pathological cases, learning capability among individuals is similar', so that 'it is possible to envisage a body of general principles of teaching' that are relevant for 'most individual pupils'. The determination, or identification, of such general principles must comprise the objects of pedagogical study and research (Stones, 1979, p. 453).

One further point may be made at the start. The term 'pedagogy' itself implies structure. It implies the elaboration or definition of specific means adapted to produce the desired effect – such-and-such learning on the part of the child. From the start of the use of the term, pedagogy has been concerned to relate the process of teaching to that of learning on the part of the child. It was this approach that characterised the work of Comenius, Pestalozzi and Herbart.

Both the conditions defined above are today very widely accepted among leading psychologists directly concerned with education and with research into human cognitive development. When Bruner claimed, in a striking and well-known statement, that 'any subject can be taught to anybody at any age in some form that is both interesting and honest', he was basing himself on a positive assessment of human capacity for learning, and deliberately pointing to the need to link psychology with pedagogy. In an essay aimed at persuading American psychologists of the need to concern themselves with education – to provide assistance in elucidating the learning process for practising educators – he stressed his central point, 'that developmental psychology without a theory of pedagogy was as empty an enterprise as a theory of pedagogy that ignored the nature of growth'. 'Man is not a naked ape', writes Bruner, 'but a culture clothed human being, hopelessly ineffective without the prosthesis provided by culture'. Education itself can be a powerful cultural influence, and educational experiences ordered and structured to enable people more fully to realise their humanity and powers, to bring about social change – and so create a world according to their felt and recognised objectives. The major problem humanity faces is not the general development of skill and intelligence, but 'devising a society that can use it wisely' (Bruner, 1972, pp. 18, 131, 158).

When writing this, Bruner was clearly concerned with social change, and with the contribution that pedagogical means might make to this, as we must be in Britain in face of the dramatic social challenge that technological change now presents. And in considering the power of education, rightly ordered, to play a central part in this, it may be as well to recall that, while the simplified and certainly over-mechanist interpretations of the associationist psychologists of the nineteenth century are no longer acceptable in the form, for instance, expressed by Alexander Bain (and his predecessors), yet the concept of learning as a process involving the formation of new connections in the brain and higher nervous systems has in fact not only retained its force, but been highly developed by neuro-physiologists and psychologists specifically concerned to investigate learning. Among these, perhaps the greatest contribution has been made by A. R. Luria in a series of works relevant to teaching, education and human development generally; but perhaps particularly in his work on the role of language in mental development, and in his theory of the formation of what he calls 'complex functional systems' underlying learning (Luria, 1962).

> It is now generally accepted that in the process of mental development there takes place a profound qualitative reorganisation of human mental activity, and that the basic characteristic of this reorganisation is that elementary, direct activity is replaced by complex functional systems, formed on the basis of the child's communication with adults in the process of learning. These functional systems are of complex construction, and are developed with the close participation of language, which as the basic means of communication with people is simultaneously one of the basic tools in the formation of human mental activity and in the regulation of behaviour. It is through these complex forms of mental activity . . . that new features are acquired and begin to develop according to new laws which displace many of the laws which govern the formation of elementary conditioned reflexes in animals.

The work and thinking of both Luria and Bruner (as representative of their respective traditions) point in a similar direction – towards a renewed understanding both of the power of education to effect human change and especially cognitive development, and of the need for the systematisation and structuring of the child's experiences in the process of learning. And it is precisely from this standpoint that a critique is necessary of certain contemporary standpoints, dichotomies and ideologies, and, in particular, of the whole trend towards so-called 'child-centred' theories, which have dominated this area in Britain basically since the early 1920s, to reach its apotheosis in what is best called the 'pedagogic romanticism' of the Plowden Report, its most recent, and semi-official expression.

It may be unfashionable, among educationists, to direct attention specifically to this point, more particularly because a critique of 'progressivism' was central to the outlook expressed in the Black Papers in the late sixties and early seventies; but to make such a critique does not imply identification with the essentially philistine and a-theoretical standpoint of the Black Paperites, as I hope to establish. Indeed the dichotomies which these and other critics sought to establish, for instance between progressive and traditional approaches, between the 'formal' and 'informal', do not reflect the options now available, nor even contemporary practice as it really is.

The basic tenets of child-centred education derive in particular from the work of Froebel who held that children are endowed with certain characteristics or qualities which will mature or flower given the appropriate environment. The child develops best in a 'rich' environment. The teacher should not interfere with this process of maturation, but act as a 'guide'. The function of early education, according to Froebel, is 'to make the inner outer' (Froebel, 1912, p. 94). Hence the emphasis on spontaneity, as also on stages of development, and the concomitant concept of 'readiness' – the child will learn specific skills and mental operations only when he is 'ready'.

That there is a fundamental convergence between this view and the theories (or assumptions) embodied in Intelligence Testing has been overlooked; nevertheless it is the close similarity between both sets of views as to the nature of the child which made it possible for both to flourish together in the period following World War I and after. Intelligence Testing also embodied the view that the child is endowed with certain innate characteristics; in this case a brain and higher nervous system of a given power or force – Spearman's 'Mental Energy or Noegenetics' (Spearman, 1927), and that the process of education is concerned to actualise the given potential, that is, to activate and realise the 'inner' (in Froebel's sense). Both views in fact deny the creative function of education, the formative power of differential educational (or life) experiences. The two trends come together strikingly, for instance, in the work of Susan Isaacs who, on the one hand, firmly believed in the scientific truth of the doctrines of Intelligence Testing, and, on the other, forcefully propagated Froebelian approaches, which she considered particularly appropriate for advanced (middle-class) children with high 'intelligence' (Isaacs, 1932, pp. 25, 28–29; 1963, pp. 41–42).

The theoretical, or pedagogical stance of the Plowden Report represents an extension of these ideas. In their re-interpretation of the conclusions derived from psychometry they reject the concept of total hereditary, or genetic, determination. Development is seen as an interactional process, in which the child's encounters with the environment are crucial. Yet Plowden takes the child-centred approach to its logical limits, insisting on the principle of the complete individualisation of the teaching/learning process as the ideal (even though, from a pedagogic standpoint, this is not a practical possibility in any realistic sense). In their analysis the hereditary/environmental interactional process is interpreted as exacerbating initial differences so greatly that each child must be seen to be unique, and be treated as such. The matter is rendered even more complex by their insistence that each individual child develops at different rates across three parameters, intellectual, emotional and physical; and that in determining her approach to each individual child each of these must be taken into account by the teacher. The result is that the task set the teacher, with an average of 35 children per class when Plowden reported, is, in the words of the report itself, 'frighteningly high' (Plowden, 1967, I paras 75, 875).

I want to suggest that, by focusing on the individual child ('at the heart of the educational process lies the child'), and in developing the analysis from this point, the Plowden Committee created a situation from which it was impossible to derive an effective pedagogy (or effective pedagogical means). If each child is unique, and each requires a specific pedagogical approach appropriate to him or her and to no other, the construction of an all-embracing pedagogy, or general principles of teaching becomes an impossibility. And indeed research has shown that primary school teachers who have taken the priority of individualisation to heart, find it difficult to do more than ensure that each child is in fact engaged on the series of tasks which the teacher sets up for the child; the complex management problem which then arises takes the teacher's full energies. Hence the approach of teachers who endeavour to implement these prescripts is necessarily primarily didactic ('telling') since it becomes literally impossible to stimulate enquiry, or to 'lead from behind', as Plowden held the teacher should operate in the classroom. Even with a lower average of 30 children per class, this is far too complex and time-consuming a role for the teacher to perform.[8]

The main thrust of the argument of this chapter is this: that to start from the standpoint of individual differences is to start from the wrong position. To develop effective pedagogy means starting from the opposite standpoint, from what children have in common as members of the human species; to establish the general principles of teaching and, in the light of these, to determine what modifications of practice are necessary to meet specific individual needs. If all children are to be assisted to learn, to master increasingly complex cognitive tasks, to develop increasingly complex skills and abilities or mental operations, then this is an objective that schools must have in common; their task becomes the deliberate development of such skills and abilities in all their children. And this involves importing a definite structure into the teaching, and so into the learning experiences provided for the pupils. Individual differences only become important, in this context, if the pedagogical means elaborated are found not to be appropriate to particular children (or groups of children) because of one or other aspect of their individual development or character. In this situation the requirement becomes that of modifying the pedagogical means so that they become appropriate for all; that is, of applying general principles in specific instances.

What is suggested here is that the starting point for constructing the curriculum, or children's activities in school, insofar as we are concerned with cognitive development (the schools may reasonably have other aims as well) lies in definition of the objectives of teaching, which forms the ground base from which pedagogical means are defined and established, means or principles which underlie specific methodological (or experiential) approaches. It may well be that these include the use of co-operative group work as well as individualised activities – but these are carefully designed and structured in relation to the achievement of overall objectives. This approach, I am arguing, is the opposite of basing the educational process on the child, on his immediate interests and spontaneous activity, and providing, in theory, for a total differentiation of the learning process in the case of each individual child. This latter approach is not only undesirable in principle, it is impossible of achievement in practice.[9]

In a striking phrase Lev Vygotsky summed up his outlook on teaching and learning. Pedagogy, he wrote, 'must be oriented not towards the yesterday of development but towards its tomorrow'. Teaching, education, pedagogic means, must always take the child forward, be concerned with the formation of new concepts and hierarchies or concepts, with the next stage in the development of a particular ability, with ever more complex forms of mental operations. 'What the child can do today with adult help', he said, 'he will be able to do independently tomorrow.' This concept, that of the 'zone of next (or "potential") development' implies in the educator a clear concept of the progression of learning, of a consistent challenge, of the mastery by the child of increasingly complex forms – of never standing still or going backwards. 'The only good teaching is that which outpaces development', insisted Vygotsky.[10] Whether the area is that of language development, of concepts of number and mathematics – symbolic systems that underlie all further learning or whether it covers scientific and technological concepts and skills as well as those related to the social sciences and humanities, appropriate pedagogical means can and should be defined, perhaps particularly in areas having their own inner logical structures. In this sense, psychological knowledge combined with logical analysis forms the ground base from which pedagogical principles can be established, given, of course, effective research and experiment.

This chapter has been strictly concerned with cognitive development, since it is here that technological/scientific and social changes will make their greatest impact and demands. But for successful implementation of rational procedures and planning, in the face of the micro-processor revolution, more than this needs consideration. There is also the question, for instance, of the individual's enhanced responsibility for his own activities; the development of autonomy, of initiative, creativity, critical awareness; the need on the part of the mass of the population for access to knowledge and culture, the arts and literature, to mention only some aspects of human development. The means of promoting such human qualities and characteristics cannot simply be left to individual teachers, on the grounds that each individual child is unique so that the development of a pedagogy is both impracticable and superfluous. The existing teaching force of half a million have, no doubt, many talents, but they need assistance in the pursuit of their common objective the education of new generations of pupils. The new pedagogy requires carefully defined goals, structure, and adult guidance. Without this a high proportion of children, whose concepts are formed as a result of their everyday experiences, and, as a result, are often distorted and incorrectly reflect reality, will never even reach the stage where the development of higher cognitive forms of activity becomes a possibility. And this implies a massive cognitive failure in terms of involvement and control (responsible participation) in the new social forms and activities which the future may bring.

## Notes

1. The English failure to take pedagogy seriously is stressed in an article on the subject in an educational encyclopaedia of a century ago. Interest in pedagogy 'is not held in much honour among us English'. The lack of a professional approach to teaching means that 'pedagogy is with us at a discount'. This, it is held, 'is unquestionably a most grievous national loss . . . Without something like scientific discussion on educational subjects, without pedagogy, we shall never obtain a body of organised opinion on education' (Fletcher, 1889, pp. 257–258).

2. An exception here was R. H. Quick, author of *Essays On Educational Reformers* (1869), a public schoolmaster himself who fought hard for professional training and who appears to have been largely instrumental in setting up the Cambridge Syndicate which organised (prematurely) the first systematic set of lectures on education in an English university; those delivered at Cambridge in 1879–1880 (see Storr, 1889, pp. 349–388). For a young teacher's experience of 'learning on the job' in the 1930s see Worsley, 1967, Chapter 1.

3. See, for instance, Arnold (1874) which devotes a lengthy chapter to the professional training of schoolmasters for the *gymnasia* and *realschule* in Prussia (Chapter 5).

4. I have analysed developments in this period in detail in Simon (1965).

5. See especially Legge (1929) on Liverpool, and Gosden and Sharp (1978, pp. 77 ff.) on the West Riding.

6. Percy Nunn was Principal of the University of London Institute of Education from 1922 to 1936. His textbook went through over 20 reprintings between its publication in 1920 and 1940; it was required reading for many graduates training as teachers. For an acute critique of Nunn's biologism, see Gordon and White (1979, pp. 207–213).

7. This position is concisely reflected in a statement by Cyril Bun in 1950: 'Obviously in an ideal community, our aim should be to discover what ration of intelligence nature has given to each individual child at birth, then to provide him with an appropriate education, and finally to guide him into the career for which he seems to have been marked out' (Burt, 1950).

8. These points are argued in detail, supported by empirical evidence derived from systematic classroom observation, in Galton, Simon and Croll (1980).

9. For a critique of this approach by a psychologist who has worked closely with Piaget (regarded as the authority for individualisation, for instance, in the Plowden Report), see Duckworth (1979).

10. See Vygotsky, 1963; see also Vygotsky, 1962, 1967. For Vygotsky's views on education, 'Teaching and Development: a Soviet Investigation', Special Issue of *Soviet Education*. Vol. 19, nos. 4–6, 1977.

## References

Arnold, M. (2nd edn 1874) *High Schools and Universities In Germany*, London, Macmillan.

Bain, A. (1879) *Education as a Science*, London, Kegan Paul.

Bruner, J. S. (1972) *The Relevance of Education*, London, Allen & Unwin.

Burt, C. (1921) *Mental and Scholastic Tests*, London, Staples Press.

Burt, C. (1950) 'Testing intelligence', *The Listener*, 16 November.

Duckworth, E. (1979) 'Either we're too early and they can't learn it or we're too late and they know it already: The dilemma of "applying Piaget"', *Harvard Educational Review*, 49, 3.

Fletcher, A. E. (ed.) (2nd edn 1889) *Cyclopaedia of Education*, Swan Sonnenschein.

Galton, M., Simon, B. and Croll, P. (1980) *Inside the Primary Classroom*, London, Routledge & Kegan Paul.

Gordon, P. and White, J. (1979) *Philosophers as Educational Reformers*, London, Routledge & Kegan Paul.

Froebel, F. (1912) *The Education of Man*, New York & London, Appleton.

Gosden, P. H. J. H. and Sharp, P. R. (1978) *The Development of an Education Service the West Riding 1889–1974*, Oxford, Martin Robertson.

Honey, J. R. de S. (1977) *Tom Brown's Universe*, London, Millington.

Isaacs, S. (1932) *The Children We Teach: 7 to 11 Years*, London, University of London Press.

Isaacs, S. (1963) *The Psychological Aspects of Child Development*, London, Evans.

Legge, J. G. (1929) *The Rising Tide*, Oxford, Blackwell.

Luria, A. R. (1962) *Voprosy Psikhologii* 1962, 4.

Murphy, G. (1938) *Historical Introduction to Modern Psychology*, New York, Harcourt, Brace.

Plowden Report, the (1967) *Children and their Primary Schools*, London, HMSO.

Quick, R. H. (1869) *Essays on Educational Reformers*, London, Longmans Green.

Simon, B (1965) *Education and the Labour Movement, 1870–1920*, London, Lawrence & Wishart.

Spearman, C. (1927) *The Nature of 'Intelligence' and the Principles of Cognition*, London, Macmillan.

Stones, E (1979) *Psychopedagogy: Psychological Theory and the Practice of Teaching*, London, Methuen.

Storr, F. (ed.) (1889) *Life and Remains of the Rev. R. H. Quick*, Cambridge, Cambridge University Press.

Vygotsky, L. S. (1962) *Thought and Language*, London, Wiley.

— (1963) 'Learning and mental development at school age', in B. Simon and J. Simon (eds) *Educational Psychology in the USSR*, London, Routledge & Kegan Paul.

— (1967) Vygotskyan Memorial Issue of *Soviet Psychology and Psychiatry*, 5, 3.

Worsley, T. C. (1967) *Flannelled Fools*, London, Alan Ross.

# 4

# Pedagogy, Culture, Language, and Race: A Dialogue

## Paulo Freire and Donaldo P. Macedo

The following is part of an ongoing dialogue that Donaldo Macedo and Paulo Freire have been having since 1983. [T]his dialogue not only challenges the frequent misinterpretations of his leading philosophical ideas by conservative and some liberal educators, but also embrace[s] contemporary educational issues [discussing] what it means to educate for critical citizenry in the ever-increasing multiracial and multicultural world of the twenty-first century.

*MACEDO:* In their attempt to cut the chains of oppressive educational practices, many North American educators blindly advocate the dialogical model, creating, in turn, a new form of methodological rigidity laced with benevolent oppression – all done under the guise of democracy with the sole excuse that it is for the students' own good. As educators, many of us have witnessed pedagogical contexts in which we are implicitly or explicitly required to speak, to talk about our experiences, as an act of liberation. We all have been at conferences where speakers have been chastised because they failed to locate themselves in history. In other words, the speakers failed to give primacy to their experiences in addressing issues of critical democracy. It does not matter that the speakers had important and insightful things to say. [. . .] Another form of rigidity manifested in these educational practices modeled on your leading ideas is the process in which teachers relinquish their authority to become what is called a facilitator. Becoming a facilitator signals, in the view of many educators, a democratization of power in the classroom. Can you speak about these issues and perhaps clarify them?

*FREIRE:* Donaldo, let me begin responding by categorically saying that I consider myself a teacher and always a teacher. I have never pretended to be a facilitator. What I want to make clear also is in being a teacher, I always teach to facilitate. I cannot accept the notion of a facilitator who facilitates so as not to teach.

The true comprehension of dialogue must differentiate the role that only facilitates from the role that teaches. When teachers call themselves

---

This chapter has been edited

facilitators and not teachers, they become involved in a distortion of reality. To begin with, in de-emphasizing the teacher's power by claiming to be a facilitator, one is being less than truthful to the extent that the teacher turned facilitator maintains the power institutionally created in the position. That is, while facilitators may veil their power, at any moment they can exercise power as they wish. The facilitator still grades, still has certain control over the curriculum, and to deny these facts is to be disingenuous. I think what creates this need to be a facilitator is the confusion between authoritarianism and authority. What one cannot do in trying to divest of authoritarianism is relinquish one's authority as teacher. In fact, this does not really happen. Teachers maintain a certain level of authority through the depth and breadth of knowledge of the subject matter that they teach. The teacher who claims to be a facilitator and not a teacher is renouncing, for reasons unbeknownst to us, the task of teaching and, hence, the task of dialogue.

Another point worth making is the risk of perceiving facilitators as nondirective. I find this to be a deceitful discourse; that is, a discourse from the perspective of the dominant class. Only in this deceitful discourse can educators talk about a lack of direction in teaching. I do not think that there is real education without direction. To the extent that all educational practice brings with it its own transcendence, it presupposes an objective to be reached. Therefore, practice cannot be nondirective. There is no educational practice that does not point to an objective; this proves that the nature of educational practice has direction. The facilitator who claims that 'since I respect students I cannot be directive, and since they are individuals deserving respect, they should determine their own direction', does not deny the directive nature of education that is independent of his own subjectivity. Rather, this facilitator denies himself or herself the pedagogical, political, and epistemological task of assuming the role of a subject of that directive practice. This facilitator refuses to convince his or her learners of what he or she thinks is just. This educator, then, ends up helping the power structure. To avoid reproducing the values of the power structure, the educator must always combat a laissez-faire pedagogy, no matter how progressive it may appear to be.

Authoritarian educators are correct, even though they are not always theoretically explicit, when they say that there is no education that is nondirective. I would not disagree with these educators; but, I would say that no claim to be a facilitator is authoritarian to the extent that the facilitators make their own objectives and dreams the directives that they give to learners in their educational practice. Facilitators are authoritarian because, as subjects of the educational practice, they reduce learners to objects of the directives they impose.

While educators divest of an authoritarian educational practice, they should avoid falling prey to a laissez-faire practice under the pretext of facilitating. On the contrary, a better way to proceed is to assume the authority as a teacher whose direction of education includes helping learners get involved in planning education, helping them create the critical capacity to consider and participate in the direction and dreams of education, rather than merely following blindly. The role of an educator who is pedagogically and critically radical is to avoid being indifferent, a characteristic of the facilitator who promotes a laissez-faire education. The radical educator has to be an active presence in educational practice. But, educators should never allow their active and curious presence to transform the learners' presence into a shadow of the educator's presence. Nor can educators be a shadow of their learners. The educator who dares to teach has to stimulate learners to live a critically conscious presence in the pedagogical and historical process.

*MACEDO:* I believe that to renounce the task of teaching under the guise of facilitating is part and parcel of a paternalistic ideology.

*FREIRE:* Exactly. The true issue behind the act of facilitating remains veiled because of its ideological nature. In the end, the facilitator is renouncing his or her duty to teach – which is a dialogical duty. In truth, the teacher turned facilitator rejects the fantastic work of placing an object as a mediator between him or her and the students. That is, the facilitator fails to assume his or her role as a dialogical educator who can illustrate the object of study. As a teacher, I have the responsibility to teach, and in order to teach, I always try to facilitate. In the first place, I am convinced that when we speak of dialogue and education, we are speaking, above all, about practices that enable us to approach the object of knowledge. In order to begin to understand the meaning of a dialogical practice, we have to put aside the simplistic understanding of dialogue as a mere technique. Dialogue does not represent a somewhat false path that I attempt to elaborate on and realize in the sense of involving the ingenuity of the other. On the contrary, dialogue characterizes an epistemological relationship. Thus, in this sense, dialogue is a way of knowing and should never be viewed as a mere tactic to involve students in a particular task. We have to make this point very clear. I engage in dialogue not necessarily because I like the other person. I engage in dialogue because I recognize the social and not merely the individualistic character of the process of knowing. In this sense, dialogue presents itself as an indispensable component of the process of both learning and knowing.

*MACEDO:* I could not agree with you more. I am reminded of how educators who embrace your notion of dialogue mechanistically reduce the epistemological relationship of dialogue to a vacuous, feel-good comfort zone. For instance, in a graduate class I taught last semester in which we discussed extensively an anti-racist pedagogy, many White teachers felt uncomfortable when the non-White students made connections between the assigned theoretical readings and their own lived experience with racism. In discussing her feelings of discomfort, a White teacher remarked that 'we should spend at least three weeks getting to know each other so as to become friends before taking on sensitive issues such as racism'. In other words, this White teacher failed to recognize her privileged position that enabled her to assume she can negotiate the terms under which classmates from oppressed groups can state their grievances. It is as if in order to be able to speak the truth about racism or to denounce racist structures, non-Whites must first befriend their White classmates. The inability of this White teacher to acknowledge her privileged position in demanding to negotiate her comfort zone before grievances against racism are made makes her unable to realize that, in most instances, certain groups such as African Americans are born and live always without any comfort zone, much less the privilege to assume they can negotiate the appropriate comfort zone within a graduate course.

*FREIRE:* All of this leads us to consider another dimension that is implicit, but not always clear, in relation to the concept of dialogue. That is to say, the dialogue about which we are now speaking, the dialogue that educators speak about, is not the same as the dialogue about a walk up the street, for example, which becomes no more than the object of mere conversation with friends in a bar. In this case, people are not necessarily engaged in a search for the delimitation of a knowable object. Here I am speaking with respect to dialogue in a strictly epistemological perspective. What then does dialogue require as a sine qua non condition?

*MACEDO:* If in this sense the object of knowledge is the fundamental goal, the dialogue as conversation about individuals' lived experiences does not truly constitute dialogue. In other words, the appropriation of the notion of dialogical teaching as a process of sharing experiences creates a situation in which teaching is reduced to a form of group therapy that focuses on the psychology of the individual. [. . .] Simply put, I do not think that the sharing of experiences should be understood in psychological terms only. It invariably requires a political and ideological analysis as well. That is, the sharing of experiences must always be understood within a social praxis that entails both reflection and political action. In short, dialogue as a process of learning and knowing must always involve a political project with the objective of dismantling oppressive structures and mechanisms prevalent both in education and society.

Part of the reason why many teachers who claim to be Freire-inspired end up promoting a laissez-faire, feel-good pedagogy is because many are only exposed to, or interpret, your leading ideas at the level of cliché. By this I mean that many professors who claim to be Freire-inspired present to their students a watered-down translation of your philosophical positions in the form of a lock-step methodology. Seldom do these professors require their students to read your work as a primary source and, in cases where they do read, let's say, *Pedagogy of the Oppressed*, they often have very little knowledge of other books that you have published. For example, I have been in many educational contexts throughout the country where students ask me, 'Why is it that my professors are always talking about Freire and the dialogical method and yet they never ask us to read Freire?'

This point was made poignant some time ago in a workshop when a teacher began the presentation of her project by saying, 'My project is Freirean inspired. I'll be talking about Freire even though I haven't read his books yet'. Assigning students secondary or tertiary sources is very common within education programs in the United States. The end result is that professors become translators of the primary source's leading ideas. In so doing, they elevate their status by introducing translated materials that students almost blindly consume as innovative and progressive and, in some instances, also begin to identify these translated ideas with the professor-translator and not with the original author. This occurs because students have been cut off from the primary source. On the other hand, the professor-translator assumes falsely that the primary source is too difficult for students, which points to the paternalistic notion that future teachers are not capable of engaging with complex, theoretical readings. This false assumption leads, unfortunately, to the total deskilling of teachers in that it kills epistemological curiosity.

*FREIRE:* You are absolutely correct. I think that your posture indicates clearly that you understand very well the difference between dialogue as a process of learning and knowing and dialogue as conversation that mechanically focuses on the individual's lived experience, which remains strictly within the psychological sphere.

*MACEDO:* In the United States, even many educators who like your work mistakenly transform your notion of dialogue into a method, thus losing sight of the fact that the fundamental goal of dialogical teaching is to create a process of learning and knowing that invariably involves theorizing about the experiences shared in the dialogue process. [. . .] By overindulging in the legacy and importance of their respective voices and experiences, these educators often fail to move beyond a notion of difference structured in polarizing binarisms and uncritical appeals to the discourse of experience. I believe that it is for this reason that some of these educators invoke a romantic pedagogical mode that exoticizes discussing lived experiences as a process of coming to voice. At the same time, educators who misinterpret your notion of dialogical teaching also refuse to link experiences to the politics of culture and critical democracy, thus reducing their pedagogy to a form of middle-class narcissism. This creates, on the one hand, the transformation of dialogical teaching into a method invoking conversation that provides participants with a group therapy space for stating their grievances. On the other hand, it offers the teacher as facilitator a safe pedagogical zone to deal with his or her class guilt. It is a process that bell hooks characterizes as nauseating in that it brooks no dissent.

*FREIRE:* Yes, yes. In the end, what these educators are calling dialogical is a process that hides the true nature of dialogue as a process of learning and knowing. What you have described can provide certain dialogical moments, but, in general, it is a mere conversation overly focused on the individual and removed from the object of knowledge. Understanding dialogue as a process of learning and knowing establishes a previous requirement that always involves an epistemological curiosity about the very elements of the dialogue.

*MACEDO:* I agree; there has to be a curiosity about the object of knowledge. Otherwise, you end up with dialogue as conversation, where individual lived experiences are given primacy. I have been in many contexts where the over-celebration of one's own location and history often eclipses the possibility of engaging the object of knowledge by refusing to struggle directly, for instance, with the readings, particularly if these readings involve theory.

*FREIRE:* Yes. Curiosity about the object of knowledge and the willingness and openness to engage theoretical readings and discussions is fundamental. However, I am not suggesting an over-celebration of theory. We must not negate practice for the sake of theory. To do so would reduce theory to pure verbalism or intellectualism. By the same token, to negate theory for the sake of practice, as in the use of dialogue as conversation, is to run the risk of losing oneself in the disconnectedness of practice. It is for this reason that I never advocate either a theoretic elitism or a practice ungrounded in theory, but the unity between theory and practice. In order to achieve this unity, one must have an epistemological curiosity – a curiosity that is often missing in dialogue as conversation.

Returning to my original point, I would like to reiterate that human beings are, by nature, curious beings. They are ontologically curious. In order to be more rigorous, I would venture to say that curiosity is not a phenomenon exclusively human, but exclusively vital. That is, life is curious, without which life cannot survive. Curiosity is as fundamental to our survival as is pain. Without the ability to feel pain, and I am here referring to physical pain and not moral pain, we could possibly jump from a fourth-floor apartment without anticipating the consequences. The same would be true if we put our hands in fire. Pain represents one of the physical limitations on our practices. Thus, dialogue, as a process of learning and knowing, presupposes curiosity. It implies curiosity.

Teachers who engage in an educational practice without curiosity, allowing their students to avoid engagement with critical readings, are not involved in dialogue as a process of learning and knowing. They are involved, instead, in a conversation without the ability to turn the shared experiences and stories into knowledge. What I call epistemological curiosity is the readiness and eagerness of a conscious body that is open to the task of engaging an object of knowledge.

The other curiosity without which we could not live is what I call spontaneous curiosity. That is, along the lines of aesthetics, I may find myself before a beautiful tall building and I spontaneously exclaim its beauty. This curiosity does not have as its fundamental objective the apprehension and the understanding of the raison d'etre of this beauty. In this case, I am gratuitously curious.

As you pointed out earlier, Donaldo, one of the difficulties often con-
fronted by an educator in assuming an epistemologically curious posture is
that, at certain moments, the educator falls prey to the bureaucratization of
the mind, becoming a pure methodologist. The bureaucratized educator is
the one who assigns time slots for students to take turns speaking in a
bureaucratized, if not vulgarized, democracy without any connection with
the object of knowledge. In this case, the educator turned facilitator becomes mechanical, mechanizing the entire dialogue as a process of learning
and knowing so as to make it a mechanical dialogue as conversation. In a
bureaucratized dialogue as conversation, both students and teacher speak
and speak, all convinced that they are engaged in a substantive educational
practice just because they are all participating in an unknown bureaucratized discourse that is not connected to an object of knowledge. This
pattern is not dialogical because you cannot have dialogue without a posture that is epistemologically curious. The educator who wants to be dialogical cannot relinquish his or her authority as a teacher, which requires
epistemological curiosity, to become a facilitator who merely orchestrates
the participation of students in pure verbalism.

*MACEDO:* This bureaucratized dialogical process orchestrated by the facilitator who falsely relinquishes his or her authority as teacher ends up
being a process that gives rise to politics without content.

*FREIRE:* In my view, each class is a class through which both students and
teachers engage in a search for the knowledge already obtained so they can
adopt a dialogical posture as a response to their epistemological inquietude
that forces the revision of what is already known so they can know it better.
At the same time, it is not easy to be a dialogical teacher because it entails a
lot of work. What is easy is to be a pure descriptivist.

*MACEDO:* You can also have the other extreme: A descriptive dialogue.

*FREIRE:* Of course you can.

*MACEDO:* This is what happens a lot with those teachers who relinquish
their authority in order to become facilitators and, in the process, impose
their bureaucratized dialogical method in a rigid manner that may require,
for example, that all students must speak even if they choose not to do so.
This rigidity transforms dialogical teaching, not into a search for the object
of knowledge, but into a superficial form of democracy in which all students must forcefully participate in a turn-taking task of 'blah-blah-blah'. I
have had the experience of students suggesting to me that I should monitor
the length of time students talk in class in order to insure equal participation for all students. In most instances, these suggestions are raised without
any concern that the turn-at-talk be related to the assigned readings. In
fact, in many cases, students go through great lengths to over-emphasize
the process of turn-taking while de-emphasizing the critical apprehension
of the object of knowledge. In the end, their concerns attempt to reduce
dialogue to a pure technique. I want to make it clear that in criticizing the

mechanization of turn-at-talk I do not intend to ignore the voices that have been silenced by the inflexible, traditional method of lecturing. What is important to keep in mind is not to develop a context whereby the assignment of turn-taking to give voice to students results in a new form of rigid imposition. Instead, it is important to create pedagogical structures that foster critical engagement as the only way for the students to come to voice. The uncritical license to take equal turns speaking in a rigid fashion gives rise to a 'blah-blah-blah' dialogue resulting in a form of silencing while speaking. Critical educators should avoid at all costs the blind embracing of approaches that pay lip-service to democracy and should always be open to multiple and varied approaches that will enhance the possibility for epistemological curiosity with the object of knowledge. The facile and uncritical acceptance of any methodology regardless of its progressive promise can easily be transformed into a new form of methodological rigidity that constitutes, in my view, a form of methodological terrorism. A vacuous dialogue for conversation only is pernicious to the extent that it deskills students by not creating pedagogical spaces for epistemological curiosity, critical consciousness, and agency, which is the only way through which one can transcend valorized experience to embrace new knowledge in order to universalize one's own experience.

*FREIRE:* Exactly. This is where dialogical teaching ceases to be a true process of learning and knowing to become, instead, pure formalism; everything but dialogue. It represents a process to bureaucratize the mind. The educator who is really dialogical has a tiring task to the extent that he or she has to 1) remain epistemologically curious, and 2) practice in a way that involves epistemological curiosity that facilitates his or her process of learning and knowing. The problem lies in the fact that students often have not sufficiently developed such habits. It is for this reason that many students end up reading only mechanically and can easily spend an entire semester doing so because they were not able to transcend the spontaneity of curiosity you spoke of earlier so as to engage the epistemological curiosity that involves methodological rigor. Students today find it difficult to engage in this type of educational rigor precisely because they are often not challenged to engage in a rigorous process of learning and knowing. The end result is that they often remain at the periphery of the object of knowledge. Their curiosity has not yet been awakened in the epistemological sense. It is for this reason that we now witness more and more a disequilibrium between chronological age and epistemological curiosity. In many cases, epistemological curiosity remains truncated, giving rise to students who are intellectually immature.

What dialogical educators must do is to maintain, on the one hand, their epistemological curiosity and, on the other hand, always attempt to increase their critical reflection in the process of creating pedagogical spaces where students become apprentices in the rigors of exploration. Without an increased level of epistemological curiosity and the necessary apprenticeship in a new body of knowledge, students cannot truly be engaged in a dialogue.

*MACEDO:* I think this is a very important point that needs to be highlighted. That is, when students lack both the necessary epistemological curiosity and a certain conviviality with the object of knowledge under study, it is difficult to create conditions that increase their epistemological curiosity so as to develop the necessary intellectual tools that will enable them to apprehend and comprehend the object of knowledge. If students are not able to transform their lived experiences into knowledge and to use the already acquired knowledge as a process to unveil new knowledge, they will never be able to participate rigorously in a dialogue as a process of learning and knowing. In truth, how can you dialogue without any prior apprenticeship with the object of knowledge and without any epistemological curiosity? For example, how can you dialogue about linguistics if the teacher refuses to create the pedagogical conditions that will apprentice students into the new body of knowledge? By this I do not mean that the apprenticeship process should be reduced to the authoritarian tradition of lecturing without student input and discussion.

*FREIRE:* As you can see, Donaldo, my pedagogical posture always implies rigor, and never a laissez-faire dialogue as conversation orchestrated by facilitators. A mere appearance does not transform itself into the concreteness and substanticity of the actual object. Then, you cannot realistically have a dialogue by simply thinking that dialogue is a kind of verbal ping-pong about one's historical location and lived experiences.

*MACEDO:* Unfortunately, that is what happens too frequently.

*FREIRE:* The problem that is posed concerning the question of location is important. I do not think that anyone can seriously engage in a search for new knowledge without using his or her point of view and historical location as a point of departure. This does not mean, however, that I should remain frozen in that location, but, rather, that I should seek to universalize it. The task of epistemological curiosity is to help students gain a rigorous understanding of their historical location so they can turn this understanding into knowledge, thus transcending and universalizing it. If one remains stuck in his or her historical location, he or she runs the risk of fossilizing his or her world disconnected from other realities.

[. . .]

*MACEDO:* Paulo, if you don't mind, I would like to turn at this point to what I believe to be one of the most pressing educational challenges we face as we approach the end of this century. I would like to turn to the issue of multiculturalism. You mentioned to me a talk you gave in Jamaica where you stressed the need to find unity in diversity. How do you propose to achieve this noble goal when multicultural conflicts are intensifying everywhere?

*FREIRE:* A very first step is to understand the nature of multicultural coexistence so as to minimize the glaring ignorance of the cultural other. Part of this understanding implies a thorough understanding of the history that engenders these cultural differences. We need to understand that: a) there are intercultural differences that exist due to the presence of such factors as class, race, and gender and, as an extension of these, you have national differences; and b) these differences generate ideologies that, on the one hand, support discriminatory practices and, on the other hand, create resistance.

The culture that is discriminated against does not generate the discriminatory ideology. Discrimination is generally generated by the hegemonic culture. The discriminated culture may give rise to an ideology of resistance that, as a function of its experience with struggle, adopts cultural behavior patterns that are more or less pacifist. In other instances, resistance is manifested in rebellious forms that are more or less indiscriminately violent. However, sometimes resistance emerges as a critical reflection leading toward the re-creation of the world. There is an important point that needs to be underlined: to the extent that these relations between these ideologies are dialectical, they interpenetrate each other. These relations do not take place in pure form and they can change from person to person. For example, I can be a man as I am and not necessarily be a *machista*. I can be Black, but in defending my economic interests, I might become complicit with White discrimination.

[. . .]

[*FREIRE:*] These ideologies, whether discriminatory or resistant, embody themselves in special forms of social or individual behavior that vary from context to context. These ideologies express themselves in language – in the syntax and the semantics – and also in concrete forms of acting, of choosing, of valuing, of dressing, and even in the way one says hello on the street. These relations are dialectical. The level of these relations, their contents, their maximum dose of power revealed in the superior air one demonstrates, the distance, the coldness with which those in power treat those without power, the greater or lesser degree of accommodation or rebellion with which the dominated people respond to oppression – all of these are fundamental in the sense of overcoming the discriminatory ideologies so we can live in utopia; no more discrimination, no more rebelliousness or accommodation, but Unity in Diversity.

It is impossible to think, however, of overcoming oppression, discrimination, passivity, or pure rebellion without first acquiring a critical comprehension of history in which these intercultural relations take place in a dialectical form. Thus, they are contradictory and part of a historical process. Second, we cannot think of overcoming oppression without political pedagogical projects that point to the transformation or the reinvention of the world.

Let's speak a little about the first question, the comprehension of the history that we have. As historical beings, our actions are not merely historical, but also are historically conditioned. Sometimes, without wanting to, in acting we are consciously clear with respect to the conception of history that defines us. Hence, I recognize the importance of discussions in courses of teacher preparation concerning the different ways we comprehend history that makes us as we make it.

Let's talk succinctly of some different ways we reflect on our presence in the world and in which we find ourselves. One way of seeing ourselves is as spiritual beings, endowed with reason and the ability to make judgements, capable of distinguishing between good and bad, marked by original sin, thus needing to avoid at all costs falling into sin. From this perspective, falling into sin is viewed as always being preceded by strong temptations and the research for the road to salvation. Here sin and its negation become such that the former signals absolute weakness and the latter a facile cry of victory, in which human existence, reduced to this struggle, ends up almost losing itself in the fear of freedom or in the Puritanical hypocrisy that is a form of staying with the ugliness and rejecting the beauty of purity. History, in truth, is the history of the search for the beauty of purity, the salvation of the soul through the escape from sin. The prayers, the penitences, and promises are the principal arms and fundamental methods of action for those who idealistically experiment with this conception of history. Liberation theology signifies a radical rupture with this magical-mystical religiosity discussed above and, by putting its roots in the concrete context of experiences of women and men, God's people, it speaks of another comprehension of history that is, in reality, made by us. According to this interpretation of history, God is a presence. However, his presence does not prevent people from making their own history. On the contrary, God pushes people not only to make history, but to do so without negating the rights of others just because they are different from us.

With relation to the future, I would like to highlight two other comprehensions of history. Both are immobilizing and deterministic. The first has in the future a mere repetition of the present. In general, this is how the dominant class thinks. The tomorrow for them is always their present, as dominance is reproduced only with adverbial alterations. There is no place in this historical conception for a substantive overcoming of racial, sexual, linguistic, and cultural discrimination.

Blacks continue to be considered inferior, but now they can sit anywhere on the bus . . . Latin Americans are good people, but they are not practical . . . Maris is an excellent young woman; she is Black *but* she is intelligent . . . In the three examples, the adversative co-function *but* is impregnated with ideology that is authoritarianly racist and discriminatory.

Another conception of history is, just as much as the others, at very least conditioned by practices regardless of the area. The cultural, educational, and economic relations among nations, and the environmental, scientific, technological, artistic, and communication areas reduce the tomorrow to a given fact. The future is predetermined, a type of fate, of destiny. The future is not problematic. On the contrary, it is unyielding. The dialectic that this vision of history reclaims, and has its origin in a certain Marxist dogmatism, is the domesticated dialectics. We know synthesis before we experience the dialectical collision between thesis and antithesis.

Another way of understanding history is to submit it to the caprice of individual will. The individual, from whom the social is dependent, is the subject of history. His or her conscience is the arbitrary maker of history. For this reason, the better education shapes individuals, that much better are their hearts, that much more will they who are full of beauty make the ugly world become beautiful. According to this vision of history, the role of women and men in the world is to take care of their hearts, leaving out, untouched, the social structures.

I see history exactly as do the liberation theologians, among whom I feel very good, and am in total disagreement with the other comprehensions of history I have discussed. For me, history represents a time of possibilities and not determinism. And if it is a time of possibilities, the first conse-quence that comes to the fore is that history does not only exist, but also requires freedom. To struggle for freedom is possible when we insert our-selves in history so as to make ourselves equally possible. Instead of being the constant persecutor of sin in order to be saved, we need to view history as possibility so we can both liberate and save ourselves. This is possible only through a historical perspective in which men and women are capable of assuming themselves, as both objects and subjects of history, capable of reinventing the world in an ethical and aesthetic mold beyond the cultural patterns that exist. This makes sense when we discuss communication as a new phase of continuous change and innovation. This, then, necessitates the recognition of the political nature of this struggle.

To think of history as possibility is to recognize education as possibility. It is to recognize that if education cannot do everything, it can achieve some things. Its strength, as I usually say, resides in its weakness. One of our challenges as educators is to discover what historically is possible in the sense of contributing toward the transformation of the world, giving rise to a world that is rounder, less angular, more humane, and in which one prepares the materialization of the great Utopia: Unity in Diversity.

*MACEDO:* After your public lecture at Harvard University in November of 1994, an African American woman talked impatiently to me inquiring why it is that your work on liberation struggles does not ever address the race issue in general, and the African American plight in particular. Can you address this criticism and attempt to clarify how your pedagogy takes on the role of race in liberation struggles?

*FREIRE:* In the first place, when I wrote the *Pedagogy of the Oppressed*, I tried to understand and analyze the phenomenon of oppression with re-spect to its social, existential, and individual tendencies. In doing so, I did not focus specifically on oppression marked by specificities such as color, gender, race, and so forth. I was extremely more preoccupied with the oppressed as a social class. But this, in my view, does not at all mean that I was ignoring the racial oppression that I have denounced always and strug-gled against even as a child. My mother used to tell me that when I was a child, I used to react aggressively, not physically, but linguistically, against any manifestation of racial discrimination. Throughout my life, I have worked against all forms of racial oppression, which is in keeping with my desire and need to maintain coherence with my political posture. I could not write on the defense of the oppressed while being a racist, just as I could not be a *machista* either.

In the second place, I would like to point out that today I have spoken and written a great deal about the question of race in my deep quest to fight against any form of discrimination. You need to keep in mind that my work is not limited to the *Pedagogy of the Oppressed*, and that all my writings are not available in English. It is exactly because of my growing awareness over the years concerning the specificities of oppression along the lines of language, race, gender, and ethnicity that I have been defending the fundamental thesis of Unity of Diversity, so that the various oppressed groups can become more effective in their collective struggle against all forms of oppression. To the extent that each specificity of oppression contains itself within its historical location and accepts the profile that was created by the oppressor, it becomes that much more difficult to launch an effective fight that will lead to victory. For example, when the oppressors speak of the minorities, in this process they hide the basic element of oppression. The label 'minority' distorts and falsifies the reality if we keep in mind that the so-called minorities actually constitute the majority, while the oppressors generally represent the dominant ideology of a minority.

*MACEDO:* This is how language is used to distort reality so as to make social discrimination invisible. The same ideological mechanisms operate with the label *people of color*, which has even been embraced by many racial and ethnic groups to designate themselves. By calling non-White racial and ethnic groups 'people of color', one is proposing that white is not a color, even though colorless white as a proposition is a semantic impossibility. Ideologically, 'people of color' functions as a mechanism to make 'White' as an ideological category invisible. However, it is precisely through this invisibility that the dominant White supremacy makes the ideological distinction against which all non-White groups are measured so as to be devalued and denigrated. This process facilitates the continued dance with bigotry without having to take responsibility for the poisonous effects of racism.

*FREIRE:* You are absolutely right. That is why I argue that the oppressed groups cannot and should not accept the dominant class's categorization of them as 'minority' and, in the process, remain divided along race, class, gender, language, and ethnicity lines. Such divisions may lead not only to a form of essentialism, but also make it more difficult for these groups to dismantle the oppressive structures that rob them of their humanity. By noting this, I do not want to minimize the specific historical location of oppression. In fact, it is only through one's historical location that one is able to develop the critical tools to understand the globality of oppression. What I want to make very clear to all oppressed groups, including racial, gender, linguistic, and ethnic groups, is that I maintain a great solidarity with their struggles against their oppressive conditions and that I have been expressing this more and more explicitly in my work.

# SECTION 2
# TRANSFORMING KNOWLEDGE

# Introduction

## Jenny Leach and Bob Moon

The chapters in this section explore contemporary debates about what constitutes teacher knowledge and how this knowledge should be developed. Lee Shulman has had a major impact on thinking about teaching and learning. Looking at a range of teacher education programmes in the early 1980s he came to question the separation of pedagogy and content in preservice and professional development courses.

Shulman (Chapter 5) argues that teachers are members of a scholarly community. As such they must understand the structure and conceptual organization of the subject-matter, the institutional settings and resources within which teaching occurs, the inherited empirical understanding of teaching and learning, and the formal and informal 'wisdom of practice' passed down from one generation of teachers to another.

Central to Shulman's argument is a model of 'pedagogical reasoning and action' which is based around the linked processes of comprehension, transformation, instruction, evaluation and reflection. At the core of this theory of pedagogy is the notion of transformation – the decisions that teachers make when they create pedagogic settings. For Shulman the key to understanding the knowledge base of teaching 'lies at the intersection of content and pedagogy, in the capacity of a teacher to transform the content knowledge he or she possesses into forms that are pedagogically powerful and yet adaptive to the variations in ability and background presented by the students'. Given the importance of the transformation process Shulman argues that pedagogical reasoning is as much a part of teaching as is the actual performance itself. One of the major sources for creating a knowledge base for teachers, he suggests, is 'scholarship in the content disciplines'. This is a theme centrally addressed in the next chapter.

Howard Gardner's book *Frames of Mind* (1983) has been one of the most influential psychological texts of recent years. There he advanced the idea of multiple intelligences – the notion that intelligence is multifaceted rather than singular. In subsequent years a number of school programmes, mostly in the USA, have sought to use this underlying idea as the basis for a reformed approach to schooling and pedagogy (see Gardner, 1983). Gardner and Boix-Mansilla (Chapter 6) suggest that learners need a range of pedagogical approaches to facilitate the engagement of their intelligences with any particular subject-matter. To achieve this requires teachers with a structured knowledge of the concepts, methods and perspectives of disciplinary understanding and the means by which this can be presented. In many respects Gardner and Boix-Mansilla are echoing Lee Shulman's analysis, although they go further than Shulman in their advocacy of the importance of the established discipline of knowledge.

Chapter 7 elaborates on Shulman's and Gardner and Boix-Mansilla's ideas, drawing also on situated learning theory and the writings of some contemporary European writers in seeking a synthesis of practical value to teacher education and development programmes. The authors argue for a reconceptualization of the relationship between knowledge and pedagogy, one which places a personal view of the purposes of teaching and learning at its centre and offer a framework through which this can be achieved. The chapter goes on to examine some of the implications of the framework for the process of regulatory curriculum building now practised by a majority of national education systems. In doing this the relationship between pedagogy and didactics is discussed.

Didactics, a long-established focus of study in Europe, is rarely considered in the USA or the wider English-speaking world where the word hardly appears in the educational lexicon. In Chapter 8, Peter Menck analyses the German tradition of didactics in posing the question, 'What exactly is the content of classroom instruction?' He explains the German concept of *Bildung*, of acquiring human understanding, and after looking at the relevance of historical figures such as Comenius for current thinking, suggests that work in classrooms should be conceptualized as interpretation, an approach which resonates with the perspectives set out in Section 1 of this volume.

Birgit Pepin in Chapter 9 demonstrates how European cultural traditions influence the representation of knowledge and styles of pedagogy. In an ethnographic study of secondary mathematics teachers in England, France and Germany, Pepin suggests, echoing Simon's concerns, that teachers in England hold to a very individualistic view of the learner. By contrast, she argues, French and German teachers adopt a more communal class-orientated approach. The Menck and Pepin chapters, juxtaposed with the North American perspectives of Shulman and Gardner, hold out interesting possibilities for analysis and synthesis across the different educational research communities.

# References

Gardner, H. (1983) *Frames of Mind*, New York, Basic Books.
Gardner, H. (1993) *Multiple Intelligences: The Theory in Practice*, New York, Basic Books.

# 5

# Knowledge and Teaching: Foundations of the New Reform

## Lee S. Shulman

[ . . . ]

The claim that teaching deserves professional status [ . . . ] is based on a [ . . . ] fundamental premise: that the standards by which the education and performance of teachers must be judged can be raised and more clearly articulated. The advocates of professional reform base their arguments on the belief that there exists a 'knowledge base for teaching' – a codified or codifiable aggregation of knowledge, skill, understanding, and technology, of ethics and disposition, of collective responsibility as well as a means for representing and communicating it. [ . . . ]

The rhetoric regarding the knowledge base, however, rarely specifies the character of such knowledge. It does not say what teachers should know, do, understand, or profess that will render teaching more than a form of individual labor, let alone be considered among the learned professions.

In this [chapter], I present an argument regarding the content, character, and sources for a knowledge base of teaching that suggests an answer to the question of the intellectual, practical, and normative basis for the professionalization of teaching. The questions that focus the argument are: What are the sources of the knowledge base for teaching? In what terms can these sources be conceptualized? What are the implications for teaching policy and educational reform?[1]

In addressing these questions I am following in the footsteps of many eminent scholars, including Dewey (1904), Scheffler (1965), Green (1971), Fenstermacher (1978), Smith (1980), and Schwab (1983), among others. Their discussions of what qualities and understandings, skills and abilities, and what traits and sensibilities render someone a competent teacher have continued to echo in the conference rooms of educators for generations.

[ . . . ]

What follows is a discussion of the sources and outlines of the required knowledge base for teaching. I divide this discussion into two distinct analyses. First, after providing an overview of one framework for a knowledge base for teaching, I examine the *sources* of that knowledge base, that is, the domains of scholarship and experience from which teachers may draw their

---

This chapter has been edited

understanding. Second, I explore the processes of pedagogical reasoning and action within which such teacher knowledge is used.


## The Knowledge Base

Begin a discussion on the knowledge base of teaching, and several related questions immediately arise: What knowledge base? Is enough known about teaching to support a knowledge base? Isn't teaching little more than personal style, artful communication, knowing some subject matter, and applying the results of recent research on teaching effectiveness? Only the last of these, the findings of research on effective teaching, is typically deemed a legitimate part of a knowledge base.

The actions of both policymakers and teacher educators in the past have been consistent with the formulation that teaching requires basic skills, content knowledge, and general pedagogical skills. Assessments of teachers in most states consist of some combination of basic-skills tests, an examination of competence in subject matter and observations in the class-room to ensure that certain kinds of general teaching behavior are present. In this manner, I would argue, teaching is trivialized, its complexities ig-nored, and its demands diminished. Teachers themselves have difficulty in articulating what they know and how they know it.

Nevertheless, the policy community at present continues to hold that the skills needed for teaching are those identified in the empirical research on teaching effectiveness. This research, summarized by Brophy and Good (1986), Gage (1986) and Rosenshine and Stevens (1986), was conducted within the psychological research tradition. It assumes that complex forms of situation-specific human performance can be understood in terms of the work-ings of underlying generic processes. In a study of teaching context, the re-search, therefore, seeks to identify those general forms of teaching behavior that correlate with student performance on standardized tests, whether in descriptive or experimental studies. The investigators who conduct the re-search realize that important simplifications must be made, but they believe that these are necessary steps for conducting scientific studies. Critical features of teaching, such as the subject matter being taught, the classroom context, the physical and psychological characteristics of the students, or the accomplish-ment of purposes not readily assessed on standardized tests, are typically ignored in the quest for general principles of effective teaching.

When policymakers have sought 'research-based' definitions of good teaching to serve as the basis for teacher tests or systems of classroom observation, the lists of teacher behaviors that had been identified as effec-tive in the empirical research were translated into the desirable competen-cies for classroom teachers. They became items on tests or on classroom-observation scales. They were accorded legitimacy because they had been 'confirmed by research'. While the researchers understood the findings to be simplified and incomplete, the policy community accepted them as sufficient for the definitions of standards.

For example, some research had indicated that students achieved more when teachers explicitly informed them of the lesson's objective. This seems like a perfectly reasonable finding. When translated into policy however, classroom-observation competency-rating scales asked whether the teacher had written the objective on the blackboard and/or directly told the student the objectives at the beginning of class. If the teacher had not, he or she was marked off for failing to demonstrate a desired competency. No effort was made to discover whether the withholding of an objective might have been consistent with the form of the lesson being organized or delivered.

Moreover, those who hold with bifurcating content and teaching processes have once again introduced into policy what had been merely an act of scholarly convenience and simplification in the research. Teaching processes were observed and evaluated without reference to the adequacy or accuracy of the ideas transmitted. In many cases, observers were not expected to have content expertise in the areas being observed, because it did not matter for the rating of teacher performance. Thus, what may have been an acceptable strategy for research became an unacceptable policy for teacher evaluation.

In this [chapter] I argue that the results of research on effective teaching, while valuable, are not the sole source of evidence on which to base a definition of the knowledge base of teaching. Those sources should be understood to be far richer and more extensive. Indeed, properly understood, the actual and potential sources for a knowledge base are so plentiful that our question should not be, Is there really much one needs to know in order to teach? Rather, it should express our wonder at how the extensive knowledge of teaching can be learned at all during the brief period allotted to teacher preparation. Much of the rest of this [chapter] provides the details of the argument that there exists an elaborate knowledge base for teaching.

## A View of Teaching

I begin with the formulation that the capacity to teach centers around the following commonplaces of teaching, paraphrased from Fenstermacher (1986). A teacher knows something not understood by others, presumably the students. The teacher can transform understanding, performance skills, or desired attitudes or values into pedagogical representations and actions. These are ways of talking, showing, enacting, or otherwise representing ideas so that the unknowing can come to know, those without understanding can comprehend and discern, and the unskilled can become adept. Thus, teaching necessarily begins with a teacher's understanding of what is to be learned and how it is to be taught. It proceeds through a series of activities during which the students are provided specific instruction and opportunities for learning,[2] though the learning itself ultimately remains the responsibility of the students. Teaching ends with new comprehension by both the teacher and the student.[3] Although this is certainly a core conception of teaching, it is also an incomplete conception. Teaching must properly be understood to be more than the enhancement of understanding; but if it is not even that, then questions regarding performance of its other functions remain moot. The next step is to outline the categories of knowledge that underlie the teacher understanding needed to promote comprehension among students.

## Categories of the Knowledge Base

If teacher knowledge were to be organized into a handbook, an encyclopedia, or some other format for arraying knowledge, what would the category headings look like?[4] At minimum, they would include:

- content knowledge;
- general pedagogical knowledge, with special reference to those broad principles and strategies of classroom management and organization that appear to transcend subject matter;
- curriculum knowledge, with particular grasp of the materials and programs that serve as 'tools of the trade' for teachers;
- pedagogical content knowledge, that special amalgam of content and pedagogy that is uniquely the province of teachers, their own special form of professional understanding;
- knowledge of learners and their characteristics;
- knowledge of educational contexts, ranging from the workings of the group or classroom, the governance and financing of school districts, to the character of communities and cultures; and
- knowledge of educational ends, purposes, and values, and their philosophical and historical grounds.

Among those categories, pedagogical content knowledge is of special interest because it identifies the distinctive bodies of knowledge for teaching. It represents the blending of content and pedagogy into an understanding of how particular topics, problems, or issues are organized, represented, and adapted to the diverse interests and abilities of learners, and presented for instruction. Pedagogical content knowledge is the category most likely to distinguish the understanding of the content specialist from that of the pedagogue. While far more can be said regarding the categories of a knowledge base for teaching, elucidation of them is not a central purpose of this [chapter].

## Enumerating the Sources

There are at least four major sources for the teaching knowledge base: (1) scholarship in content disciplines, (2) the materials and settings of the institutionalized educational process (for example, curricula, textbooks, school organizations and finance, and the structure of the teaching profession), (3) research on schooling, social organizations, human learning, teaching and development, and the other social and cultural phenomena that affect what teachers can do, and (4) the wisdom of practice itself. Let me elaborate on each of these.

*Scholarship in content disciplines.* The first source of the knowledge base is content knowledge – the knowledge, understanding, skill, and disposition that are to be learned by school children. This knowledge rests on two foundations: the accumulated literature and studies in the content areas, and the historical and philosophical scholarship on the nature of knowledge in those fields of study. For example, the teacher of English should know English and American prose and poetry, written and spoken language use and comprehension, and grammar. In addition, he or she should be familiar with the critical literature that applies to particular novels or epics that are under discussion in class. Moreover, the teacher should understand alternative theories of interpretation and criticism, and how these might relate to issues of curriculum and of teaching.

Teaching is, essentially, a learned profession. A teacher is a member of a scholarly community. He or she must understand the structures of subject matter, the principles of conceptual organization, and the principles of inquiry that help answer two kinds of questions in each field: What are the important ideas and skills in this domain? and How are new ideas added and deficient ones dropped by those who produce knowledge in this area? That is, what are the rules and procedures of good scholarship or inquiry? These questions parallel what Schwab (1964) has characterized as knowledge of substantive and syntactic structures, respectively. This view of the sources of content knowledge necessarily implies that the teacher must have not only depth of understanding with respect to the particular subjects taught, but also a broad liberal education that serves as a framework for old learning and as a facilitator for new understanding. The teacher has special responsibilities in relation to content knowledge, serving as the primary source of student understanding of subject matter. The manner in which that understanding is communicated conveys to students what is essential about a subject and what is peripheral. In the face of student diversity, the teacher must have a flexible and multifaceted comprehension, adequate to impart alternative explanations of the same concepts or principles. The teacher also communicates, whether consciously or not, ideas about the ways in which 'truth' is determined in a field and a set of attitudes and values that markedly influence student understanding. This responsibility places special demands on the teacher's own depth of understanding of the structures of the subject matter, as well as on the teacher's attitudes toward and enthusiasms for what is being taught and learned. These many aspects of content knowledge, therefore, are properly understood as a central feature of the knowledge base of teaching.

*Educational materials and structures.* To advance the aims of organized schooling, materials and structures for teaching and learning are created. These include: curricula with their scopes and sequences; tests and testing materials; institutions with their hierarchies, their explicit and implicit systems of rules and roles; professional teachers' organizations with their functions of negotiation, social change, and mutual protection; government agencies from the district through the state and federal levels; and general mechanisms of governance and finance. Because teachers necessarily function within a matrix created by these elements, using and being used by them, it stands to reason that the principles, policies, and facts of their functioning comprise a major source for the knowledge base. There is no need to claim that a specific literature undergirds this source, although there is certainly abundant research literature in most of these domains. But if a teacher has to 'know the territory' of teaching, then it is the landscape of such materials, institutions, organizations, and mechanisms with which he or she must be familiar. These comprise both the tools of the trade and the contextual conditions that will either facilitate or inhibit teaching efforts.

*Formal educational scholarship.* A third source is the important and growing body of scholarly literature devoted to understanding the processes of schooling, teaching, and learning. This literature includes the findings and methods of empirical research in the areas of teaching, learning, and human development, as well as the normative, philosophical, and ethical foundations of education.

The normative and theoretical aspects of teaching's scholarly knowledge are perhaps most important. Unfortunately, educational policymakers and staff developers tend to treat only the findings of empirical research on teaching and learning as relevant portions of the scholarly knowledge base. But these research findings, while important and worthy of careful study, represent only one facet of the contribution of scholarship. Perhaps the most enduring and powerful scholarly influences on teachers are those that enrich their images of the possible: their visions of what constitutes good education, or what a well-educated youngster might look like if provided with appropriate opportunities and stimulation.

The writings of Plato, Dewey, Neill, and Skinner all communicate their conceptions of what a good educational system should be. In addition, many works written primarily to disseminate empirical research findings also serve as important sources of these concepts. I count among these such works as Bloom's (1976) on mastery learning and Rosenthal and Jacobson's (1968) on teacher expectations. Quite independent of whether the empirical claims of those books can be supported, their impact on teachers' conceptions of the possible and desirable ends of education is undeniable. Thus, the philosophical, critical, and empirical literature which can inform the goals, visions, and dreams of teachers is a major portion of the scholarly knowledge base of teaching.

A more frequently cited kind of scholarly knowledge grows out of the empirical study of teaching effectiveness. This research has been summarized recently by Gage (1978, 1986), Shulman (1986a), Brophy and Good (1986), and Rosenshine and Stevens (1986). The essential goal of this program of research has been to identify those teacher behaviors and strategies most likely to lead to achievement gains among students. Because the search has focused on generic relationships – teacher behaviors associated with student academic gains irrespective of subject matter or grade level – the findings have been much more closely connected with the management of classrooms than with the subtleties of content pedagogy. That is, the effective-teaching principles deal with making classrooms places where pupils can attend to instructional tasks, orient themselves toward learning with a minimum of disruption and distraction, and receive a fair and adequate opportunity to learn. Moreover, the educational purposes for which these research results are most relevant are the teaching of skills. Rosenshine (1986) has observed that effective teaching research has much less to offer to the teaching of understanding, especially of complex written material; thus, the research applies more to teaching a skill like multiplication than to teaching critical interpretations of, say, the *Federalist Papers*.

There are a growing number of such generic principles of effective teaching, and they have already found their way into examinations such as the National Teachers Examination and into state-level assessments of teaching performance during the first teaching year. Their weakness, that they essentially ignore the content-specific character of most teaching, is also their strength. Discovering, explicating, and codifying general teaching principles simplify the otherwise outrageously complex activity of teaching. The great danger occurs, however, when a general teaching principle is distorted into prescription, when maxim becomes mandate. Those states that have taken working principles of teaching, based solely on empirical studies of generic teaching effectiveness, and have rendered them as hard, independent criteria for judging a teacher's worth, are engaged in a political process likely to injure the teaching profession rather than improve it.

The results of research on learning and development also fall within the area of empirical research findings. This research differs from research on teaching by the unit of investigation. Studies of teaching typically take place in conventional classrooms. Learning and development are ordinarily studied in individuals. Hence, teaching studies give accounts of how teachers cope with the inescapable character of schools as places where groups of students work and learn in concert. By comparison, learning and development studies produce principles of individual thought or behavior that must often be generalized to groups with caution if they are to be useful for schoolteaching.

The research in these domains can be both generic and content-specific. For example, cognitive psychological research contributes to the development of understanding of how the mind works to store, process, and retrieve information. Such general understanding can certainly be a source of knowledge for teachers, just as the work of Piaget, Maslow, Erikson, or

Bloom has been and continues to be. We also find work on specific subject matter and student developmental levels that is enormously useful; for example, we learn about student misconceptions in the learning of arithmetic by elementary school youngsters (Erlwanger, 1975) or difficulties in grasping principles of physics by university and secondary school students (for example, Clement, 1982). Both these sorts of research contribute to a knowledge base for teaching.

*Wisdom of practice.* The final source of the knowledge base is the least codified of all. It is the wisdom of practice itself, the maxims that guide (or provide reflective rationalization for) the practices of able teachers. One of the more important tasks for the research community is to work with practitioners to develop codified representations of the practical pedagogical wisdom of able teachers. As indicated above, much of the conception of teaching embodied in this [chapter] is derived from collecting, examining, and beginning to codify the emerging wisdom of practice among both inexperienced and experienced teachers.

[ . . . ] As we organize and interpret such data, we attempt to infer principles of good practice that can serve as useful guidelines for efforts of educational reform. We attempt to keep the accounts highly contextualized, especially with respect to the content-specificity of the pedagogical strategies employed. In this manner we contribute to the documentation of good practice as a significant source for teaching standards. We also attempt to lay a foundation for a scholarly literature that records the details and rationales for specific pedagogical practice.

One of the frustrations of teaching as an occupation and profession is its extensive individual and collective amnesia, the consistency with which the best creations of its practitioners are lost to both contemporary and future peers. Unlike fields such as architecture (which preserves its creations in both plans and edifices), law (which builds a case literature of opinions and interpretations), medicine (with its records and case studies), and even unlike chess, bridge, or ballet (with their traditions of preserving both memorable games and choreographed performances through inventive forms of notation and recording), teaching is conducted without an audience of peers. It is devoid of a history of practice.

Without such a system of notation and memory the next steps of analysis, interpretation, and codification of principles of practice are hard to pursue. We have concluded from our research with teachers at all levels of experience that the potentially codifiable knowledge that can be gleaned from the wisdom of practice is extensive. Practitioners simply know a great deal that they have never even tried to articulate. A major portion of the research agenda for the next decade will be to collect, collate, and interpret the practical knowledge of teachers for the purpose of establishing a case literature and codifying its principles, precedents, and parables (Shulman. 1986b). [ . . . ]

A knowledge base for teaching is not fixed and final. Although teaching is among the world's oldest professions, educational research, especially the systematic study of teaching, is a relatively new enterprise. We may be able to offer a compelling argument for the broad outlines and categories of the knowledge base for teaching. It will, however, become abundantly clear that much, if not most, of the proposed knowledge base remains to be discovered, invented. and refined. As more is learned about teaching, we will come to recognize new categories of performance and understanding that are characteristic of good teachers, and will have to reconsider and redefine other domains. Our current 'blueprint' for the knowledge base of teaching has many cells or categories with only the most rudimentary place-holders, much like the chemist's periodic table of a century ago. As we proceed, we will know that something can be known in principle about a particular aspect of teaching, but we will not yet know what that principle or practice entails. At base, however, we believe that scholars and expert teachers are able to define, describe, and reproduce good teaching.

## The Processes of Pedagogical Reasoning and Action

The conception of teaching I shall discuss has emerged from a number of sources both philosophical and empirical. A key source has been the several dozen teachers whom we have been studying in our research during the past three years. Through interviews, observations, structured tasks, and examination of materials, we have attempted to understand how they commute from the status of learner to that of teacher,[5] from being able to comprehend subject matter for themselves, to becoming able to elucidate subject matter in new ways, reorganize and partition it, clothe it in activities and emotions, in metaphors and exercises, and in examples and demonstrations, so that it can be grasped by students.

As we have come to view teaching, it begins with an act of reason, continues with a process of reasoning, culminates in performances of imparting, eliciting, involving, or enticing, and is then thought about some more until the process can begin again. In the discussion of teaching that follows, we will emphasize teaching as comprehension and reasoning, as transformation and reflection. This emphasis is justified by the resoluteness with which research and policy have so blatantly ignored those aspects of teaching in the past.

Fenstermacher (1978, 1986) provides a useful framework for analysis. The goal of teacher education, he argues, is not to indoctrinate or train teachers to behave in prescribed ways, but to educate teachers to reason soundly about their teaching as well as to perform skillfully. Sound reasoning requires both a process of thinking about what they are doing and an adequate base of facts, principles, and experiences from which to reason. Teachers must learn to use their knowledge base to provide the grounds for choices and actions. Therefore, teacher education must work with the beliefs that guide teacher actions, with the principles and evidence that underlie the choices teachers make. Such reasons (called 'premises of the practical argument' in the analysis of Green, 1971, on which Fenstermacher bases his argument) can be predominantly arbitrary or idiosyncratic ('It sure seemed like the right idea at the time!' 'I don't know much about teaching, but I know what I like.'), or they can rest on ethical, empirical, theoretical, or practical principles that have substantial support among members of the professional community of teachers. Fenstermacher argues that good teaching not only is effective behaviorally, but must rest on a foundation of adequately grounded premises.

When we examine the quality of teaching, the idea of influencing the grounds or reasons for teachers' decisions places the emphasis precisely where it belongs: on the features of pedagogical reasoning that lead to or can be invoked to explain pedagogical actions. We must be cautious, however, lest we place undue emphasis upon the ways teachers reason to achieve particular ends, at the expense of attention to the grounds they present for selecting the ends themselves. Teaching is both effective and normative; it is concerned with both means and ends. Processes of reasoning underlie both. The knowledge base must therefore deal with the purposes of education as well as the methods and strategies of educating.

This image of teaching involves the exchange of ideas. The idea is grasped, probed, and comprehended by a teacher, who then must turn it about in his or her mind, seeing many sides of it. Then the idea is shaped or tailored until it can in turn be grasped by students. This grasping, however, is not a passive act. Just as the teacher's comprehension requires a vigorous interaction with the ideas, so students will be expected to encounter ideas actively as well. Indeed, our exemplary teachers present ideas in order to provoke the constructive processes of their students and not to incur student dependence on teachers or to stimulate the flatteries of imitation.[6]

Comprehension alone is not sufficient. The usefulness of such knowledge lies in its value for judgment and action. Thus, in response to my aphorism. 'those who can, do: those who understand, teach' (Shulman, 1986b p. 14), Petrie (1986) correctly observed that I had not gone far enough. Understanding, he argued, must be linked to judgment and action, to the proper uses of understanding in the forging of wise pedagogical decisions.

## Aspects of Pedagogical Reasoning

I begin with the assumption that most teaching is initiated by some form of 'text': a textbook, a syllabus, or an actual piece of material the teacher or student wishes to have understood. The text may be a vehicle for the accomplishment of other educational purposes, but some sort of teaching material is almost always involved. The following conception of pedagogical reasoning and action is taken from the point of view of the teacher, who is presented with the challenge of taking what he or she already understands and making it ready for effective instruction. The model of pedagogical reasoning and action is summarized in Table 5.1.

Given a text, educational purposes, and/or a set of ideas, pedagogical reasoning and action involve a cycle through the activities of comprehension, transformation, instruction, evaluation, and reflection.[7] The starting point and terminus for the process is an act of comprehension.

*Comprehension.* To teach is first to understand. We ask that the teacher comprehend critically a set of ideas to be taught.[8] We expect teachers to understand what they teach and, when possible, to understand it in several ways. They should understand how a given idea relates to other ideas within the same subject area and to ideas in other subjects as well.

Comprehension of purposes is also central here. We engage in teaching to achieve educational purposes, to accomplish ends having to do with student literacy, student freedom to use and enjoy, student responsibility to care and care for, to believe and respect, to inquire and discover, to develop understandings, skills and values needed to function in a free and just society. As teachers, we also strive to balance our goals of fostering individual excellence with more general ends involving equality of opportunity

Table 5.1   *A model of pedagogical reasoning and action*

*Comprehension*
Of purposes, subject matter structures, ideas within and outside the discipline

*Transformation*
Preparation: critical interpretation and analysis of texts, structuring and segmenting, development of a curricular repertoire, and clarification of purposes
Representation: use of a representational repertoire which includes analogies, metaphors, examples, demonstrations, explanations, and so forth
Selection: choice from among an instructional repertoire which includes modes of teaching, organizing, managing, and arranging
Adaptation and Tailoring to Student Characteristics: consideration of conceptions, preconceptions, misconceptions, and difficulties, language, culture, and motivations, social class, gender, age, ability, aptitude, interests, self-concepts, and attention

*Instruction*
Management, presentations, interactions, group work, discipline, humor, questioning, and other aspects of active teaching, discovery or inquiry instruction, and the observable forms of classroom teaching

*Evaluation*
Checking for student understanding during interactive teaching
Testing student understanding at the end of lessons or units
Evaluating one's own performance, and adjusting for experiences

*Reflection*
Reviewing, reconstructing, reenacting and critically analyzing one's own and the class's performance, and grounding explanations in evidence

*New Comprehensions*
Of purposes, subject matter, students, teaching, and self
Consolidation of new understandings, and learnings from experience

and equity among students of different backgrounds and cultures Although most teaching begins with some sort of text, and the learning of that text can be a worthy end in itself, we should not lose sight of the fact that the text is often a vehicle for achieving other educational purposes. The goals of education transcend the comprehension of particular texts, but may be unachievable without it.

Saying that a teacher must first comprehend both content and purposes, however, does not particularly distinguish a teacher from non-teaching peers. We expect a math major to understand mathematics or a history specialist to comprehend history. But the key to distinguishing the knowledge base of teaching lies at the intersection of content and pedagogy, in the capacity of a teacher to transform the content knowledge he or she possesses into forms that are pedagogically powerful and yet adaptive to the variations in ability and background presented by the students. We now turn to a discussion of transformation and its components.

*Transformation.* Comprehended ideas must be transformed in some manner if they are to be taught. To reason one's way through an act of teaching is to think one's way from the subject matter as understood by the teacher into the minds and motivations of learners. Transformations, therefore, require some combination or ordering of the following processes, each of which employs a kind of repertoire: (1) preparation (of the given text materials) including the process of critical interpretation, (2) representation of the ideas in the form of new analogies, metaphors, and so forth, (3) instructional selections from among an array of teaching methods and models, and (4) adaptation of these representations to the general characteristics of the children to be taught, as well as (5) tailoring the adaptations to the specific youngsters in the classroom. These forms of transformation, these aspects of the process wherein one moves from personal comprehension to preparing for the comprehension of others, are the essence of the act of pedagogical reasoning, of teaching as thinking, and of planning – whether explicitly or implicitly – the performance of teaching.

Preparation involves examining and critically interpreting the materials of instruction in terms of the teacher's own understanding of the subject matter (Ben-Peretz, 1975). That is, one scrutinizes the teaching material in light of one's own comprehension and asks whether it is 'fit to be taught'. This process of preparation will usually include (1) detecting and correcting errors of omission and commission in the text, and (2) the critical processes of structuring and segmenting the material into forms better adapted to the teacher's understanding and, in prospect, more suitable for teaching. One also scrutinizes educational purposes or goals. We find examples of this preparation process in a number of our studies. Preparation certainly draws upon the availability of a curricular repertoire, a grasp of the full array of extant instructional materials, programs, and conceptions.

Representation involves thinking through the key ideas in the text or lesson and identifying the alternative ways of representing them to students. What analogies, metaphors, examples, demonstrations, simulations, and the like can help to build a bridge between the teacher's comprehension and that desired for the students? Multiple forms of representation are desirable. We speak of the importance of a representational repertoire in this activity.[9]

Instructional selections occur when the teacher must move from the reformulation of content through representations to the embodiment of representations in instructional forms or methods. Here the teacher draws upon an instructional repertoire of approaches or strategies of teaching. This repertoire can be quite rich, including not only the more conventional alternatives such as lecture, demonstration, recitation, or seatwork, but also a variety of forms of cooperative learning, reciprocal teaching, Socratic dialogue, discovery learning, project methods, and learning outside the classroom setting.

Adaptation is the process of fitting the represented material to the characteristics of the students. What are the relevant aspects of student ability, gender, language, culture, motivations, or prior knowledge and skills that will affect their responses to different forms of representation and presentation? What student conceptions, misconceptions, expectations, motives, difficulties, or strategies might influence the ways in which they approach, interpret, understand, or misunderstand the material? Related to adaptation is tailoring, which refers to the fitting of the material to the specific students in one's classrooms rather than to students in general. When a teacher thinks through the teaching of something, the activity is a bit like the manufacture of a suit of clothing. Adaptation is like preparing a suit of a particular style, color, and size that can be hung on a rack. Once it is prepared for purchase by a particular customer, however, it must be tailored to fit perfectly.

Moreover, the activity of teaching is rarely engaged with a single student at a time. This is a process for which the special term 'tutoring' is needed. When we speak of teaching under typical school circumstances, we describe an activity which brings instruction to groups of at least fifteen – or more typically, twenty-five to thirty-five – students. Thus, the tailoring of instruction entails fitting representations not only to particular students, but also to a group of a particular size, disposition receptivity, and interpersonal 'chemistry'.

All these processes of transformation result in a plan, or set of strategies, to present a lesson, unit, or course. Up to this point, of course, it is all a rehearsal for the performances of teaching which have not yet occurred. Pedagogical reasoning is as much a part of teaching as is the actual performance itself. Reasoning does not end when instruction begins. The activities of comprehension, transformation, evaluation, and reflection continue to occur during active teaching. Teaching itself becomes a stimulus for thoughtfulness as well as for action. We therefore turn next to the performance that consummates all this reasoning in the act of instruction.

*Instruction.* This activity involves the observable performance of the variety of teaching acts. It includes many of the most crucial aspects of

pedagogy: organizing and managing the classroom; presenting clear explanations and vivid descriptions; assigning and checking work; and inter-
acting effectively with students through questions and probes, answers and
reactions, and praise and criticism. It thus includes management, explanation, discussion, and all the observable features of effective direct and
heuristic instruction already well-documented in the research literature on
effective teaching.

[ . . . ]

*Evaluation.* This process includes the on-line checking for understanding
and misunderstanding that a teacher must employ while teaching interac-
tively, as well as the more formal testing and evaluation that teachers do to
provide feedback and grades. Clearly, checking for such understanding
requires all the forms of teacher comprehension and transformation described above. To understand what a pupil understands will require a deep
grasp of both the material to be taught and the processes of learning. This
understanding must be specific to particular school subjects and to individual topics within the subject. This represents another way in which what we
call pedagogical content knowledge is used. Evaluation is also directed at
one's own teaching and at the lessons and materials employed in those
activities. In that sense it leads directly to reflection.

*Reflection.* This is what a teacher does when he or she looks back at the
teaching and learning that has occurred, and reconstructs, reenacts, and/or
recaptures the events, the emotions, and the accomplishments. It is that set
of processes through which a professional learns from experience. It can be
done alone or in concert, with the help of recording devices or solely
through memory. Here again, it is likely that reflection is not merely a
disposition (as in, 'she's such a reflective person!') or a set of strategies, but
also the use of particular kinds of analytic knowledge brought to bear on
one's work (Richert, in preparation). Central to this process will be a
review of the teaching in comparison to the ends that were sought.

*New comprehension.* Thus we arrive at the new beginning, the expectation that through acts of teaching that are 'reasoned' and 'reasonable' the
teacher achieves new comprehension, both of the purposes and of the
subjects to be taught, and also of the students and of the processes of
pedagogy themselves. There is a good deal of transient experiential learning among teachers, characterized by the 'aha' of a moment that is never
consolidated and made part of a new understanding or a reconstituted
repertoire (Brodkey, 1986). New comprehension does not automatically
occur, even after evaluation and reflection. Specific strategies for documentation, analysis, and discussion are needed.

Although the processes in this model are presented in sequence, they are
not meant to represent a set of fixed stages, phases, or steps. Many of the
processes can occur in different order. Some may not occur at all during
some acts of teaching. Some may be truncated, others elaborated. In elementary teaching, for example, some processes may occur that are ignored
or given short shrift in this model. But a teacher should demonstrate the

capacity to engage in these processes when called upon and teacher education should provide students with the understandings and performance abilities they will need to reason their ways through and to enact a complete act of pedagogy, as represented here.

[ . . . ]

## Notes

1. Most of the empirical work on which this essay rests has been conducted with secondary-school teachers, both new and experienced. While I firmly believe that much of the emphasis to be found here on the centrality of content knowledge in pedagogy holds reasonably well for the elementary level as well, I am reluctant to make that claim too boldly. Work currently underway at the elementary level, both by Leinhardt (1983) and her colleagues (for example, Leinhardt & Greeno, 1985; Leinhardt & Smith, 1986) and by our own research group, may help clarify this matter.

2. There are several aspects of this formulation that are unfortunate, if only for the impression they may leave. The rhetoric of the analysis, for example, is not meant to suggest that education is reduced to knowledge transmission, the conveying of information from an active teacher to a passive learner, and that this information is viewed as product rather than process. My conception of teaching is not limited to direct instruction. Indeed, my affinity for discovery learning and inquiry teaching is both enthusiastic and ancient (for example, Shulman & Keislar, 1966). Yet even in those most student-centered forms of education, where much of the initiative is in the hands of the students, there is little room for teacher ignorance. Indeed, we have reason to believe that teacher comprehension is even more critical for the inquiry-oriented classroom than for its more didactic alternative.

Central to my concept of teaching are the objectives of students learning how to understand and solve problems, learning to think critically and creatively as well as learning facts, principles, and rules of procedure. Finally, I understand that the learning of subject matter is often not an end in itself, but rather a vehicle employed in the service of other goals. Nevertheless, at least at the secondary level, subject matter is a nearly universal vehicle for instruction, whatever the ultimate goal.

3. This formulation is drawn from the teacher's perspective and, hence, may be viewed by some readers as overly teacher-centered. I do not mean to diminish the centrality of student learning for the process of education, nor the priority that must be given to student learning over teacher comprehension. But our analyses of effective teaching must recognize that outcomes *for teachers* as well as pupils must be considered in any adequate treatment of educational outcomes.

4. I have attempted this list in other publications, though, admittedly, not with great cross-article consistency (for example, Shulman, 1986b; Shulman & Sykes, 1986; Wilson, Shulman & Richert, in press).

5. The metaphor of commuting is not used idly. The journey between learner and teacher is not one-way. In the best teachers, as well as in the more marginal, new learning is constantly required for teaching.

6. The direction and sequence of instruction can be quite different as well. Students can literally initiate the process, proceeding by discovering, inventing, or inquiring, to prepare their own representations and transformations. Then it is the role of the teacher to respond actively and creatively to those student initiatives. In each case the teacher needs to possess both the comprehension and the capacities for transformation. In the student-initiated case, the flexibility to respond, judge,

nurture, and provoke student creativity will depend on the teacher's own capacities for sympathetic transformation and interpretation.

7. Under some conditions, teaching may begin with 'given a group of students'. It is likely that at the early elementary grades, or in special education classes or other settings where children have been brought together for particular reasons, the starting point for reasoning about instruction may well be at the characteristics of the group itself. There are probably some days when a teacher necessarily uses the youngsters as a starting point.

8. Other views of teaching will also begin with comprehension, but of something other than the ideas or text to be taught and learned. They may focus on comprehension of a particular set of values, of the characteristics, needs, interests, or propensities of a particular individual or group of learners. But some sort of comprehension (or self-conscious confusion, wonder, or ignorance) will always initiate teaching.

9. The centrality of representation to our conception of pedagogical reasoning is important for relating our model of teaching to more general approaches to the study of human thinking and problem solving. Cognitive psychologists (for example, Gardner, 1986; Marton, 1986; Norman, 1980) argue that processes of internal representation are key elements in any cognitive psychology. 'To my mind, the major accomplishment of cognitive science has been the clear demonstration of the validity of positing a level of mental representation: a set of constructs that can be invoked for the explanation of cognitive phenomena, ranging from visual perception story comprehension' (Gardner, 1986, p. 383). Such a linkage between models of pedagogy and models of more general cognitive functioning can serve as an important impetus for the needed study of teacher thinking.

# References

Ben-Peretz, M. (1975). The concept of curriculum potential. *Curriculum Theory Network, 5*, 151–159.

Bloom, B. S. (1976). *Human characteristics and school learning.* New York: McGraw-Hill.

Brodkey, J. J. (1986). *Learning while teaching: Self-assessment in the classroom.* Unpublished doctoral dissertation, Stanford University.

Brophy, J. J., & Good, T. (1986). Teacher behavior and student achievement. In M. C. Wittrock (Ed.), *Handbook of research on teaching* (3rd ed., pp. 328–375). New York: Macmillan.

Clement, J. (1982). Students' preconceptions in introductory mechanics. *American Journal of Physics, 50*, 67–71.

Dewey, J. (1904). The relation of theory to practice in education. In C. A. McMurry (Ed.), *The relation of theory to practice in the education of teachers* (Third Yearbook of the National Society for the Scientific Study of Education, Part I). Bloomington, IL: Public School Publishing.

Erlwanger, S. H. (1975). Case studies of children's conceptions of mathematics, Part I. *Journal or Children's Mathematical Behavior, 1*, 157–283.

Fenstermacher, G. (1978). A philosophical consideration of recent research on teacher effectiveness. In L. S. Shulman (Ed.), *Review of research in education* (Vol. 6. pp. 157–185). Itasca. IL: Peacock.

Fenstermacher, G. (1986). Philosophy of research on teaching: Three aspects. In M. C. Wittrock (Ed.), *Handbook of research on teaching* (3rd ed., pp. 37–49). New York: Macmillan.

Gage, N. L. (1978). *The scientific basis of the art of teaching.* New York: Teachers College Press.

Gage, N. L. (1986). *Hard gains in the soft sciences: The case of pedagogy.* Bloomington, IN: Phi Delta Kappa.

Gardner, H. (1986). *The mind's new science: A history of cognitive revolution.* New York: Basic Books.

Green, T. F. (1971). *The activities of teaching,* New York: McGraw-Hill.

Lcinhardt, G. (1983). Novice and expert knowledge of individual student's achievement. *Educational Psychologist, 18,* 165–179.

Leinhardt, G., & Greeno, J. G. (1985). The cognitive skill of teaching. *Journal of Educational Psychology, 78,* 75–95.

Leinhardt. G., & Smith. D. A. (1985). Expertise in mathematics instruction: Subject matter knowledge. *Journal of Educational Psychology, 77,* 247–271.

Marton, F. (1986). *Towards a pedagogy of content.* Unpublished manuscript. University of Gothenburg, Sweden.

Norman, D. A. (1980). What goes on in the mind of the learner? In W. J. McKeachie (Ed.), *New directions for teaching and learning: Learning, cognition. and college teaching* (Vol. 2). San Francisco: Jossey-Bass.

Petrie, H. (1986, May). *The liberal arts and sciences in the teacher education curriculum.* Paper presented at the Conference on Excellence in Teacher Preparation through the Liberal Arts, Muhlenberg College, Allentown, PA.

Richert, A. (in preparation). *Reflex to reflection: Facilitating reflection in novice teachers.* Unpublished doctoral dissertation in progress, Stanford University.

Rosenshine, B. (1986, April). *Unsolved issues in teaching content: A critique of a lesson on Federalist Paper No. 10.* Paper presented at the meeting of the American Educational Research Association, San Francisco, CA.

Rosenshine, B., & Stevens, R. S. (1986). Teaching functions. In M. C. Wittrock (Ed.) *Handbook of research on teaching* (3rd ed., pp. 376–391). New York: Macmillan.

Rosenthal, R., & Jacobson, L. (1968). *Pygmalion in the classroom.* New York: Holt, Rinehart & Winston.

Scheffler, I. (1965). *Conditions of knowledge: An introduction to epistemology and education.* Chicago: University of Chicago Press.

Schwab, J. J. (1964). The structure of the disciplines: Meanings and significances. In G. W. Ford & L. Pugno (Eds.), *The structure of knowledge and the curriculum.* Chicago: Rand McNally.

Schwab, J. J. (1983). The practical four: Something for curriculum professors to do. *Curriculum Inquiry, 13,* 239–265.

Shulman, L. S. (1986a). Paradigms and research programs for the study of teaching. In M. C. Wittrock (Ed.), *Handbook of research on teaching* (3rd ed., pp. 3–36). New York: Macmillan.

Shulman, L. S. (1986b). Those who understand: Knowledge growth in teaching. *Educational Researcher 15*(2), 4–14.

Shulman, L. S., & Keislar, E. R. (Eds.). (1966). *Learning by discovery: A critical appraisal.* Chicago: Rand McNally.

Shulman, L. S., & Sykes, G. (1986, March). *A national board for teaching? In search of a bold standard* (Paper commissioned for the Task Force on Teaching as a Profession, Carnegie Forum on Education and the Economy).

Smith, B. O. (1980). *A design for a school of pedagogy.* Washington, DC: U.S. Department of Education.

Sykes. G. (1986). *The social consequences of standard-setting in the professions* (Paper commissioned for the Task Force on Teaching as a Profession, Carnegie Forum on Education and the Economy).

Wilson, S. M., Shulman, L. S.. & Richert, A. (in press). '150 different ways' of knowing: Representations of knowledge in teaching. In J. Calderhead (Ed.), *Exploring teacher thinking.* Sussex, Eng.: Holt, Rinehart & Winston.

# 6

# Teaching for Understanding in the Disciplines – and Beyond

## Howard Gardner and Veronica Boix-Mansilla

[. . .]

## Introduction: Discipline Defended

The notion of *discipline* is doubly dual-edged. The popular version of discipline denotes the requirement that individuals behave according to a strict regimen. While many in our culture recognize the need for disciplined training ('that child needs discipline'), few (except perhaps for masochists) wax enthusiastic about a disciplined life. The academic version of discipline refers to domains of knowledge or competence within a society; individuals enroll in scholastic or informal apprenticeships and eventually achieve a certain degree of expertise in a discipline. While most educators recognize the need for the acquisition of academic disciplines, a rather widespread conviction obtains that such disciplines are good for you ('that child needs to master the disciplines before going to college'), rather than enjoyable to pursue, ultimately useful, or essential for full development.

In this [chapter] we adopt a positive view of both disciplinary terrains. We believe that individuals will be most fully engaged and most productive when they lead a life in which disciplined training has become a regular, predictable feature. Relatedly, we maintain that the scholarly disciplines represent the formidable achievements of talented human beings, toiling over the centuries, to approach and explain issues of enduring importance. Shorn of disciplinary knowledge, human beings are quickly reduced to the level of ignorant children, indeed, to the ranks of barbarians.

One hundred years ago, a defense of the disciplines would have been completely unnecessary. In the current climate, however, there has been much criticism of the organization of precollegiate curricula, and the disciplines have often been a flashpoint for that criticism. Criticism of the disciplines in schools typically takes several forms: sometimes it becomes a call for interdisciplinary or thematic curricula, even at times when students

---

This chapter has been edited

78

could not yet have mastered individual disciplines; at times it suggests that disciplines are an outmoded way of organizing knowledge, and are better replaced by a focus on 'ways of knowing', 'learning styles', or even 'intelligences'. Finally, criticism of the disciplines cites shifting definitions of disciplines or 'blurring of genres' as additional reasons for discarding a disciplinary focus in the curriculum.

More responsible critics do recognize the contributions of the disciplines, but often their critiques lead educators to conclude that the disciplines constitute a significant part of the problem in schools today. We, in contrast, find the disciplines to be indispensable in any quality education, and we urge individuals not to throw away the 'disciplinary baby' with the 'subject matter' bathwater.

While adopting this decidedly more benign view, we do concur in one respect with those who harbor reservations about discipline. We assert that disciplinary competence is hard to come by, indeed much more difficult than observers have hitherto believed. Indeed, so powerful are our early 'predisciplinary' ways of knowing that the achievement of genuine disciplinary mastery proves highly demanding.

In what follows, we undertake three principal tasks. To begin with, we review the accumulated evidence that disciplinary knowledge represents an impressive yet elusive attainment. Next, we sketch out an educational approach designed to engender effective understanding within and across the disciplines. We illustrate this 'ideal type' sketch by reporting preliminary results from a study in which teachers are attempting to enhance student understanding across the disciplines. This discussion includes a brief consideration of understanding that transcends individual disciplines – hence, the 'and beyond' of our title. Finally, we return to the practical difficulties that arise in attempting to educate for understanding and indicate how some of these obstacles might be dealt with.

## The Power of the Unschooled Mind

While most observers would endorse the goal of 'teaching for understanding', there have been only scattered attempts to define what is meant by this phrase and set up programs that explicitly address this goal. In our own work, we define 'understanding' as the capacity to use current knowledge, concepts, and skills to illuminate new problems or unanticipated issues. So long as one is drawing on such knowledge only to illuminate issues that have already been encountered, it is not possible to tell how much genuine understanding has been achieved. But one can with some confidence conclude that genuine understanding has been achieved if an individual proves able to apply knowledge in new situations, without applying such knowledge erroneously or inappropriately; and if he or she can do so spontaneously, without specific instruction to do so.

Copious research documents how difficult it is to demonstrate such understanding in even our best students. Wherever one looks in the curriculum, one finds very little evidence of deep understanding. At most, students show extremely threadbare forms of understanding. In the sciences, misconceptions abound. Students of physics believe in forces that can be mysteriously transmitted from one substance or agent to another; students of biology think of evolution as a planful, teleological process, culminating in the perfect human being; students of algebra plug numbers into an equation with hardly a clue as to what the equation means or when (and when *not*) to invoke it; students of history insist on applying the simplest stereotypical models to the elucidation of events that are complex and multifaceted; students of literature and the arts prefer works that are simple, realistic, and sentimental over those that deal with philosophical issues or treat subject matter that is not overtly beautiful.

Why the robustness of these unproductive habits of mind? Why does it prove so difficult to educate for understanding? We argue that, during the early years of life, children form extremely powerful theories or sets of beliefs about how the world works – theories of mind, theories of matter, theories of life. Some aspects of children's early understanding of the world, such as their genuine questions and inquisitive spirit, provide a promising grounding for future disciplinary understanding. However, many other aspects constitute obstacles to be overcome. Children construct powerful stereotypes about persons and events (people who look different from oneself are seen as more likely to be evil; events are conceived as having single causes or are interpreted from self-centered perspectives). They establish habits of learning facts and procedures in a reflexively syntactic manner, overlooking the meaning or implications of particular statements or processes; the result is ritualistic memorization of meaningless facts and disembodied procedures.

These theories, ideas, and procedures become so deeply entrenched in the human mind that they prove very difficult to eradicate in favor of the more comprehensive and more veridical views that have been painstakingly constructed in and across the disciplines. Rather, like the proverbial Trojan Horse, these powerful yet erroneous notions remain quietly in hiding during the school years until their opportunistic moment arises: at that point they rise up and assert themselves with considerable force – in the process documenting an enduring lack of genuine understanding on the part of most students.

To educate the unschooled mind, two kinds of disciplines are necessary. First of all, the classical academic disciplines, ranging from physics to poetry, offer well-established means for understanding the world. If individuals pursue these disciplines assiduously, they ought to be able to replace their misconceptions with more appropriate ideas and practices. Indeed, experts may be thought of as individuals who really do succeed in replacing their earlier, imperfect notions with more serviceable ones. Such experts exemplify cases in which intuitive and commonsense ideas that were once engraved on the mind/brain have been gradually smoothed away; ultimately these initial configurations have come to be replaced by a new and more appropriate set of engravings. To achieve such expertise, students require ample doses of discipline in the alternative sense of the term: regular practice, with feedback, in applying those habits of mind that yield understanding.

It is important to specify what we mean by disciplines. Disciplines consist of approaches devised by scholars over the centuries in order to address essential questions, issues, and phenomena drawn from the natural and human worlds; they include methods of inquiry, networks of concepts, theoretical frameworks, techniques for acquiring and verifying findings, appropriate images, symbol systems, vocabularies, and mental models. Over the centuries, human beings have developed these particular ways to look at the past, to understand biological beings, or to understand ourselves, that now proceed under the label of history, biology, or psychology. Disciplines are dynamic. Their objects, methods, theories, or accounts stimulate controversy and evolve in time. In order to socialize our youngsters into these bodies of knowledge and practices we need to focus on the disciplines' essential features at this point in history, while acknowledging their dynamic and evolving nature.

Defining disciplinary boundaries is a complex epistemological and sociological enterprise that lies beyond the scope of this [chapter]. Whereas some concepts and methods are prototypical features of specific disciplines, others are shared by two or more disciplines. Assumptions about the nature of knowledge as well as particular theoretical positions within disciplines shape the discussion about disciplinary boundaries. Despite these wrinkles, we believe one can still identify the essential questions that each of these disciplinary approaches is trying to address as well as the 'rules of the game' that help students develop appropriate habits of mind and understanding.

Disciplines are not the same as subject matters or Carnegie units. At best there is a rough correspondence between any list of school subjects and the disciplines that underlie them. Whereas subject matters are seen as collections of contents that students need to learn, disciplines entail particular modes of thinking or interpreting the world that students need to develop. In disciplinary work, concepts or theories are not disembodied from the knowledge building process through which they emerge.

With reference to these disciplinary considerations, what actually happens in most schools, for most students, is a curious form of détente. Certainly, students do learn facts, memorize concepts, come to master practices and performances in the classroom or in the laboratory. However, by and large such 'subject-matter knowledge' is superficial. Students master knowledge encoded in textbooks and spew that knowledge back in tests that are yoked to the textbook. Teachers and students agree to honor the 'correct answer compromise'. That is, both partners in the educational conversation agree to accept certain formulations as evidence of mastery,

ɛ not pushing one another any further on what the particular issue in
stion genuinely entails: 'If you don't push me on what energy (or photo-
thesis or a negative number, or the Russian Revolution) really means, I
wun't hold you accountable for such sophisticated understanding on the
final exam.'

And, finally, many teachers succumb to what one might term the
'teacher's fallacy'; in its most familiar form, this fallacy entails the chain of
reasoning 'I taught a great class; therefore the students must have understood'. In truth, of course, unless the teacher has the opportunity to look
carefully at student work, to probe for both understandings and nonunder-
standings, it is just not possible to ascertain how successful one's teaching
has actually been. In our view, even teachers who know a great deal about
their disciplines and about general learning principles need to diagnose
students' conceptions regularly if they are to gauge the effectiveness of
their teaching.

Despite this searing indictment of most schools in most countries, we
believe that there are schools in which teaching for understanding does
occur. In general, such institutions aim for 'uncoverage' rather than for
'coverage'; they embrace the contemporary aphorism that 'less is more'.
Certainly, the greatest enemy of understanding is coverage – the com-
pulsion to touch on everything in the textbook or the syllabus just because
it is there, rather than taking the time to present materials from multiple
perspectives, allowing students to approach the materials in ways that are
initially congenial to them but that ultimately challenge them, and assessing understandings in as direct and flexible a manner as possible. To the
extent that various schools, ranging from English boarding schools to
French lycées to John Dewey's progressive schools, have adopted a less
frenetic and more thoughtful approach to the curriculum, the opportunities
to educate for understanding can be seized.

## Teaching for Understanding in the Disciplines: An Ideal View

At least in the United States, much of what happens inside classrooms
happens for reasons unconnected to educational effectiveness: Teaching
content is determined by an externally mandated syllabus; practices endure
because they had been carried out in the past, or because they satisfy the
putative requirements of the College Board, a regimen of Carnegie units,
or the curricular ideas endorsed by the local school board.

It is possible to envision an education that assumes a totally different
form. In such an approach, one rooted in the progressive tradition of John
Dewey, Theodore Sizer, and others, the curriculum is built from the first
around gritty central questions or generative issues. These are issues that
thoughtful human beings all over the world have posed, issues for which

answers of various degrees of adequacy have been promulgated over the centuries in diverse cultures.

These basic questions are articulated by young children, on the one hand, and by seasoned philosophers, on the other; they are addressed by the disciplines created by the scholars, the roles adopted in the society, the artwork, poetry, and religion forged by the culture. Among the essential questions, grouped roughly by conceptual domains, are these:

*Identity and history*   Who am I? Where do I come from? Who is my family? What is the group to which I belong? What is the story of that group?

*Other people, groups*   Who are the other people around me, and in other parts of the world? How are they similar to and different from me? How do they look? What do they do? What is their story?

*Relations to others*   How should you treat other people? How should they treat you? What is fair? What is moral? How do you cooperate? How do you handle conflicts? Who is the boss and why?

*My place in the world*   Where do I live? How did I get here? How do I fit into the universe? What will happen to me when I die?

*The psychological world*   What is my mind? Do others have minds? Are they like mine? What are thoughts, dreams, feelings? Where do my emotions come from? How can I handle them? How do I remember things? How do I communicate?

*The biological world*   What about other creatures? What does it mean to be alive? Dead? Do animals think? What about plants? How are animals related to one another, to the world of plants, to humans? Is there a substance of life? How is it created?

*The physical world*   What is the world made up of? Why do things move? What do we know about the sun, the stars, the waters, the rocks – their origins, their fate?

*Forms, patterns, sizes*   Why do things look and feel the way that they do? What regularities are there in the world? How do they come about? What is big, biggest? How can you tell?

In an education geared toward understanding, such issues are introduced in forms that reflect relevant aspects of disciplinary inquiry from the earliest ages. Youngsters approach these questions in ways appropriate to their age, developmental stage, and learning style. Much if not most of the curriculum is tied directly to these questions; students and parents, as well as teachers, should be able readily to discern the connections among today's homework assignment, tomorrow's projects, and the questions that have animated them. Indeed, in a school geared toward understanding, one should be able to stop anyone in the halls, find out what he or she is doing, and beyond that individual relating a current activity to the questions that inspired it and to the long-term goal of achieving a sophisticated understanding of that question. This state of affairs can come about only if there is agreement across the grade levels on the principal understandings to be achieved.

How does one introduce the perennial tasks of education into a framework organized around questions? To begin with, students encounter instances of individuals (preferably 'live', but if necessary on film or transmitted electronically) who are themselves addressing these issues in a serious and engaged way. These include disciplinary experts, of course, but also ordinary men and women at work as well as individuals featured in works of art. If a society values the question 'What are human beings made of?' the student in that society should observe basic scientists attempting to answer that question; and to the extent that meaningful approaches to this question are being pursued by artists, technologists, spiritual leaders, or philosophers, these perspectives should be on ready display as well.

Having seen experts at work contemplating or solving these problems and questions, what should children do? Certainly it is important for students to master the basic literacies – to be able to read, write, and compute, with increasing ease, confidence, and automaticity. However, such literacies need to be seen as *means* – means for approaching the questions, means for learning the disciplines that represent the society's sustained attempts to tackle basic questions. This is the genius of 'whole language' classrooms or of 'project-based education' – students have the opportunity of acquiring literacies and disciplines not as unmotivated ends themselves, but rather as part of an effort to gain leverage on questions with which thoughtful persons have long wrestled. However, there are attendant risks to such holistic methods: To the extent that such projects do not build on the literacies and the disciplinary curriculum, to the extent that they wander off in other directions, the school is functioning in a fragmented fashion. In an integrated educational environment literacies and disciplinary knowledge readily make their way into students' projects and exhibitions. Even for those who have mastered the basic literacies, the road to disciplinary mastery is by no means uncluttered. Indeed, in thinking about the skills that individuals require to approach essential questions in an increasingly sophisticated way, we find it important to isolate several distinct approaches to knowing.

## Early Common Sense

From the very first, youngsters are able to utilize their incipient theories and explanatory frameworks in order to approach essential questions. We see these simple notions at work when the child explains the movement of the cloud in terms of a motor contained within it or the breath of a flying monster propelling it across the sky. Early common sense is a wonderful capacity, and it can both charm and disarm. Its exercise reflects the species' proclivity of using available symbolic forms to make sense of our surrounding world. Yet, as the philosopher Nelson Goodman once quipped, much of common sense is actually common nonsense, and it needs to be recognized as such.

## Enlightened Common Sense

Still at the level of common sense, yet more sophisticated than the garden-variety common sense of the toddler, is what we term 'enlightened common sense'. This variety is a result of experience in the culture and incipient habits of reflection and questioning. It develops spontaneously with little need for specific instruction. The difference between the eight-year-old and the four-year-old is not so much the greater disciplinary knowledge of the eight-year-old but rather his or her potential for reflecting critically on an answer, for drawing on relevant daily experience, for engaging in discussion and dialogue and benefitting from such interchange.

## Proto-disciplinary Knowledge

By the middle years of elementary school, most children are ready to adopt some of the habits of the disciplinary thinker. As budding scientists, they can think about empirical claims and the evidence that supports or undercuts them; as incipient historians, they can understand the difference between a historical and a fictional account and appreciate the role of records and texts in the creation of a historical account; as aspiring artistic practitioners, they can assume the role of the critic as well as that of the creator.

We term this approach 'proto-disciplinary' because it does not require a full-fledged immersion in the texts and the methods of the disciplines. Indeed, the roots of proto-disciplinary knowledge lie in the habits of common sense as leavened by discourse with other persons and by casual attention to the practices of reflective adults. Proto-disciplinary knowledge extends beyond common sense in that it includes some of the salient features of a discipline-based approach. At this point, there is no need for a formal delineation of disciplines – and indeed the disciplinary terrain at this point consists of but a handful of distinct approaches to knowledge. Gross distinctions between understanding in the social realm (social studies) and understanding the natural world (natural science) may be enough. In further developing disciplinary understanding, finer distinctions among disciplines (history, sociology, political science) will emerge. Given certain literate or scholarly environments, one can count on some youngsters to achieve proto-disciplinary knowledge without direct tutelage; such an expectation is not realistic when it comes to the mastery of 'normal' disciplinary knowledge.

## Normal Disciplinary Knowledge

Scholars over the centuries have accumulated the knowledge, the theories, the concepts, and above all, the methods that constitute the disciplines of today. It would be clearly impossible for any individual starting from scratch to assemble and organize that knowledge on his or her own.

Therefore, schools are in a privileged position to introduce students to
normal disciplinary knowledge – its texts, its problem sets, its ritualized
procedures – since it would be unrealistic to expect youngsters to achieve
such understandings on their own. Normal disciplinary knowledge constitutes the main course of middle school and beyond. And it is regularly
enacted 'discipline', in the aforementioned popular sense of the term,
that allows individuals to move toward disciplinary mastery.

Most schools achieve a measure of success in conveying to most students
the procedures of the major disciplines. However, as we have argued
above, disciplines tend to be conveyed (or at least, to be apprehended) in a
superficial way. Often, the focus falls on the mastery of facts, and facts, it
turns out, are remarkably bereft of genuine disciplinary content. That is, to
know the atomic weight of fluorine does not differ epistemologically from
knowing the date of the fall of Constantinople or the materials out of which
the murals on the ceiling of the Sistine Chapel were painted. Thus, so long
as the correct cues or frames are presented, it looks as though students
genuinely understand the disciplines – or at least have mastered the required subject matter. But once a question or issue is phrased in an unfamiliar way, or posed at an unexpected time, one is likely to find that
genuine understanding is absent. In fact, as has been amply documented,
when facing new situations, even students who score well on standard tests
fall back on the kinds of answers given by the five-year-old 'unschooled'
mind. Disciplinary tactics and terminology are likely to stick, but disciplinary understanding has not been achieved.

## On Beyond the Disciplines

The distinct approaches to knowledge described above suggest a developmental trend from early common sense to disciplinary understanding. It is
worth noticing that this development is not linear. A single individual may
elicit different simultaneous approaches within or across specific disciplines
depending on factors such as mastery of a particular topic, the context in
which he or she works, or the extent of scaffolding received.

In moving beyond the disciplines, three additional forms of knowing
need to be kept in mind: multi-, inter-, and meta-disciplinary knowledge.
Because performing understanding in these realms requires mastery in
specific disciplines, these forms of knowing are not often achieved successfully in the precollegiate educational systems.

## *Multidisciplinary Work*

It is possible to approach a topic or issue by employing, *seriatim*, a number
of disciplines. An individual interested in the Renaissance who approaches

this era first as a historian, then as a scientist, then as an artist, is employing a multiplicity of disciplines. And yet, so long as no attempt is made at synthesis, the whole will not be greater than the sum of its parts.

## Interdisciplinary Work

An individual who not only applies more than one discipline but actually strives to combine or synthesize these stances is engaging in that rare but precious practice called interdisciplinary work. Many questions or problems can be approached only in a pluri-disciplinary way, and many of our most honored thinkers are those who can synthesize disciplines. However, it is crucial to note that interdisciplinary work can be carried out legitimately *only* after the individual has become at least somewhat conversant in the relevant disciplines. Much of what is termed interdisciplinary or multidisciplinary work in the early grades is actually pre-disciplinary work – drawing chiefly on common sense.

## Meta-disciplinary Work

In meta-disciplinary work, rather than using disciplines to illuminate a topic or question, one focuses on the nature of disciplinary thought itself – of what the disciplines consist, how they interact, to what uses they can be put, and allied meta-cognitive concerns. It is possible to be an excellent disciplinarian without engaging in meta-disciplinary work; yet some reflectiveness about the nature of disciplinary activity should aid most students. For instance, students can receive a variety of insights when they compare a historical novel or film with a piece of historical writing or a cinematic documentary; and such a meta-disciplinary stance is certainly at a premium in the reading and writing of a [chapter] like this.

While this sequence is suggestive rather than lock-step, it is not easy – and not advisable – to speed up or to alter it. In a single high school class, one might well have students who are pre-disciplinary as well as ones who have already become deeply involved in the discipline. Moreover, the same student may be a pre-disciplinary thinker in one domain, yet exhibit considerable disciplinary understanding in another. Each student needs to be addressed at his or her level of disciplinary sophistication. At the same time, however, it is advisable to expose students of all degrees of sophistication to genuine disciplinary work, so that they receive an image of what it is like to use one's disciplinary knowledge – one's developed mind – in a productive manner. While the disciplinary sequence may be developmental, the educational setting should be holistic.

[. . .]

# Conclusion

During the past decade there has been mounting concern expressed, both in the United States and abroad, about the quality of education for all students. The so-called first wave of reform concentrated on the acquisition of basic skills and the need for higher standards. There was at best limited achievement of these goals; moreover, even when a higher level of skill was apparently achieved, it soon became evident that students were not using these skills to illuminate their understanding or to motivate them to learn further on their own.

The second wave of reform addressed issues of professionalization and management. It was considered important to place more responsibility for school at the level of the building and the principal, and to enhance the professional development of teachers. It is too early to pass judgment on this phase, but the results so far have been scattered at best.

We believe that there has been an almost purposeful avoidance of the most crucial set of questions: What is education for? How can we tell whether we have achieved success in attaining this goal? In this [chapter], which signals the need for a 'third wave', we have argued that the purpose of education should be to achieve understanding. We provided evidence that such understanding is hard to achieve, both because educators have little accumulated knowledge of how to teach for it and because students harbor many potent habits of mind that stand in the way of performances of understanding.

Still, it is premature to despair. It is possible to envision an education that places understanding centrally in the curriculum. Once the decisive step has been taken, it becomes possible – despite many obstacles – to move in the direction of greater understanding. One must activate two powerful allies: the disciplines of knowledge that have developed painstakingly over the centuries, and the habits in which students work regularly and determinedly to master knowledge and skills and to activate them in the service of understanding. The distinguished British educator Paul Hirst once argued that disciplines do not train the mind; rather, they let us see what it is to have a mind. And that is certainly a goal worth aiming for, and, perhaps, even an end to which one might meaningfully devote one's life.

[. . .]

# 7

# New Understandings of Teachers' Pedagogic Knowledge

## Frank Banks, Jenny Leach and Bob Moon

## Introduction

How significant is content or subject knowledge for creative and effective teaching? What links can be made between a teacher's knowledge and the associated pedagogic strategies and practices to ensure successful learning? How important is the updating of a teacher's knowledge base? What form should this take?

These questions illustrate a theme in teacher education that is increasingly catching the attention of policy-makers. In England and Wales, for example, in the 1990s some regulatory requirements were placed on the first degree required for entry to a postgraduate teacher training course. Secondary teachers were required to have at least two years of their first degree in the subject they wished to teach. More recent legislation (DfEE, 1998) statutorily requires that all entrants to the teaching profession demonstrate very detailed requirements relating to a specialist subject both at primary and secondary level.

The question of content, subject or disciplinary knowledge can also easily become embroiled in some of the petulant political rhetoric around education. In the USA, as in other countries, there is a continuous polemic associated with the place of disciplines in school reform. Advocacy of this importance has become linked to a particular political stance as the debate surrounding Bloom's *The Closing of the American Mind* (1987), a polemic against the contemporary curriculum of the universities, illustrated. In England and Wales a traditionalist subject-based approach to the National Curriculum attracted widespread opposition (Haviland, 1988). In the 1990s the debate has continued, again with a sometimes confusing mixture of political, epistemological and pedagogic interpretations. The frequent revisions to the National Curriculum in England and Wales since 1987 and the recently increasingly vigorous debate about how to teach it have been indicative of this.

The relationship between knowledge and pedagogy is, however, an important one and needs further exploration. Does a degree in archaeology provide a basis for teaching contemporary history? Is the high-flying physicist able to teach adequately the biology of a general science course? Can a primary teacher successfully work across the whole of the primary curriculum even though his or her subject expertise may lie in one or two areas? Does the phrase 'the best way to learn is to teach' really underpin the teaching role?

In this chapter we want to explore these issues, to describe some of the debates and research taking place, to suggest a reconceptualization of the field and to set out some preliminary research with preservice students using the model identified. The aim is to stimulate debate around an important area, not least in providing a stronger theoretical framework against which policy and regulatory proposals can be described, analysed and critiqued.

## The Subject Knowledge Debate

In debating these questions we have formulated a distinction between the terms knowledge, school knowledge and pedagogy. Our focus, therefore, is on the definitions and inter-relations of these three concerns for teacher education. We acknowledge the wider concerns that influence and constrain the manifestations of each within the development of teacher knowledge and expertise. We are sympathetic, for example, to Walter Doyle's (1983, p. 377) assertion that he 'continues to be impressed by the extent to which classroom factors push the curriculum around'. The concern here, however, is with a specific focus on the relation of knowledge to pedagogy.

In seeking a stronger theoretical foundation to this work we have been working with three clusters of ideas: the curriculum-orientated work of Shulman (1986), the cognitive approach of Gardner (1983; 1991) and the inter-related tradition of didactics and pedagogy in continental Europe (Verret, 1975; Chevellard, 1991). Having identified key areas of professional knowledge, we have also considered how a teacher's professional development is also centrally formed by the 'community of practice' of schools and subject communities. We review each of these ideas in turn.

## The Curriculum Perspective

Since the mid-1980s there has been a growing body of research into the complex relationship between subject knowledge and pedagogy (Shulman, 1986; Shulman and Sykes, 1986; Wilson *et al.*, 1987; MacNamara, 1991). Shulman's original work in this field has been an obvious starting point, arising from the pertinent question: 'how does the successful college student transform his or her expertise into the subject matter form that high school students can comprehend?' (Shulman, 1986, p. 5). His conceptual framework is based on the now well-known distinction between *subject content knowledge, curricular knowledge* and the category of *pedagogic content knowledge*. This complex analysis has spawned a plethora of subject-specific research (e.g. Leinhardt and Smith, 1985; Wilson and Wineberg, 1988; Grossman *et al.*, 1989; McDiarmid *et al.*, 1989).

Whilst our exploration of professional knowledge has acknowledged Shulman's analysis as an important and fruitful starting point, it has offered only partial insight into the complex nature of subject expertise for teaching. We are critical in particular of Shulman's implicit emphasis on professional knowledge as a static body of content somehow lodged in the mind of the teacher. Shulman's work, we would argue, is informed by an essentially objectivist epistemology. In this tradition academic scholars search for ultimate truths, whilst teachers 'merely seek to make that privileged representation accessible to ordinary mortals' (McKewan and Bull, 1991). Pedagogical content knowledge as defined by Shulman (1986, p. 6) requires the subject specialist to know 'the most useful forms of analogies, illustrations, examples, explanations, and demonstrations – in a word, the ways of representing and formulating the subject in order to make it comprehensible to others'. From this perspective, Shulman's work leans on a theory of cognition that views knowledge as a contained, fixed and external body of information but also on a teacher-centred pedagogy which focuses primarily on the skills and knowledge that the teacher possesses, rather than on the process of learning:

> The key to distinguishing the knowledge base of teaching lies at the intersection of content and pedagogy, in the capacity of *a teacher to transform the content knowledge he/she possesses* into forms that are pedagogically powerful and yet adaptive to the variations in ability and background presented by the students.
>
> (Shulman, 1987, p. 15)

## The Learner Perspective

Gardner's (1983) work by contrast provides us with a perspective on professional knowledge which is rooted in a fundamental reconceptualization of knowledge and intelligence. His theory of multiple intelligences, centrally informed by the sociocultural psychology of Bruner (1986; 1996), encourages a perspective on pedagogy that places emphasis on student understanding. The focus shifts from teachers' knowledge to learners' understandings, from techniques to purposes. The five entry points which Gardner (1991) proposes for approaching any key concept, narrational, logical-quantitative, foundation, experiential and aesthetic, do not simply represent a rich and varied way of mediating a subject. Rather they emphasize the process of pedagogy and a practice which seeks to promote the highest level of understanding possible (Gardner and Boix-Mansilla, 1994). At the same time, Gardner's work places discipline and domain at the core of pedagogy. Drawing extensively from Dewey, he argues that understanding through

disciplinary knowledge is indispensable: 'Organised subject matter represents the ripe fruitage of experiences . . . it does not represent perfection or
infallible vision; but it is the best at command to further new experiences
which may, in some respects at least, surpass the achievements embodied in
existing knowledge and works of art' (*ibid.*, p. 198). Gardner's espousal of
disciplinary knowledge has, in earlier exchanges, been criticized. Gardner,
says Egan (1992, p. 403), seems to offer progressive programmes to achieve
traditionalist aims, and he goes on (*ibid.*, p. 405) to argue that Gardner's
solution

> appears to assume that effective human thinking is properly more disciplined,
> more coherent and more consistent than seems to me to be the case. This is not
> an argument on behalf of greater in-discipline, incoherence and inconsistency,
> but a speculation that human thinking operates very effectively with a consider-
> able degree of those characteristics, and that attempting to reduce them to
> greater conformity with what seems like rules of disciplinary understanding –
> whose provisionalness and unclarity should not be underestimated – will more
> likely reduce our humanity or enhance it.

He further states: 'the danger of letting disciplinary understanding call the
educational tune was, for Dewey, no less than an attack on democracy
itself. It inevitably lead to an aristocracy, or meritocracy, and so to the
kinds of social divisions America was founded to prevent' (*ibid.*).

Gardner (1992) is quick to retort and, in return, also quotes extensively
from Dewey to back up his claim for the pre-eminence of understanding
through disciplinary knowledge in reforming teaching and schooling:
'Organised subject matter represents the ripe fruitage of experiences . . . it
does not represent perfection or infallible vision; but it is the best at command to further new experiences which may, in some respects at least,
surpass the achievements embodied in existing knowledge and works of art.'

Gardner's work has been critical in challenging views of cognition
based on the concept of 'intelligence', and his work is central to an endeavour to challenge widely held notions of ability as fixed and unchang-
ing (see Gardner, 1983). His espousal of disciplines and exploration of
curricula which are rooted in, but which move beyond, disciplines into
'generative themes' has given rise to some important work (Project Zero
– Sizer, 1992; Gardner, 1983). However it has little epistemological analytical underpinning.

## The Pedagogical Perspective

For this we have turned to the work of Verret (1975) and Chevellard
(1991). The concept of didactic transposition, a process by which subject
knowledge is transformed into school knowledge, an analytical category in
its own right, permits us both to understand and question the process by
which disciplinary transformations take place. The range of historical

examples in Verret's work also provides for the social and ideological dimensions of the construction of knowledge. *La transposition didactique* of Chevellard is defined as a process of change, alteration and restructuring which the subject-matter must undergo if it is to become teachable and accessible to novices or children. As this work is less known and less accessible to English-speaking discourse we will give a little more space to explanation. Verret's original thesis was that school knowledge, in the way it grows out of any general body of knowledge, is inevitably codified, partial, formalized and ritualized. Learning in that context is assumed to be programmable, defined in the form of a text, syllabus or national curriculum, with a conception of learning that implies a beginning and an end, an initial state and a final state. Verret argues that knowledge in general cannot be sequenced in the same way as school knowledge and that generally learning is far from being linear. Such a model, he suggests, in ways that predate Gardner, lacks cognitive validity as it does not take into account the schemes, constructed representations and personal constructs of the learner.

Verret's thesis is illustrated by a range of historical examples. He describes, for instance, the transformation of literature and divinatory magic into the scholastic forms of Confucian schooling and of Christian metaphysics into school and university philosophy. He looks in detail at the version of Latin that was constructed for the French schools of the seventeenth century and the way this evolved didactically in the centuries that follow.

For Chevellard, as with Verret, 'didactic objects', which we have termed school knowledge, are under constant interpretation and reinterpretation, a process which operates at a number of different levels. Didactic transformation of knowledge, therefore, becomes for Tochan and Munby (1993, pp. 206–7):

> a progressive selection of relevant knowledge, a sequential transmission involving a past and a future, and a routine memory of evolutionary models of knowledge. Because didactics is a diachronic anticipation of contents to be taught it is essentially prepositional. It names teaching experience in propositional networks and so involves a mediation of time.

The process of didactics is carefully distinguished from pedagogy (*ibid.*):

> Some research on novice teaching suggests that they have abilities to plan but encounter problems during immediate interactions. They seem to identify their role as a mainly didactic one. Their way of organising time has no flexibility; it is not synchronic . . . Though action research and reflection reveals the existence of basic principles underlying practical classroom experience, no matter what rules might be inferred pedagogy still remains an adventure.

## Understanding Teachers' Pedagogic Knowledge

Figure 7.1 represents in diagrammatic form our synthesis of the inter-relation of subject knowledge, school knowledge and pedagogic

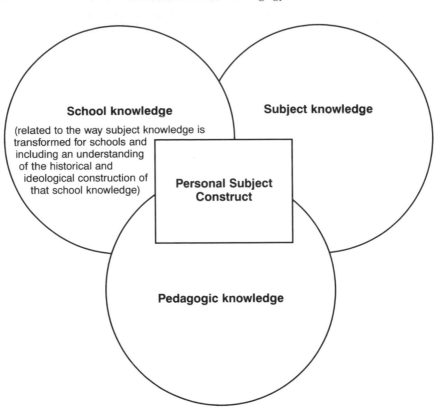

School knowledge

(related to the way subject knowledge is
transformed for schools and
including an understanding
of the historical and
ideological construction of
that school knowledge)

Subject knowledge

Personal Subject
Construct

Pedagogic knowledge

Figure 7.1   *Teachers' professional knowledge*

knowledge, our starting point for conceptualizing teacher professional
knowledge. Shulman's category of subject content knowledge we have
retained, but we denote it simply as *subject knowledge*. In doing so we wish
to emphasize the dynamic, process-driven nature of subject knowledge
which encompasses essential questions, issues and phenomenon drawn
from the natural and human world, methods of inquiry, networks of concepts, theoretical frameworks, techniques for acquiring and verifying findings . . . symbol systems, vocabularies and mental models (Gardner, 1994).
*School knowledge*, we suggest, is an analytic category in its own right,
subsuming the curricular knowledge of Shulman. We have, therefore, split
the category of pedagogic content knowledge as defined by Shulman to
gain a greater hold on this important epistemological construct. By 'school
knowledge' we do not mean a knowledge of the school context. Rather we
view it as the transposition of subject knowledge referred to above.

Our third category which we call *pedagogic knowledge* we see as going
beyond the generic set of beliefs and practices that inform teaching and
learning. Although these exist, and rightly form an important part of the
development of teacher expertise, they are insufficient we would argue,

unless integrated into an understanding of the crucial relationship between subject knowledge and school knowledge.

One might initially see 'school knowledge' as being intermediary between subject knowledge (knowledge of technology as practised by different types of technologists, for example) and pedagogic knowledge as used by teachers ('the most powerful analogies, illustrations, example, explanations and demonstrations'). This would be to underplay the dynamic relationship between the categories of knowledge implied by the diagram. For example, a teacher's subject knowledge is transformed by his or her own pedagogy in practice and by the resources which form part of his or her school knowledge. It is the active interaction of subject knowledge, school knowledge and pedagogical understanding and experience that brings teacher professional knowledge into being.

Lying at the heart of this dynamic process are the *personal constructs* of the teacher, a complex amalgam of past knowledge, experiences of learning, a personal view of what constitutes 'good' teaching and belief in the purposes of the subject. This all underpins a teacher's professional knowledge and holds good for any teacher. A student teacher needs to question his or her personal beliefs about his or her subject as he or she works out a rationale for classroom practice. But so must those teachers who, although more expert, have experienced profound changes of what contributes 'school knowledge' during their career.

## The Model in Use

This model has been discussed with a number of professionals groups in the UK and in other parts of the world such as Spain, The Netherlands, Sweden and South Africa (Banks *et al.*, 1996; Leach and Banks, 1996; Moon and Banks, 1996; Banks, 1997). These professionals have been different groups of school teachers of design and technology and of English, teacher educators and researchers. The reaction to the model across this spectrum of professional expertise has been remarkably similar. We have noticed the following points:

- The different aspects of teacher knowledge are recognized by all these groups as being meaningful. Teachers, in particular, are excited by the categories and value the model as a way of easily articulating what they know and are able to do. The model has a spin-off for mentoring and initial teacher education, facilitating explicit discussion about the nature of professional knowledge.
- School knowledge is often misunderstood as knowledge of the context for teaching. This illustrates the importance of this category in framing the teacher's role.
- The model can be interpreted at different levels. Some see it as a tool for categorizing personal understanding. Others see it as being useful for planning in-service development for a group of teachers.

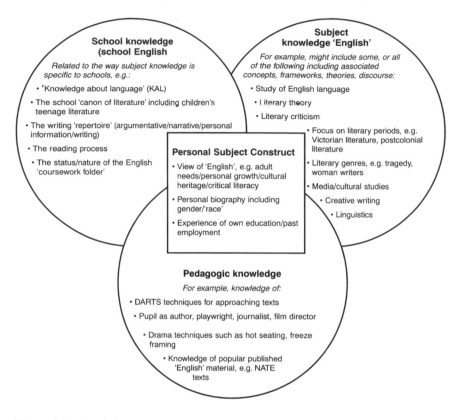

Figure 7.2    *English teachers' professional knowledge*

Figure 7.2 illustrates the way in which the model was developed by one group of English teachers. They recognized a strong distinction between 'English' as conceived for example by university and college courses and 'school English'. In most schools much of the English literature studied involves knowledge of authors, themes and styles (texts written for children or teenagers, or deemed suitable for the younger reader) distinctively different from literature studied in universities and colleges. And few English courses at degree level currently incorporate knowledge about the reading process, but this is a statutory part of school 'English' in the UK.

We would argue that the development of professional knowledge is a dynamic process. It depends on the interaction of the elements we have identified, but is brought into existence by the learning context itself – learners, setting, activity and communication as well as context in its broadest sense. In order to illustrate this socially situated, essentially participatory process (Lave and Wenger, 1991), we present two case studies. The first illustrates the dilemmas presented for a new student teacher where the elements described by our model are still incompletely formed, certainly an inevitable experience for student teachers in the early part of training. The vignette focuses on two technology students at the *beginning teaching* (Furlong and Maynard, 1995) phase of development. It illustrates both the developmental nature of professional knowledge and the difficulty novice students face in combining the complex but distinctive elements of this process. The second illustration focuses on a student teacher of English in the final stage of her initial training, raising further issues for our model in practice.

## Case Study 1: Emerging Professional Knowledge – Issues and Problems

Although they are at the *beginning teaching* phase of their course, Alun and Geoff have already planned and begun to pair-teach a series of lessons for their placement school. The department was concerned that the existing school scheme of work which was offered in Year 7 did not yet include aspects of simple electronics. The mentor asked Alun and Geoff, working as a pair, to organize the teaching of this. Significantly, the mentor herself lacked subject knowledge in this area (having a business studies background) and asked the students to come up with the resources for a project which the whole department could use. She thought that a knowledge of subject should enable the students to produce an adequate resource.

Although some advice was given by the science department, the students were largely left to themselves. Using their own ideas and curriculum materials such as textbooks and electronic kits already in the school, the students decided to organize their teaching around the development of a face mask with flashing eyes. They found this a very difficult exercise. A particular lesson concerned the pupils investigating which materials were conductors and which insulators. To do this the student teachers employed a standard kit called *Locktronics* but talked about the circuit by drawing diagrams on the chalkboard.

### Subject Knowledge

The students' own understanding of simple electricity was sufficient, but lacked the flexible and sophisticated (McDiarmid *et al.*, 1989) features to ensure it was conveyed clearly. They understood electricity themselves, but were unsure of the depth and nature of the topic in this design-and-make task. For example, a description of current flow also involved a confusing discussion of electron flow. A picture of a battery was combined (incorrectly) with a diagram of the electrical symbols. The rather unsatisfactory chalkboard illustration shown in Figure 7.3 was the result.

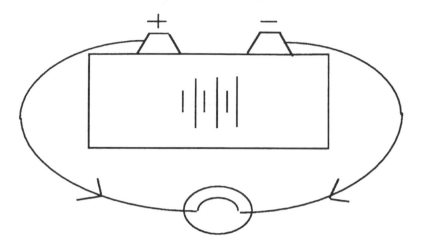

Figure 7.3   *Current flow/electron flow*

## School Knowledge

The purpose of the project was unclear in the minds of the student teachers. When describing the task they would sometimes see it as means to teach design and making (a practical 'capability task'). However, the functional aspects of wearing the mask were not thought through. For example, the students had not considered the weight or where the battery would be located on the mask, or how it would be supported. They also recognized practical skills such as soldering as being central but had not allowed enough time to develop such skills. In practice, the face mask became a means to teach aspects of electronics.

They thought that an understanding of $V = IR$ was important, but the science department had suggested that the use of such an equation was too difficult for 11-year-old pupils. Their desire to teach the *science* subject background, such as (in this lesson) conductors and insulators and the existence of electrons, cut down on the time for making. They were unclear if the overall purpose of the activity was designing, acquiring specific skills or a seeing-is-believing confirmation of scientific principles. Overall, their understanding of school technology was poor without the necessary pedagogic rationale or appropriate strategies.

## Pedagogic Knowledge

Only Geoff had used the electronics kits before as a pupil, and both student teachers were unfamiliar with the way they could be used in the classroom. The pupils had some difficulty in manipulating the components and in interpreting the circuits which they had constructed on the boards. For

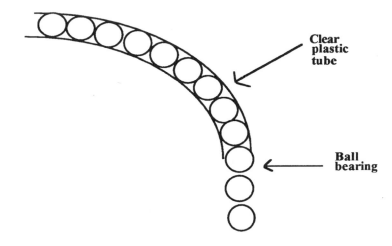

Figure 7.4     *Electrons*

example the pupils did not easily link up the connectors to make the bulb light as they invariably first constructed a loop of wire to the bulb before connecting the power supply (referred to as a battery in the original explanation by the student teacher). Later the pupils did not see how the kit could be adapted to accommodate different-shaped rods of various materials in an experiment to clarify 'conductors' and 'insulators'.

As these students were not able to enlist the experience of their mentor, they drew on their own embryonic pedagogic knowledge to formulate teaching activities for the project. They naturally used analogies to try to convey ideas about electrical flow. For example, Geoff talked about how it is easier to walk around a hill, rather than walk over it, in an attempt to cover quickly the idea of a short circuit. As they considered a knowledge of electrons an essential prerequisite to an understanding of conductors and insulators, Alun showed the following real model and then talked about it using the chalkboard diagram given in Figure 7.4:

The actual tube, shown to the pupils later, represented the wire, and the ball bearings were the electrons. It is unclear what the pupils thought about the size of electrons and the need for a conductor for electron flow! Alun was asked where the analogy came from:

*Alun:*       Well I picked it up from a book but er    yeah, I don't think I've ever seen anything like that, I just thought if I used the analogy it would be helpful rather than just explaining it.

*Interviewer:*  There were a number of analogies that were used in the lesson in general. Where did the idea of using analogies for electricity come from, I mean, why do it like that? For example, Geoff was talking about would you go round the hill or would you go over the top of the hill . . .

*A:*         I don't know where he got that from.

*I:*          Have you ever heard anything like that before?

A:          Yes. Yeah, yeah . . . er, electricity flowed through the easiest part
            and water would have sound and things like that, I've come across
            them yes. I can . . . I've got a bit of an idea, never thought of using it
            but he brought it into the context quite well. Um . . . I don't know,
            do you learn these things through life? Possibly so. Reading . . .

and Geoff, separately, reinforced this didactic role, missing the fact that the
pedagogy employed in the lesson was having limited success (see Tochan
and Munby, 1993):

I:          How did you come up with what to do when?
Geoff:      Well, we sort of sat down. I had a project that I'd seen a friend of mine
            had done a few years back – he's a teacher, now – so we had that to
            start. It was a different project but it was electronics. It was a different
            circuit but basically . . . slightly different, but we had the way he's
            structured it, we had a look at that and said, 'Right, what's good about
            this, what's missing?' and what have you. We also went through a lot of
            books, different books, and if you read them they're all basic electricity
            or electronic books, they're all a bit much the same. They all go
            through the same steps as well. You've got to start at the beginning, so
            if you haven't done anything on what electrons are or what a conductor
            is, then how do you explain to them why it's flowing later on? We've
            got . . . if you just stick the circuit up there, you're going backwards and
            we decided . . . what is the basics of it? What are the mechanics of any
            circuit, and come through it that way.

The student teachers wished to scaffold the learning of the pupils and they
believed a hands-on approach was appropriate. However they found it difficult to leave the pupils to experiment with the kits, and continually inter-
vened to move them on as time was felt to be so short. Too much was
attempted too quickly and some pupils became confused then bored. The
students did not have the pedagogical knowledge to know which aspects of
electricity are difficult to convey. Indeed, they were unsure of how all this
fitted into school knowledge of technology as they were unclear about why
they were teaching this in relation to this particular design-and-make project.

## Personal Subject Constructs

Both Geoff and Alun have a personal subject construct moulded by experience in industry which strongly influences their direction and orientation to
how and why pupils should learn technology. They both see hands on as
being vital (although they get side tracked by a belief that detailed theoretical science concepts are an inevitable precursor to understanding of school
technology) and wish to emphasize a link to marketing the face-mask
product (although that aspect is not made explicit to the pupils):

Alun:       I've a belief that everyone should follow technology with a business and a
            legal aspect, i.e. unless you know how much it's gonna cost, it's pointless
            designing something . . . Can we make it? Far too often we find we design
            things which do not take into the remit . . . realistic targets. So I'd like to
            relate technology to more . . . creative depth within the curriculum. We
            could include mathematics, i.e. costs, working out costs of things, what
            it's going to cost you. Er . . . Perhaps I've deviated slightly there, I don't
            know. My own views I think you've got there.

## Case Study 2: Developing Professional Knowledge – Issues and Possibilities

Our second case study focuses a student in the *autonomous* phase of her teacher education course. It describes the beginning of a sequence of English lessons prepared and taught by Lucy in her final school experience and illustrates the way in which a more experienced student is beginning to combine the different elements of professional knowledge. This case study presents the student's own selected reflection on her first experience of teaching an A-Level English group; a group studying at a level closer to her own level of understanding. The transcript is deliberately juxtaposed with other data drawn from written assignments to attempt to illustrate the variety of knowledge and experience she is synthesizing in this account:

### Teaching A-Level English for the first time

Whan that April with his showres soote
The droughte of March hath perced to the root
And bathed every veyne in swich licour
Of which vertu engendered is the flour;
When Zephirus eek with his sweete breath
Inspired hath in every holt and heeth
The tendre croppes, and the yonge sonne
Hath in his ram his halve course
And smale fowles maken melodye
That slepen al the nyght with open Ye
and (So pricketh hem nature in hir courages);
Thanne longen folk to goon pilgrimages.

From Chaucer's *Prologue to the Canterbury Tales*

I had this sixth form . . . an exam class. Their set book for this part of the term was Chaucer's 'Prologue' . . . I hadn't done Chaucer for about . . . since . . . 1975 and er I thought 'Gosh! I can't remember this book', the idea of going back to study and look at the background information . . . and all that . . . and the idea of having to experiment with a sixth form class was a new experience I was trying to look for. And based on that what I did first was to try to find out what kind of students they were . . . what level they were at . . . what was the method of teaching the sixth form? And I discovered that most of the time for sixth formers was too staid, too strict and too formal and I thought, teaching them Chaucer, which is an entirely different language from the normal present-day English, I had to bring it out in a very interesting way and make them go into it without scaring them off, like I was scared when I was doing it in the sixth form.

So *what my mentor and I* decided to do was to go about it in a fun way. *We decided* that my first lesson was going to be a kind of . . . group work, all the lessons were group work except for when they were going to write, and *we decided* that *we should ask them* to plan a modern pilgrimage, just kind of break them into the idea of pilgrimages and the motive behind pilgrimages.

My mentor's an extremely imaginative person, don't know how she gets all the ideas, and it just comes like that, I get my ideas basically from her and from . . . classes I observed during my teaching practice. So my mentor was really quite instrumental towards all the ideas I had.

Vygotsky's theory of social constructivism emphasises 'human potential and educability' which does not recognise any notion of absolute imitation. This theory emphasises 'the crucial role of human culture in the development and direction of learning' . . . there is great emphasis here on the role of language in learning. [ . . . ] (Written assignment)

I asked them to come together in groups of fours, think of characters within this country for example who might go on a protest – animal rights, or something like that, characters within the groups, the genuine ones and the ones with different motives, then draw the characters, what they're wearing and why they think they're wearing this outfit and give them dialogue. So *we did that* and they presented it to the class and it really was very good!

With that *I* was now able to come into Chaucer and talk about Chaucer as a person, who he was, his background and then what the society was then, in medieval times, and . . . what *I* felt Chaucer's motive was in writing the 'General Prologue' and that kind of, the kind of activity they'd done gave them the basics and they were able to look at . . . in that light without just looking at it in terms of the text book, but looking at it in terms of life itself and how they can actually assimilate what's been happening in this present life and what's been happening in medieval times. It was quite successful because after the first lesson, there was a parents' evening. I didn't even know what had happened and when I came back the following day my mentor said to me 'What did you teach them? Show me what you did'. And the kids had gone to tell their parents that they had a very exciting lesson in Chaucer.

At T School, in English lessons, students are often placed in a variety of contexts in which they are speaking and listening, reading and writing contemporaneously . . . the department recognises the central importance of speaking and listening which, in real life are the most used elements of language. In most of my lessons speaking preceded writing and reading.

(Final written assignment)

My partner school is situated at the edge of Coventry. A high percentage of children come from the neighbouring council estates but also from the privately owned housing around the area. Asian Moslems and Brethren children from the city centre attend because their parents prefer a single sex school.                                        (Written assignment)

Lucy:   Then after that, *we did* . . . *we took* the first 42 lines which was introduc-
        tion, basically and did it *together as a group* so they could have that sense
        of security . . . because I wasn't feeling too secure myself . . . (laughs) . . .
        so it was kind of a '*get it together*' and then we did the translation
        *together*. And *I* introduced them to reference books that they could use.
        After that *I* gave them homework, that they were to go back and use the
        CD-ROM, use the library, and do research into Chaucer's background
        the historical perspective, sociological and geographical . . . They went

and did a lot of research . . . because without that most of the information would be lost to them and they would not be able to understand and empathise with what Chaucer was trying to do and what society was like then. And that was quite good as well!

By the time they came back, *I* had found a tape, a tape of 'The Canterbury Tales' and *I* thought 'this is good', it's going to take the pressure off me because I don't know how to pronounce this and the kids are now going to listen, get the meaning without worrying about the pronunciation! *We would* have spent so much time on . . . that would have done them in actually in terms of their confidence . . . and that worked . . . *we listened* to the tape (which was very funny because of the pronunciation) and then we *stopped* it intermittently to discuss the issues and then *we went back* to their groups and started sketching. Sketching the characters *as we read* them . . . the picture that came to them and how they saw those characters and they were able to present it together as a kind of display to the class . . . And that was how *we did it*.

> Teachers in T School English Department share knowledge with other members of staff. There are regular INSET programmes for staff and special provision is made to newly qualified staff to enable them to develop confidence and versatility – they have quite a number of resources in the department. I looked through them and picked out what I thought was going to be useful to me.
> (Written assignment)

> Even the map for the route to Canterbury . . . that I gave to the students, somebody in the department gave me that too.

## Subject Knowledge

Lucy has been required, in the sequence of lessons she describes, to introduce an A-Level English group to Chaucer's *General Prologue*, a set examination text. Her subject knowledge includes this text, but she has done additional work to ensure that she gets to grips with the text in detail; she uses a study guide, for example, to help her refresh her knowledge of the work. Lucy recognizes, however, that she will be out of her depth in reading Middle English aloud, so she ensures she obtains an audiotape to help her. Her existing knowledge of Chaucer does not prevent her from feeling nervous about tackling it for the first time with A-Level students, but she has enough confidence to see that the task demands a joint interrogation of the text. She also sees the need to be flexible enough to encourage students to form their own interpretations which requires them to give evidence for their views: 'Using prying questions helped them to focus, constantly reminding them of the need for quotation to prove their point of view' (mentor notes).

The mentor's notes underline Lucy's strong and developing subject knowledge: 'Lucy explains and draws together – emphasises main points again – showing thorough preparation and knowledge. Points out missing information from group 1 – 'Amor vincit omnia' – asks group the significance rather than explaining straight away – good. Groups have access to other groups' sheets – benefit from others' research.'

## School Knowledge

As with the technology lesson the 'school English' demands decisions about a variety of complex concepts and a selection from her own subject knowledge. Lucy has to use her knowledge of the conventions of teaching A-Level and its 'set book' demands to decide, for example, when and how to introduce the language and form of the poem, concepts such as setting, character, theme, tone, authorial voice, and skills such as use of textual evidence. The knowledge demanded also cuts across school disciplines – in this case history and sociology. She has to decide whether to introduce the historical and cultural context of the text. In her lesson-planning notebook she writes 'it is possible to enjoy Chaucer without the knowledge of the social and cultural background, but much would be lost. The context will be missed.'

## Pedagogic Knowledge

Lucy, like the technology students, draws on analogy. She transfers the notion of a pilgrimage into a modern 'protest'. This is fairly standard methodology for English teachers but she uses it quite subtly so that the analogy works at several levels. First it allows the pupils to choose a 'cause' they feel committed to, thus enabling the pupils to 'get inside' the notion of pilgrimage successfully. Secondly, by underlining that they should choose different 'characters' with differing motives she simultaneously prepares them for Chaucer's intensely visual, vivid characterization of the pilgrims, as well as their multifarious motives. The group task thus enables the pupils to be autonomous and gives free rein to their own ideas drawing on known contexts, whilst preparing them for varied concepts of pilgrimage, character, motive and authorial viewpoint including irony and hyperbole.

Use is made of curricular materials prepared by the department (e.g. map of Canterbury, audiotape of poem) in addition to her own structured materials for groupwork. She also establishes what materials are available in the library and on CD-ROM.

Lucy's account illustrates the way in which the different elements of her professional knowledge intersect. She sees her pupils as young intellectuals and has the highest expectations for them: 'productive lesson – ALL had to work hard!, weaker students supported by more able' (Mentor notes).

## *Personal and Collective Subject Constructs*

Lucy worked as an unqualified teacher in Nigeria before her four children were born. Lucy's personal construct of English is centrally informed by the fact that English is her second language:

> *Lucy:* I think . . . English to me would . . . means a mode of expression . . . expressing oneself. It's communication . . . the language of . . . speech . . . erm . . . business . . . er . . . instruction . . . A language! It's a mode that takes you out of isolation into a kind of community where you can communicate with other people. That's as far as I think it is. Because to me . . . English is . . . because English is not my first language . . . I probably look at English from a different point of view from an English person, because I speak other languages as well. So English to me is just another way of communicating with people in a language they understand . . . and . . . um . . . English is not much different from what you're doing in other classes . . . you're concentrating on the language itself as a science . . .

Lucy's transcript demonstrates that whilst this view may be the one that she articulates, other views are influential in her practice, not least the view of English teaching held by her host department and mentor in particular. Although by the middle of her third school experience she is developing in confidence and style, her mentor still sees her role as critically important. She still co-plans work with Lucy, observing many lessons carefully and providing both oral and detailed written commentary. This stands in strong contrast to the views frequently voiced by mentors in students' final school experiences that they should 'be on their own now', or that they should not be 'over-reliant on departmental schemes of work'. Students are frequently criticized at this stage and even earlier for being 'unable to come up with their own ideas'.

## Developing Teacher Professional Knowledge in Communities of Practice

As preservice teachers, Alun, Geoff and Lucy are newcomers being inducted into a setting strongly influenced by their school environment and interaction with 'old timers' – other professionals, particularly their mentor. In this sense we recognize that our conceptualization of professional knowledge needs to be rooted in a social theory of learning. Lave's (1988; 1991) research has underlined the way in which cognitive change is an attribute of situated pedagogical relationships in particular settings and contexts. Her research with adult learners engaged in new learning situations focuses on the social situation or participation framework in which such learning takes place, a process of involvement in communities of practice. She has proposed the concept of legitimate peripheral participation, a process of gradual involvement in communities of practice that is at first legitimately peripheral, gradually increasing in engagement and complexity. To become a full member of a community of practice requires access to 'a wide range of ongoing activity, old-timers, and other members of the community; and to information, resources and opportunities for participation in communities of practice' (Lave and Wenger, 1991, p. 101). Newcomers, Lave contends, can be prevented from this vital peripheral participation if they are *not given productive access to activity in the community of practitioners or if the meaning of such activities is not made transparent.*

The contrast in the way the two case studies illustrate access to the professional community of practice is marked. Lucy's account would seem to demonstrate 'productive access in a community of practitioners' and how such activity has been made transparent. The pronouns *I* and *we* that Lucy uses throughout the transcript as she talks about her planning and teaching have been deliberately highlighted. She moves imperceptibly between them. Sometimes the *we* refers to herself and her mentor, indicating the importance of the collaborative planning despite her growing confidence in solo teaching. At the beginning of the transcript, for example, it would appear as though she co-taught the first lesson with her mentor: '*What my mentor and I* decided to do was . . . so *we did that*'. It is only when she notes that her mentor 'asked me "What did you teach them?"' that it becomes clear that Lucy was teaching alone. Lucy provides clear evidence that she is working in a department that operates explicitly as a community of English teachers. Both experienced and new members of staff are encouraged to share new materials, feedback from courses, exchange views on the subject 'English' as well as supporting each other in planning new curriculum practice. Because the experienced teachers see themselves as learners, so the student is able to see departmental practice as an ongoing pedagogical 'adventure' (Tochan and Munby, 1993) of research and critical inquiry.

In the final sentence of her account, the second time she has used the phrase 'that's how *we* did it', she emphatically gathers together the *community of practice* of which she has been a part. The phrase draws together herself both as teacher and learner, her pupils, other members of the department and of course her mentor. The process of teaching and learning from this perspective has been powerfully described by Bruner (1986, p. 129) as a forum or dialogue, a constant meeting of minds in which teacher and learner engage in a negotiation of shared meaning:

> The language of education, if it is to be an invitation to reflection and culture creating, cannot be the so-called uncontaminated language of fact and objectivity. It must express stance and counter-stance and in the process leave place for reflection, for metacognition. It is this that permits one to reach higher ground, this process of objectifying in language and image what one has thought and then turning around on it and reconsidering it.

Such a process critically extends the role of teacher or mentor well beyond that of mere facilitator or coach, for the quality of the cognitive support becomes a key dimension: 'Legitimate peripheral participation places the explanatory burden . . . on the cultural practice in which the learning is taking place, on issues of access, and on the *transparency of the cultural environment with respect to the meaning of what is being learned*' (Lave and Wenger, 1991, pp. 104–5 *emphasis added*).

What Lucy initiates in this classroom is by its situated nature a singular combination of the professional knowledge and experience she brings, the context and setting, her relationship with and response to her students as well as the knowledge and experience they contribute. In her rich, if incomplete, attempt to articulate this process, she nevertheless clearly illustrates the way in which the different elements described by our framework intersect. This is a unique process which is not abstract but concrete and dynamic, inherently fraught with challenge and dilemmas (McDiarmid *et al.*, 1989). She sees herself as engaged in a community of practice. She is working alongside subject specialists who view learning itself as an interactive process of connecting pupils to the community of the discipline (English) and more broadly to critical inquiry and research.

Alun and Geoff, by contrast, are denied productive access to participation in their placement school and the 'learning curriculum' of this community (Burgess and Leach, 1996). Their mentor did not share the same specialist area within technology (being a business studies teacher) and access to observable lessons and to advice for their electronics lessons was limited:

*Interviewer*:  OK, so you haven't actually observed a lot of actual teaching, is that what you're saying?

*Alun*:      Teaching of the subject, no. Definitely not. I've been too involved myself teaching.

And Geoff's comments on the subject advice received from the science department in a different area of the school, *not* from the technology department: 'They are trying to help us out, definitely, but I mean that's like anything, they haven't got . . . They've got their own problems as well so they've limited time, so we're obviously going to miss things so that's why we're going round a few times.'

Lucy's account articulates the community of practice in which the knowledge and experience she brings can develop. The semi-detached nature of Alun and Geoff's involvement with a corresponding community of subject specialists, by contrast, reinforces the importance of this interaction in the development of critical pedagogy.

## Conclusion

In this chapter we have argued for a reconceptualization of the relationship between knowledge and pedagogy and offer a framework through which this can be achieved. We accept the limitations of any diagrammatic representation and have already, in a number of presentations, been pushed to develop a three-dimensional configuration! The aim at this stage, however, is to stimulate further debate and research. Finding a place for 'subject' is important in primary and secondary schools as well as in the 'secret garden' curriculum of further and higher education. The analysis we suggest is every bit as significant for the university lecturer as the nursery school teacher.

In teacher education it is critical that these issues are fully explored. A model of practice must evolve that acknowledges the importance of subject knowledge within the curriculum as much as the processes or pedagogies of teaching. To do this is not necessarily to reassert some traditionalist subject-centred view of the curriculum, or to adopt solely a secondary or tertiary perspective; it is rather to say that 'subject' is important.

The model points to the need for greater sophistication in the curriculum-building process that creates particular forms of school knowledge. The analysis of *la transposition didactique* (the use of transposition rather than transformation is significant) points up some of the clumsiness that goes on in building curriculum at a national level. The jockeying for space and the internal feuds of subject communities that have been associated with the building of the National Curriculum in England and Wales give scant regard to the epistemological and methodological issues raised by Verret and Chevellard. The boundary between knowledge and school knowledge, however, is more than the framing of a national curriculum. It is part of the web and weave of a teacher's daily work – whether the recollection of a metaphor or the building of a whole scheme of work the transposition of knowledge is a continuous process. Again we need to look more deeply into the issues raised. Does the English teacher who sat at the feet of Leavis thirty years ago teach differently, create different forms of learning than a younger colleague with Derrida or Foucault as a model? Does the technology teacher with a three-dimensional design background offer his or her pupils substantially different insights into product development from the one who studied mechanical engineering? Do the primary teachers who are mathematicians, scientists or musicians bring particular advantages to their class or particular attributes to their teaching? Our knowledge in these areas is limited and needs to be extended.

The central argument of this chapter is thus, that the interfaces between knowledge, school knowledge (i.e. that selection from the broader fields of knowledge that constitutes the school curriculum), pedagogic knowledge and personal construct are crucial areas of inquiry. The surprisingly separate worlds of curriculum and teaching studies, we contend, need to be brought together in any reconceptualization of practice.

We contend that teacher education also bears a major responsibility for formulating theoretical frameworks which will encourage both understanding of and evaluation of pedagogic practices. Teacher education must provide, we would argue, ongoing challenge to the educational bureaucracies which seek rather to define teachers primarily as technicians or pedagogical clerks, incapable of making important policy or curriculum decisions (Giroux, 1988). Our experience of using this model with teachers gives us optimism that it is a helpful and meaningful tool to assist in the articulation of teacher professional knowledge.

# References

Banks, F. (1997) *Assessing Technology Teacher Professional Knowledge* (proceedings of the PATT-8 Conference, Scheveningen, Netherlands, April).

Banks, F., Leach, J. and Moon, B. (1996) Knowledge, school knowledge and pedagogy; reconceptualising curricula and defining a research agenda. Paper presented at ECER '96 Conference, Seville, Spain, September.

Bloom, A. (1987) *The Closing of the American Mind*. Penguin, Harmondsworth.

Bruner, J. S. (1986) *Actual Minds, Possible Worlds*, Harvard University Press, London.

Bruner, J. S. (1996) *The Culture of Education*, Cambridge, Mass., Harvard University Press.

Burgess, H. and Leach, J. (1996) Solists and Collaborators: first experiences in teaching for novice teachers. Paper presented to British Education Research Association Conference, University of Lancaster, September 1996.

Chaucer, G. (1957) 'Canterbury Tales', in Robinson, F. N. (ed.) *The Complete Works of Geoffrey Chaucer*, Oxford University Press, London.

Chevellard, Y. (1991) *La Transposition Didactique: du savoir savant au savoir enseigné*, La Pensee Sauvage, Paris.

DfEE (1998) *Circular 4/98: Teaching: High Status, High Standards*, DFEE, London.

Doyle (1983) Academic Work, *Review of Educational Research*, Vol. 53, no. 2, pp. 159–99.

Egan, K. (1992) An Exchange, *Teachers' College Record*, Vol. 94, no. 2.

Egan, K. (1992) A review of *The Unschooled Mind*, *Teachers College Record*, Vol. 94, no. 2, pp. 397–413.

Furlong, J. and Maynard, T. (1995) *Mentoring Student Teachers*, Routledge, London.

Gardner, H. (1983) *Frames of Mind: The Theory of Multiple Intelligences*, Basic Books, New York.

Gardner, H. (1991) *The Unschooled Mind*, Basic Books, New York.

Gardner, H. (1992) A Response, *Teachers' College Record*, Vol. 94, no. 2.

Gardner, H. and Boix-Mansilla, V. (1994) Teaching for understanding in the disciplines and beyond, *Teachers' College Record*, Vol. 96, no. 2, pp. 198–218.

Giroux, H. A. (1988) *Teachers as Intellectuals: Towards a Critical Pedagogy of Learning*, New York, Bergin & Garvey Publication, Inc.

Grossman, P. L., Wilson, S. M. and Shulman, L. S. (1989) Teachers of substance: subject matter knowledge for teaching, in Reynolds, M. C. (ed.) *Knowledge Base for the Beginning Teacher*, Pergamon Press, Oxford.

Haviland, J. (1988) *Take Care, Mr Baker*, Fourth Estate, London.

Lave, J. (1988) *Cognition in Practice*, Cambridge University Press, Cambridge.

Lave, J. and Wenger, E. (1991) *Situated Learning: Legitimate Peripheral Participation*, Cambridge, Cambridge University Press, Cambridge.

Lawler, S. (1988) *Correct Case*, Centre for Policy Studies, London.

Leach, J. and Banks, F. (1996) Investigating the developing 'teacher professional knowledge' of student teachers. Paper presented at the BERA Conference, Lancaster, September.

Leinhardt, G. and Smith, D. (1985) Expertise in mathematical instruction: subject matter knowledge, *Journal of Educational Psychology*, Vol. 77, no. 3, pp. 247–71.

MacNamara, D. (1991) Subject knowledge and its application: problems and possibilities for teacher educators, *Journal of Education for Teaching*, Vol. 17, no. 2, pp. 113–28.

McDiarmid, G., Ball, D. L. and Anderson, C.W. (1989) Why staying one chapter ahead doesn't really work: subject-specific pedagogy, in Reynolds, M. C. (ed.) *Knowledge Base for the Beginning Teacher*, Pergamon Press, Oxford.

McKewan, H. and Bull, B. (1991) The pedagogic nature of subject matter knowledge, *American Educational Research Journal*, Vol. 28, no. 2, pp. 319–34.

Moon, B. and Banks, F. (1996) Secondary school teachers' development: reconceptualising knowledge and pedagogy. Paper presented at the Association for Teacher Education in Europe (ATEE) Conference, Glasgow, September.

Shulman, L. S. (1986) Those who understand: knowledge growth in teaching, *Educational Research Review*, Vol. 57, no. 1, pp. 4–14.

Shulman, L. S. (1987) Knowledge and teaching: foundations of the new reform, *Harvard Educational Review*, Vol. 57, pp. 1–22.

Shulman, L. S. and Sykes, G. (1986) *A National Board for Teaching? In Search of a Bold Standard. A Report for the Task Force on Teaching as a Profession*, Carnegie Corporation, New York.

Sizer, T. R. (1992) *Horace's School*, Houghton Mifflin, New York.

Tochan, F. and Munby, H. (1993) Novice and expert teachers' time epistemology: a wave function from didactics to pedagogy, *Teacher and Teacher Education*, Vol. 9, no. 2, pp. 205–18.

Verret, M. (1975) *Le temps des études*, Librarie Honoré Champion, Paris.

Wilson, S. M., Shulman, L. S. and Richert, A. (1987) 150 different ways of knowing: representations of knowledge in teaching, in Calderhead, J. (ed.) *Exploring Teacher Thinking*, Holt, Rhinehart & Winston, Eastbourne.

Wilson, S. M. and Wineberg, S. S. (1988) Peering at history through different lenses: the role of the disciplinary perspectives in teaching history, *Harvard Educational Review*, Vol. 89, no. 4, pp. 527–39.

# 8

# Didactics as Construction of Content[1]

## Peter Menck

In their well-known study on *The Language of the Classroom* (1968) Arno A. Bellack and his collaborators analyzed the teaching process through an analysis of the linguistic behaviour of teachers and students. They identified 'pedagogical moves' and were able to find and describe 'teaching cycles'. More precisely, they were able to reconstruct certain rules followed by participants in classroom discourse. They looked at classroom instruction as a 'language game' and interpreted it accordingly, developing concepts which enabled them to describe and interpret the game as one which indeed follows rules. The object of their study was not the classroom as a whole but classroom *discourse*.

They were also interested in 'the dimensions of meaning represented by the *content* of the messages communicated' (Bellack *et al.* 1968: 5), i.e. instructional meanings and substantive meanings, although they were not able to come up with much on this score. They identified 'substantive meanings' as the main concepts of the textbook on which the instruction is based, and 'substantive-logical meanings' as the 'cognitive processes involved in dealing with the subject matter'. However, in the end, they could do no more than count frequencies. They were astounded at the differences between classrooms in the area of substantive meanings: it was 'remarkable', 'particularly in relation to the similarities found in the pedagogical area' (Bellack *et al.* 1968: 69, 72, 83). In other words, they did not know what to make of these findings. I remember quite exactly the questions that came into my mind when I first read *The Language of the Classroom:* Why can't the content of classroom discourse be understood since the other variable can be? Why can't the findings be readily interpreted? Is classroom discourse a vague concept rather than a clearly defined variable? What might the concept 'content' mean?

## An Example by Way of Illustration of My Questions

Let us examine an example of classroom discourse more closely. I have chosen an excerpt from a lesson (Table 8.1) which John Sinclair and Malcolm Coulthard report in their *Towards an Analysis of Discourse* (1975).

This chapter has been edited

Table 8.1 *An example of classroom discourse (from Sinclair and Coulhard [1975]: 90–94)*

| Exchange Type | Opening | Act | Answering | Act | Follow-up | Act |
|---|---|---|---|---|---|---|
| Boundary | Now ^ FRAME | m | | | | |
| Direct | All eyes on me. | d | NV | rea | | |
| Direct | Put your pencils down. | d | NV | rea | | |
| Direct | Fold your arms. | d | NV | rea | | |
| Direct | Hands on your heads. | d | NV | rea | | |
| Direct | Hands on your shoulders. | d | NV | rea | | |
| Direct | Fold your arms. | d | NV | rea | | |
| Direct | Look at me. | d | NV | rea | | |
| Elicit | Hands up. | cu | | | | |
| | What's that? | el | Paper clip. | rep | A paper clip good. | e |
| | | | | | A paper clip. [1-] | acc |
| | | | | | There we are. | z |
| Elicit | And what's that? | el | A nail. | rep | A nail well done. | e |
| | Janet. | n | | | A nail. [1-] | acc |
| Elicit | And hands up. | cu | A nut and bolt. | rep | A nut and bolt good boy | e |
| | What's that one? | el | | | a nut and bolt. | |
| | That's got two names a double name. | cl | | | | |
| Elicit | And what do we call this thing? | s | A piece of metal. | rep | A piece of metal good boy. | e |
| | What's this a bit of? | el | | | | |
| | NV | b | | | | |
| | yes. | n | | | | |
| Direct | Can you point to a piece of metal in this room anybody a piece of metal in this room. | d | NV | rea | Yes. | e |
| Direct | You go and show me one David a piece of metal. | d(n) | NV | rea | Yes that's a piece of metal well done a team point you can have one. | e |
| Elicit | And this. | a | Hacksaw. | rep | A hacksaw yes a hacksaw. | e |
| | What's this is a picture of? | el | | | | |
| | Abdul. | n | | | | |
| Boundary | Find ^ FRAME | m | | | | |

| Move | Initiation | | Response | | Feedback | |
|---|---|---|---|---|---|---|
| Elicit | And the last picture of all, I've got there what's that? Danny. | əl | An axe. | rep | An axe yes it's an axe. | e |
| Boundary | Now then ∧ FRAME | n / m | | | | |
| Elicit | I've got some things here, too. Hands up. What's that what is it? | s / cu / el | Saw. | rep | It's a saw yes this is a saw. | e |
| Elicit | What do we do with a saw? | el | Cut wood. | rep | Yes. You're shouting out though. | e / com |
| Elicit | What do we do with a saw? Marvelette. | el / n | Cut wood. | rep | We cut wood. | e |
| Elicit | And, erm, what do we do with – Well first of all what is this what is it? | el / m / el | Hacksaw. | rep | It's a hacksaw. | e |
| Elicit | What do we do with a hacksaw this hacksaw? | el | Cut trees. | rep | | |
| Elicit | Do we cut trees with this? | el | No No | rep | | |
| Elicit | Hands up. What do we do with this? | cu / el | Cut wood. (INDISTINCT) | rep | | |
| Elicit | Do we cut wood with this? | el | No. | rep | | |
| Elicit | What do we do with that | el | Cut wood. | rep | We cut wood with that. | e |
| Elicit | What do we do with that? then? Sir. Cleveland. | el / b / n | Metal. | rep | We cut metal yes we cut metal. | e |
| Elicit | And, er, I've got this here. What's that? Trevor. | a / el / n | An axe. | rep | It's an axe yes. | e |
| Elicit | What do I cut with the axe? | el | Wood wood. | rep | Yes I cut wood with the axe. | e |
| Boundary | Right ∧ FRAME | m | | | | |

Our first reaction is probably annoyance at the gruesome drill, but that is not my concern here. The framework of the transcript indicates the linguistic angle from which Sinclair and Coulthard comprehend instruction, but this is not my question, either. Finally, and this is my main concern, they deal with – well, it is not easy to say. Thus:

- there are pictures of things which can cut and be cut;
- the materials are assigned to the respective cutting implements;
- categorization is commenced, with 'materials' as a generic term;
- objects are identified by their names and by their everyday uses.

Obviously, everything is somehow connected with the 'content'. The matter is complex and yet, on the other hand, wonderfully transparent:

- We have a pair of scissors, a *tool*, characterized by its everyday use;
- 'Scissors' is also a *name* which we can use to put the object at our disposal ('Give me the scissors');
- And there are the *pictures* of 'materials', which present, within a teaching context, the everyday world in which the tools are used and described.

|  |  |
| --- | --- |
| **◦ɕ:✿:( 198 ):✿:ɔ◦** | **◦ɕ:✿:( 199 ):✿:ʌ◦** |
| *XCVII.* | *Schola* 1 — Die Schul 1 |
| Schola. | est officina, in quâ — ist eine Werckstat/in welcher |
| [image: Die Schul.] | novelli animi — die jungen Gemüter |
|  | ad Virtuté formantur; — zur Tugend geformet wer- |
|  | & distinguitur — und wird abgetheilt (den; |
|  | in *Classes*. — in Classen. |
|  | *Praceptor*, 2 — Der Schulmeister/ 2 |
|  | sedet in *Cathedrâ*; 3 — sitzt auf dem Lehrstul; 3 |
|  | *Discipuli*, 4 — die Schüler/ 4 |
|  | in *Subselliis*: 5 — auf Bäncken : 5 |
|  | ille docet, — jener lehret/ |
|  | hi discunt. — diese lernen. |
|  | Quædam — Etliches |
|  | præscribuntur illis — wird ihnen vorgeschrieben |
|  | cretâ — mit der Kreide |
|  | in *Tabellâ*. 6 — an der Tafel. 6 |
|  | Quidam — Etliche |
|  | sedent ad mensam, — sitzen am Tische/ |
|  | & scribunt : 7 — und schreiben: 7 |
|  | ipse, corrigit 8 — Er/ verbässert 8 |
|  | Mendas. — die Fehler. |
|  | Quidam stant, — Etliche stehen/ |
|  | & recitant — und sagen her/ |
|  | memoriæ mandata. 9 — was sie gelernet. 9 |
|  | Quidam confabulan- — Etliche schwätzen 10 |
|  | ac gerunt se {tur, 10 — und erzeigen sich |
|  | petulantes — mutwillig |
|  | & negligentes: — und unfleissig : |
|  | hi castigantur — die werden gezüchtiget |
|  | *Ferulâ* (baculo) 11 — mit dem Backel 11 |
|  | & *Virgâ*. 12 — und der Ruhte. 12 |
|  | *Schola* | N 4        Museum. |

Figure 8.1   *Comenius's* Orbis Sensualium Pictus – *'The School'*

After my annoyance over the drill had subsided and I thought about this structure, I remembered John Amos Comenius, the renowned didactic theorist among the classic educationists, and his *Orbis Sensualium Pictus* (1658) (see Figure 8.1).

Sinclair and Coulthard are not Comenius. Their approach is pragmatic-linguistic and not didactic. But the lesson they report has exactly the same structure as Comenius' 300-year-old textbook. We see

- *pictures* which represent things, 'materials';
- the *things* being embedded in an everyday situation in which they are used according to the rule of life in society; and
- *words* in a meaningful text referring to those things.

We find the very same logic in the *Orbis Pictus* and in the lesson Sinclair and Coulthard analyse, namely the didactic logic of the correspondence of tools, their names, and their uses.

My example and my illustration from our classical didactician are intended to highlight what I am going to discuss. 'Content' exists in classroom instruction; it has been solidly elaborated in the didactic tradition. I will try to conceptualize it. What exactly is the 'content' of classroom instruction?

## The Concept of 'Bildung'

Right at the beginning we are faced with a practically insurmountable – if not untranslatable – obstacle: the term *Bildung*. It is difficult enough when German educationists try to discuss what *Bildung* means. I will try to explain it as simply as I have construed it for myself, and will choose to overlook the more subtle treatises produced by those of my colleagues who have closer links with philosophy.

We use *Bildung* as an attributive and talk about the *Bildungssystem*, which is none other than the 'educational system'. Or we complain that the government does not provide enough funds for *Bildung*, when we mean the same thing. And when we say someone has reached a certain *Bildungsstand*, we mean a level of schooling. But when we talk about *Allgemeinbildung*, or general education, we are coming closer to the specific German notion of *Bildung*.

- First, we use the term to distinguish certain schools from vocational (*berufsbildende*) schools.
- Second, the term has something of the *enkyklios paideia* of Hellenism about it, particularly the Greek formula *pan – pantes – pantos* which was Comenius's motto: 'all things – all men – all through'.

So, what exactly is *Bildung*? Let me put it this way. When a person is born, he or she is totally human, provided he or she has a human countenance or is created in God's image, however you wish to express it. But it is evident that this being is not only unable to walk, but is also unable to read, write, count – and to tell lies. It is also unaware that it could commit murder. So in the course of the next few years, this person must first acquire the attributes which make him or her human. In all cultures there are institutions which regulate this. And all of these places have initiation rites to conclude this process as soon as those human characteristics which are stipulated by the society in question as the minimum requirement have been seen to be formed. The process does not of course finish there, but it becomes a personal responsibility from that point onwards, and may be pursued or left at will.

Let us now imagine that the little green men managed to capture a specimen of the human race and take it back to Mars. What sort of specimen should it be, if it was intended to give its captors a relatively accurate picture of what 'humans' really are? Wilhelm von Humboldt (1767–1835), who left us a famous fragment on *Bildung* (*c*. 1790) and who was one of the founders of the modern *Gymnasium*, would say something along these lines: the specimen would have to be such 'that the notion of humanity, should this be our one and only example, would acquire a greatness and dignity of content' (Humboldt 1960: 236). And how does an individual, our newborn baby, achieve a state which allows this to be said of him or her? By applying his or her powers of reason, faculties of judgement, senses and – as Karl Marx would add – hands, to the assimilation of the material and intellectual world, cultivating his or her ear as a musical ear, his or her senses as human senses and his to her powers of any kind as human powers (Marx 1953: 242). To reiterate: How does a human being arrive at a state which represents, as perfectly as possible, what makes humans human? Humboldt answers simply, though somewhat obliquely, '. . . by combining our individual selves with the world in a process of most general, animated and free interaction' (Humboldt 1960: 235). Later he adds what for me is one of the central tenets of the didactic tradition based on a theory of *Bildung*:

> What man really needs is simply an object which makes interaction possible between receptivity and self-activity. If it is to succeed in occupying his whole being in its entire strength and unity, then *this object must be the world itself . . . or at least considered as such.*
>
> (237) [my emphasis]

'Considered as such', this is important to me. Half a century later in 1884, Karl Marx saw the world, the objective reality, as the reality of human faculties, as human reality and thus as the reality of humankind's own faculties; he saw all objects as the objectification of man's own self, i.e. man himself becomes the object (Marx 1953: 241). He maintained that it is only through the objectively developed assets of man's being that the assets of subjective human sensuality – a musical ear, an eye for beauty of form – become senses capable of human pleasure, become senses which prove themselves as human faculties. It is only then that they are cultivated or even engendered. For it is not only a question of the five senses but also the so-called intellectual sense, the practical senses (such as will and love). The senses become human senses only through the existence of their object, through nature seen as the objectification of human-kind. Later referring to an area with which we more readily associate him, Marx (1953: 243–244) describes the history of industry and the objectified existence of industry as 'the open book of human faculties', human psychology submitted to our senses. 'In ordinary, material industry . . . we have before us in the form of sensuous, foreign, utilitarian objects . . . the objectified faculties of humankind'.

That is what we think of when we speak of 'general education', the concept I have just explained with the thoughts of our classic educationists: the claim, or the promise, that the 'canon' of knowledge which school propagates represents what makes humans human. For me, this is one of the links between *Didaktik* and curriculum.

In 1959, Wolfgang Klafki (1964) reconstructed nothing less than the whole German didactic tradition from Pestalozzi (1746–1827) to the de-bates of the 1950s. The aim of Klafki's work was to elaborate a theory of education to serve as a foundation of a modern theory of didactic. In an essay which appeared the same year he (Klafki, 1963: 43) described the concept as follows:

> *Bildung* is the term we give to that phenomenon whereby we become directly conscious – by our own experience or by understanding other people – of the unity of the objective (material) and the subjective (formal). *Bildung* is the personal exploitation of a concrete and intellectual reality by an individual – that is the objective or material aspect. But at the same time it is the opening up of the same individual to this same reality – that is the subjective or formal aspect. This double-sided 'exploitation' occurs objectively as a revelation of . . . content, and subjectively as a dawning of . . . insights and experiences.

*Bildung*, says Klafki, is '*kategorial*' in the double sense that categories of reality have opened up to a person and at the same time, thanks to the categoric insights and experiences which the person has gained for him, the person has opened up to the reality (Klafki 1963: 44).

In my paper 'Throwing two dice' (Menck 1987: 220), I translated it thus:

> In my view, education has to aim at autonomy. With respect to teaching this means that teaching is to enable young people to recognize the possibilities of mankind as potentially their own and to appropriate them. The contribution of school and school instruction to the children's gaining autonomy can be depicted as the opening of a field that is the opening of possibilities of acting indepen-dently in their world – the 'field' being a metaphor for socially-constructed reality (Berger and Luckmann 1966). The larger this field is, and the more the pupils are aware of their mobility in it, the more easily they can move within it.

Given this, it is hardly surprising that Bellack and his collaborators could do nothing with the differences in substantive meanings they found be-tween the classrooms. Their categories were based on a simple content analysis of the textbook which the teachers followed; they had no concept of the content of classroom discourse, comparable, for example, to the concept of teaching cycles.

## The Content of Classroom Discourse as Symbolic Representation of Reality

In another step within the framework of *Bildungstheorie*, Klafki (1963, 1995) developed an instrument for the structuring of subject matter for teaching, termed '*didaktische Analyse*' (didactic analysis). More precisely he asked the question: What is the '*Bildungsgehalt*', i.e. the contribution to the pupils' *Bildung*, of a *Bildungsinhalt*, an element of the curriculum. He then subdivided this question into five *more detailed* groups of questions with which every topic of instruction has to be examined.

The answers to these questions paraphrase the '*Bildungsgehalt*'. There has been a long and fruitful (though on many occasions also unfruitful) discussion about this instrument. I will not go into it in any more detail here, as I am interested from a descriptive rather than a constructive point of view.

Now let us ask more precisely what this content of classroom work is. In the paper I mentioned earlier (Menck 1987: 220; emphasis added) I formulated it with respect to a mathematics class as follows:

> What does mathematics *mean* in this case? What do probability, outcome, pairs of numbers, frequency and so on *mean* in the context set up by this lesson (and by the lessons that preceded it)? I do not ask for the ideas within the minds of the pupils and I do not intend to look into their heads. . . . I am interested in the . . . knowledge which is constituted and stated as valid in this very lesson.

First of all, it is not reality itself which is present in classroom work but rather a symbolic representation of reality – remember the classrooms of Comenius, and Sinclair and Coulthard: texts, pictures, and all kinds of things (*realia*) which *represent* a context from which they have been removed and brought into the classroom: scissors, knives, guinea pigs and international economics. They all refer to reality to everyday life to social practice. In other words, *in the classroom the presentation of reality is exclusively coded in the language of various symbolic systems.*

In a manner of speaking, all these things are reality, they are real things within the world of school: a poem is read and does not only point to something else; a nesting box is built and does not only represent some sort of bio-economic context. This aspect is particularly important when it comes to motivation. But that is not the point I am trying to make here.

I have mentioned language and pictures, but that is rather vague. Ernst Cassirer (1956) analyzed different *symbolic forms*: myth, religion, science. We can differentiate further and think in particular of the different symbolic systems of the sciences. In Bellack's experiment, for example, it was the language of economics, and in my example with the two dice it was mathematics.

In the language of didactic we can now say that 'subject matter' is coded in symbolic forms. It is not the practice itself, not reality itself which is dealt with in the classroom, but *the subject matter refers to this reality*. I could just as well speak of 'culture' and, incidentally, mention that Theodor W. Adorno in his essay, on *Theorie der Halbbildung* defined *Bildung* as 'culture insofar as the subject has acquired it' (Adorno 1972: 94; my translation). Or, like Hegel (1770–1831) and later German philosophers I could refer to the 'objectifications of the spirit', 'cultural assets' (*Kulturgüter*), as we often say today. Yes, Hegel's concept is probably what the passage from Marx I quoted earlier was referring to. No matter how we formulate it, the concept of the symbolic representation of reality is appropriate, on the one hand, for determining precisely what subject matter in the classroom is and, on the other hand, for finding the link to the concept of *Bildung*: cultivation of humanity in the individual by acquisition of those attributes in which humanity is objectively manifested.

## Lehrplan and selection

So we now have culture, but we have not yet reached the classroom. Of course, 'humanity', however freely accessible, is not something which in its entirety is at the disposal of teaching. Heads are too small, books too slim, time too short. Moreover, there are any number of stakeholders keen on seeing a particular choice made. Apart from the more technical restrictions there are at least two selection principles: political power and pedagogical authority.

- By means of political power, those cultural assets are selected which represent the dominant culture.
- By means of pedagogical authority, a selection is made in the interests of society's young.

Here didactic meets curriculum. In German, we would speak of the theory of *Lehrplan* (curriculum), where these selection processes are elaborated theoretically and empirically researched (Menck 1989). Thus I shall now plunge straight into teaching. Just as a reminder: the subject matter which enters the classroom as the representation of humanity, i.e. of what makes humans human, has already been selected for the classroom, in the final instance by the teacher, who in one person must represent both the interests of the dominant culture and of the pupils.[2]

## Acquiring Humanity: Work in the Classroom

Evidently, the mere presence of cultural assets in a curriculum does not suffice for learning of this or any other kind, at least not in our society, even when they have been selected under pedagogical considerations. What happens with the subject matter in the classroom?

For Bellack and his collaborators, international economics was the object of 'discourse'. There were particular 'cognitive processes involved in dealing with the subject matter' (Bellack *et al.* 1968: 5) that is, analytical, empirical and evaluative processes. There are other things to 'deal with': throwing two dice, solving a system of equations, singing a song or knitting a sock. We need a concept which describes more precisely than 'deal with' what happens during instruction. In the didactic tradition we use the term *Arbeit*, work. I assume this could be the same in the US tradition. After all Georg Kerschensteiner (1912), who outlined the concept of an *Arbeitsschule*, derived his concept of *Arbeit* from John Dewey's work.

Today we read a lot about *Handlung*, action, hands-on-activity, which probably means the same as *Arbeit* or work as used in *Reformpädagogik*. In the wake of Soviet activity theory the concept of 'learning activity' (*Lerntaetigkeit*) was elaborated. I am not really satisfied with either concept. The first usually contains little more than the demand that the pupils should do something using their hands (as the German word *Handlung* would seem to suggest), while the latter might be restricted to reconstructing internal psychic processes in psychological terms and then localizing these in the 'pedagogical process', as it is termed. In other words, it is a form of 'psycho-didactics', important enough I grant, but I have difficulties linking this concept with the classroom as a pedagogical institution.

I would suggest conceptualizing work in the classroom as *interpretation*. If we try to see what pupils and teachers do during instruction under the term of work, i.e. as a medium for humankind becoming human, what do we see there? If there is a point in understanding the object of work as symbolically coded cultural assets, as I have done, then work could be fittingly conceived of as 'interpretation'. What else can we do with symbolic coded reality? What am I thinking of here?

According to my personal hermeneutic approach – grossly simplified, I admit – I understand 'interpretation' as work in which elements of a text (in the broadest sense of that word) are juxtaposed with other elements, and with contextual elements, in such a way that they are meaningful for those participating. The didactic tradition is a reservoir of actions – depending on the respective object and the interest in it – which are suitable for interpreting, understanding and acquiring the object.

The oldest and most dignified method is the Socratic dialogue, redeveloped by Johann Bernhard Basedow (1727–1790) and other philanthropists (as several progressive and enlightened educators of that time called themselves) as catechetic-Socratic discourse – both of them suitable for the interpretation in particular moral problems. Or we may think of the lecture as a means to produce ideas in the listeners' minds. Last but not least there is skilful manual work which helps to develop not only the hand but also the person as a whole by the production of a useful item.

This is just as reasonable for Bellack's international trade as for Sinclair's and Coulthard's cutting tools. But does it apply to pupils building a nesting-box, Kerschensteiner's (1912) example of *Arbeit* in a classroom? I think so.

They are interpreting, ecologically as it were, the relationship between man and animals, and economically as it were, the context of work economy. If, for example, pupils produce a street map of their town during their lessons, they are putting themselves in a spatial perspective to their homes, their routes to school and to the places in town important to them: they are interpreting themselves in their environment–geographically as it were.

Two things are particularly important for me in connection with the concept 'interpretation' in this context. First, I pinpoint the specific characteristics of the object being dealt with in instruction, of a symbolically coded reality. In other words one can speak of *the didactic construction of reality*. And, second, this concept allows individual actions to be interrelated meaningfully in teaching, as in the concept of teaching cycles, which, as we know, enables pedagogical moves to be comprehended as meaningful in their order. Soliciting and reacting, question and answer, are not to be seen as such; rather we have to see them as a step on the way at the end of which we find both the product and the '*Bildung*' of the producer. And praise or reproach are to be understood as means to keep up this pedagogical process. In this respect it does not make much sense to count the respective pedagogical moves and to interpret their frequency distributions. If we want to understand the content of classroom work – its structure and development – we have to reconstruct complex processes (Menck 1986).

## The Pedagogical Legitimation of Work in Instruction

Classroom work in school – be it conceptualized as 'interpretation' or anything else – differs in one essential characteristic from productive work in society. Hilbert L. Meyer (1980: 211), a leading advocate of the orientation of teaching to the principle of action, *Handlung*, writes:

> In hands-on-learning, teachers and pupils together try to do something with their heads, their hearts, their hands, their feet, and with all their senses. This can lead to results which are of meaningful utility value for teachers and pupils.

I think what he is forgetting here is that a classroom is – a classroom. It is good, even indispensable, that the products of work in the classroom have a meaning, a use for the children. But where exactly does this use lie? Susanna's mother, or indeed Susanna's elder brother, can embroider the tray cloths much more quickly and expertly than Susanna; nesting boxes are much cheaper in the supermarket. The *Hallelujah Chorus*, with the whole *Messiah* thrown in, is performed much better by a professional choir than by the school orchestra with Alexander playing solo. And yet we are pleased with the tray cloths, we hang up the slightly crooked nesting box, and go along to the school's Christmas recital, although we have not really got the time. Why? Surely not because of the utility value of these things? No, we go because the products are *signs* of something, because we read them as signs that our children have acquired something and at the same time have made something out of themselves. Crooked and off key they may be, but we are prepared to accept what we would never accept from a carpenter or a virtuoso, as long as we can be sure that the children have worked as though the future of the world depended on it, in other words, seriously and with dedication. And their future does depend on it as a matter of fact.

The point I am trying to make is that work is embedded in a pedagogical situation, in teaching. Its product is the touchstone of the situation and the pedagogical purpose with which it is organized. A utilitarian object for us, or for the children, could be motivating, is perhaps needed over and over again to maintain the situation, but it is not characteristic. On the contrary, talking about 'utility value' only obscures the real content and the pedagogical purpose which legitimates the work.

These reflections about the pedagogical construction of reality in school must be followed by the question, What is this reality actually like? I believe it is the task of research on teaching to analyze what comprises the content generated in the pedagogically-legitimated language game of instruction *What kind of image of the world is produced in the work done in the classroom, the image we expect the pupils to adopt as their own?*

[ . . . ]

## Acknowledgements

Gilian Horton-Krüger and Stefani Pirags translated the [chapter] into English. Ian Westbury did some final polishing with the somewhat rough draft version of the text. I thank them all. Nevertheless I have the responsibility for the product which is to be seen as such and not as a step of the author's '*Bildung*'.

## Notes

1. All the translations from German sources are mine.
2. It is the teacher who can see to it that not only the saints but also the heretics, not only the heroes but also the cowards and murderers, not only art but also *kitsch*, find their way into the classroom. I would like to recall this, just in case we forget that these, too, are what constitute man. By this I do not, of course, wish to propose that pupils should cultivate the potential murderer within themselves. but it would be good if they were able to recognize the potential murderer lurking within – and deal with this in a dignified and appropriate manner, in a human manner.

## References

Adorno, Th. W. (1972) *Soziologische Schriften I* (Frankfurt: Europaeische Verlagsanstalt).

Bellack, A. A., Kliebard, H. M., Hyman, R. T. and Smith, F. L. (1968) *The Language of the Classroom* (New York: Teachers College Press).

Berger, P. L. and Luckmann, T. (1966) *The Social Construction of Reality* (Garden City: Doubleday).

Cassirer, E. (1956) *Wesen und Wirkung des Symbolbegriffs* (Darmstadt: Wissenschaftliche Buchgesellschaft).

Comenius, J. A. (1658/1978) *Orbis sensualium pictus* (Dortmund: Harenberg Kommunikation).

Humboldt, W. von (1960) Theorie der Bildung des Menschen. In A. Flitner and K. Giel (eds) *Gesammelte Schriften*, Bd. I. (Darmstadt: Wissenschaftliche Buchgesellschaft), 234–240.

Kerschensteiner, G. (1912) *Begriff der Arbeitsschule* (Leipzig: Teubner).

Klafki, W. (1963) *Studien zur Bildungstheorie und Didaktik* (Weinheim: Beltz).

Klafki, W. (1964) *Das pädagogische Problem des Elementaren und die Theorie der kategorialen Bildung*. 3rd/4th edn (Weinheim: Beltz).

Klafki, W. (1995) Didactic analysis as the core of preparation of instruction. *Journal of Curriculum Studies*, 27 (1): 13–30.

Marx, K. (1993) *Die Fruehschriften*. Ed. by S. Landshut (Stuttgart: Kroener).

Menck, P. (1986) *Unterrichtsinhalt oder: Ein Verscuch über dis Konstrukion der Werklichkeit im Unterricht* (Frankfurt/M.: Peter Lang).

Menck, P. (1987) Throwing two dice: the content of a maths lesson. *Journal of Curriculum Studies*, 19 (3): 219–225.

Menck, P. (1989) Curriculum development in the Federal Republic of Germany: tradition or reform? *Education*, 40: 49–63.

Meyer, H. L. (1980) *Leitfaden zur Unterrichtsvorbereitung* (Koenigstein/Ts.: Sciptor).

Sinclair, J. M. and Coulthard, M. (1975) *Towards an Analysis of Discourse* (London: Oxford University Press).

# 9

# The Influence of National Cultural Traditions on Pedagogy: Classroom Practice in England, France and Germany

## Birgit Pepin

In this chapter it is argued that national cultural traditions are a large determinant and influence on mathematics teachers' pedagogies in England, France and Germany. The findings of the study on which this chapter is based showed that, although there were commonalities, there were also important differences in teachers' pedagogies which could be understood in the light of different facets of the cultural traditions of each country.

The research is based on a comparative ethnographic study of 12 mathematics teachers in English, French and German secondary schools who were 'shadowed' for a fortnight each, in order to explore teachers' pedagogies; the context in which they were working; and their beliefs concerning teaching. The underlying aim was to find out whether mathematics teachers in England, France and Germany could teach in a country other than their own.

The chapter is divided into three parts. The first part, describes the background to the study, such as the underlying question for the research undertaken and the methodology, whereas the second is concerned with the underpinning philosophies in the three countries. The third and main part presents one of the theoretical conclusions generated from the study, and it focuses on the finding which explores the influence of national cultural traditions on teachers' pedagogies. What is referred to here as 'pedagogy' consists of the 'principles, practice or profession of teaching' (Hanks *et al.*, 1986).

## Introduction

The Single European Act, introduced in each European Community country in 1987, attempts to remove all existing barriers to the objectives of the Treaty of Rome. This important treaty was based on the principle of freedom of movement of goods and services, capital, and labour. The broad educational consequences of the economic unification can be foreseen: workers, seeking scarce jobs in countries other than their own, will raise families in foreign countries and will need international job qualifications. Teachers will also become migrant workers, since a directive of the Council of the European Community of 1988 requires that professional qualifications, including teaching, are mutually recognized and that civil servant status is no longer to be used to exclude teaching from the terms of the Treaty of Rome (*Bulletin of the European Communities*, 1988, cited in McLean, 1990). Yet teachers and associated professionals still know very little about their colleagues' work in other countries. They need to be informed about teachers' pedagogies and what underpins teachers' classroom practices in terms of underpinning philosophies and national knowledge traditions. The study on which this chapter is based has attempted to do just that. It developed an understanding of mathematics teachers' work at secondary level in three European countries (England, France, Germany). The original question underlying the study was whether an English, French or German mathematics teacher would be able to work in any of the three countries (England, France or Germany). How do mathematics teachers at secondary level conceive of and carry out their tasks in England, France and Germany?

In terms of existing comparative research in mathematics education, Moon (1986) investigated the ways in which different educational systems, amongst them the English, French and German, had promoted and responded to the 'new maths' curriculum innovations since the early 1960s. There have been several international comparisons of attainment in mathematics, the most recent of them being the Third International Mathematics and Science Study (TIMSS) (reported, for example, by the National Foundation for Educational Research, 1997). Interestingly, whilst comparative work has been carried out by Broadfoot and Osborn (1993) in French and English state primary schooling, relatively little has been undertaken at secondary level in relation to mathematics teaching except for work by Burghes *et al.* as part of the Kassel Project (1996). Their research has been based on longitudinal studies of representative samples of pupils in participating countries (amongst them, England, France and Germany) by using regular testing of pupils. The emphasis has been on pupils and their achievement. Prais (1995) compared Swiss and English mathematics classrooms and Bierhoff (1996) undertook a comparison of primary school textbooks in Britain, Germany and Switzerland, supported by observation of classroom practice. In a very recent study of national cultural values and their role in learning in state primary schooling in England and France, Planel (1997) emphasized how culture influences pupils in the classrooms in their aspirations and expectations. However, there has been little sustained analysis and understanding of the nature of cultural differences and how they influence the day-to-day life in schools – in particular, how they influence teachers' work.

It is generally accepted that national cultural traditions of different countries are not an easy area to investigate. Boundaries are usually not clearly defined. However, despite complexities, it is important to recognize that there are differences (and similarities) across countries, and that they are significant and influential. Therefore, these differences (and similarities) need to be explained and their influence understood. It is assumed that cross-national comparisons help to sharpen the focus of analysis and help to reveal national cultural traditions, by comparing the known with the novelty which can lead to a deeper understanding of the issues of another culture, whilst also considering one's own country from the perspective of a skilled observer from outside.

England, France and Germany have long-standing national traditions and institutions which are the result of traditions and historical developments, and there are substantial differences in the national educational traditions of the three countries. These can be seen in the history of the education systems and historical developments in teacher education in the three countries (Pepin, 1997). Broadfoot and Osborn (1993) have shown that French and English educational values can be traced back to teachers' perceptions of their work. These cultural backgrounds permeate through to schools and, as this chapter will show, teachers' pedagogies can be understood in the light of those national traditions.

## Underpinning philosophies

According to McLean (1990) the main underpinning philosophy of the **English** education system is *humanism*, with its associated principles of individualism, morality and specialism. One of the claims about humanism is that it is anti-rational and that England has in the past given 'little weight in education to rational, methodical and systematic knowledge objectives' (Holmes and McLean, 1989). This can be understood in the light of the philosophy of humanism which assumes that to acquire knowledge is not a logical, sequential and standardized process, as rationalists would claim, but learning is regarded as 'intuitive'. Standardized, methodical, systematic learning are not reconcilable with this intuitive view of education. In addition, within the humanistic perspective rational thinking was not considered to be as important as in the encyclopaedic tradition, and mathematics and science were not as highly regarded as literature and the classics.

Inextricably linked and central to the philosophy of humanism is the concept of individualism, which encompasses methodology and pedagogy. Pedagogy is regarded as individualistic. The interaction between teacher and pupil is greatly emphasized. This individualism within the humanistic tradition permitted, in turn, connections with child-centred philosophies and teaching strategies. English child-centred education (mainly promoted in primary education, for example, by the Plowden Report in 1967) remained a pedagogy emphasizing the individual and active learning. Thus, English education is said to be *child centred* and *individualistic*.

**France** is often described as one of the heartlands of *encyclopaedism* with its associated principles of rationality, utility and universality. Rationality is seen here in the sense that those subjects which are perceived to encourage the development of rational faculties in students are regarded as most important. Therefore, subjects such as mathematics have a very high status in France. The principle of utility is based on the idea that social change and improvement of the society are possible through rational knowledge. The principle of universality means on one hand that students study broadly the same curriculum (at broadly the same time), on the other hand that they gain what is perceived as general 'valued' knowledge. Closely associated is the principle of *égalité* which aspires to remove social inequalities through education and promotes equal opportunities for all pupils. Thus, encyclopaedism, with its associated principles of *rationality*, universality and the associated *egalitarian views*, is the traditional signpost for the philosophical underpinning of French education.

**Germany** espouses mainly humanistic views. The concept of *Bildung* is based on Humboldt's ideal of *humanism*. The German *Bildung* (based on humanism) searches for 'rational understanding' of the order of the natural world as well as an 'intuitive appreciation of human morality' (McLean, 1990), and therefore incorporates encyclopaedic rationalism as well as humanist moralism. It basically promotes the unity of academic knowledge and moral education. However, within the German form of humanism the humanist rationale was never allowed to avoid the importance of the study of mathematics and science, according to the belief that scientific knowledge should be mastered in the continuing search for total understanding. Thus, the German humanism, with its associated concept of *Bildung*, reflects the main characteristics of German school knowledge traditions.

# Findings

Five theoretical conclusions were generated from the study, in order to develop a theorized understanding of mathematics teachers' work (at secondary level) in England, France and Germany. Those theories were concerned with commonalities (in terms of pedagogies) amongst mathematics teachers in the three countries; with the influence of cultural traditions on teachers' pedagogies; with the influence of varying ranges of teachers' responsibilities on their practices; with the terms and conditions under which teachers work with respect to people in the wider community; and with the influence of teachers' different beliefs about mathematics on their practices. Whilst related findings are used for reference and to illuminate the argument, in this chapter the following theoretical conclusion is discussed: that *national cultural traditions are a large determinant and influence on teachers' pedagogies in the three countries*.

One of the findings of the research was that there was a commonality amongst mathematics teachers in England, France and Germany with respect to normal desirable states of pupil activity (as defined by Brown and McIntyre, 1993), and those desirable states had common factors, such as co-operation and involvement. It was also argued that, although there might have been different understandings of how learning took place (individual, universal, for example) all teachers used whole-class teaching to a greater or lesser extent. In this chapter it is claimed that there were differences in the ways teachers used whole-class teaching in England, France and Germany; in the ways teachers liked pupils to behave (desirable states); and in the routines in which teachers were engaging. All these differences can be understood in the light of different facets of cultural traditions.

In order to understand the characteristics of a lesson in a particular country, it is necessary to give a short description of a lesson, or lesson 'profiles', for each of the three countries. There were certain features in each country that made it characteristic for the four teachers, although interestingly, the characteristics were not always shared completely by all four teachers. In Germany a distinction had to be made between *Hauptschul* and *Gymnasium* teachers; therefore similarities between teachers in each school form were taken into consideration:

> In **England** teachers focused on training pupils on mathematical concepts or skills and devoted much time to the practice of (sometimes routine) procedures. Most English teachers, unless the lesson was assigned for an 'investigation', introduced and explained a concept or skill to students, gave a worked example on the board and then expected pupils to practise on their own or in small groups, whilst the teacher attended to individual pupils. Students were divided into different achievement sets and teachers provided a different mathematical diet for different teaching groups. Situations where pupils discovered multiple solutions or investigated new solutions which required reasoning were rare and usually reserved for 'investigation' lessons, and so were practical activities.
>
> (Pepin, 1997, p. 223)

However, in England there was one teacher who had certain characteristics which were not congruent with those of her colleagues. Her characteristics were in tune with some of the more recent writings in mathematics education. This teacher was working as a school-based mentor in teacher education (in connection with a university). She gave pupils thought-provoking questions and tried to develop an argument or concept in an investigative style. But then there were other English traditions that underpinned much practice in teachers' classrooms (teacher-led introduction/practice lessons), even of 'new' teachers, which confirmed the widely held belief (Lortie, 1975, for example) that a massive influence on teachers is the ways they were taught during their time at school and the particular 'culture' of their school (in the sense of what was regarded as 'good teaching' in a particular mathematics department or school):

> In **France** teachers focused on developing mathematical thinking which included exploring, developing and understanding concepts, and mathematical reasoning.

This, in turn, had consequences for their classroom practice. French teachers spent much time preparing their lessons, in order to be able to provide the 'best' introduction and cognitive activities for pupils to discover the notion and to choose a range of exercises which helped pupils to assess their understanding. In class French teachers tried to pose thought-provoking problems and expected students to struggle with the problems for a while, before they drew together ideas from the class and discussed with the whole class the ideas and solutions of individuals. They tried to forge links between ideas, skills and (cognitive) activities on the one hand, and concepts on the other. Relatively little time was spent on routine procedures. Pupil mistakes were used to assess and subsequently deepen pupil understanding of the topic by discussing those mistakes with the whole class.

(Pepin, 1997, p. 223)

Again, not all characteristics were shared by all four teachers and there was evidence of a cultural shift in what went on in the classroom. The pressures from, for example, inspectors in France and the layout of textbooks made it clear that mathematics teachers were expected to abandon the traditional *cours magistral* (didactic teaching) and let pupils discover for themselves. New topics were expected to be introduced with a cognitive activity, and the investigative and problem-solving approach was to be used as much as possible. Yet by one particular teacher, and this was acknowledged by the teacher herself, this shift had not been made. The sorts of characteristics that seemed to be encouraged asked teachers to teach in a 'discovering' way, but there was still evidence of former traditions (*cours magistral*, for example) in which lessons would have a different set of characteristics:

In **Germany** teachers in the *Hauptschule* worked differently from those in the *Gymnasium*. What they had in common was that they all worked with the whole class in a kind of conversational style. Often pupils' mistakes in the homework or in class exercises were used to check and deepen pupil understanding. Textbooks were used during the lessons, mainly for exercises.

In the *Hauptschule* teachers often instructed pupils in a concept or skill, solved an example problem with the whole class and then let pupils practise on their own on exercises. But this procedure rarely lasted for a whole lesson. Typically, at a later stage the teacher checked pupil understanding by bringing pupils to the board and discussing their mistakes and understandings with the whole class. This discussion allowed the teacher to gain an impression of the understanding of the whole class.

In the *Gymnasium*, where expectations of achievement were higher, topics were treated in great depth and for a considerable length of time. As logical thinking was regarded as important, formulas were derived and formal reasoning conducted in lessons. The development and understanding of concepts was of paramount importance. The invention of new solutions or procedures was not encouraged. The lessons appeared quite formal and traditional in terms of their mathematical content, but were quite lively concerning their style (conversational). As mentioned before, the emphasis was on whole class interactive teaching which was conducted in a conversational style, with little emphasis on individualised work.

(*Ibid.*, p. 224)

After having presented a profile of lessons in each country, the following claims are discussed in detail: that whole-class teaching is employed differently in the three countries; that normal desirable states of pupil activity in the classroom are different in detail; and that teachers' routines are influenced by cultural traditions. Each of these claims is examined in turn and explained in the light of different national cultural traditions.

## Whole-class Teaching is Employed in Different Ways in the Three Countries

All teachers used whole-class teaching to a greater or lesser extent in England, France and Germany. However, there were differences in the ways that teachers used whole-class teaching. English teachers spent relatively little time on explaining concepts to the whole class, whereas French, and in particular German, teachers devoted a substantial proportion of the school day to whole-class teaching. In addition, teachers used this time in different ways. When English teachers used whole-class teaching, they explained a concept from the front in a more or less didactic way. German teachers used a more conversational style where they tried to involve the whole class in a discussion. French teachers used whole-class teaching in varied ways. When explaining a concept or pulling together ideas from the class, they used it in similar ways as their German colleagues. When summing up the main part of the lesson, they used a more didactic style.

The question arises about what it was that made all teachers use whole-class teaching, but in very different ways and for different lengths of time. It is argued that the underlying assumptions for teachers' ideas and practices were culturally and traditionally different.

In **England** there was the espoused view that teachers had to attend to the need of the individual child. This might have encouraged them to give up whole-class teaching after a short while and let pupils work on exercises, so that they could help pupils individually. But there were other possibilities and a range of options why English teachers might have chosen this particular practice (for example, to keep pupils busy, to be able to control them better, or they were told that they should not talk too long in front of the class). Nevertheless, it was entirely consistent with the tradition of individuality within the country that teachers did not class-teach for a prolonged period of time, but rather attended to the individual child during exercise phases.

Traditionally, teachers in **France** had been expected to teach the class as a whole in a didactic way (*cours magistral*). Following government reforms in 1989 towards a more child-centred approach, traditions have been challenged in the sense that strategies should include pedagogies where children were encouraged to 'discover' notions for themselves. However, the traditions of whole-class teaching were recognizable with all teachers. This can be understood in the light of egalitarian views in France, and French teachers expected the whole class to move forward together. Therefore, whole-class teaching in France can be understood from efforts to keep the whole class together.

**German** teachers were expected to use whole-class front-teaching (*Frontalunterricht*) most of the time. The tradition of the country encouraged them to teach the class as a whole. They were expected to consider the majority of the pupils (possibly the whole class) and to move them to a different level of cognition (understanding was the dilemma for teachers here). Those children who did not understand and who needed individual attention were regarded as being the exception to the rule. However, especially in the *Hauptschule*, more and more pupils did not respond to a teacher-led style. But teachers were not encouraged by teacher educators, for example, to change their teaching style. Front-teaching (*Frontalunterricht*) was seen as a suitable approach. Although there were courses on offer that suggested different teaching approaches, there was not a climate where teachers were encouraged to change. They tried to find ways for themselves to solve their difficulties in the classroom and felt unsupported to do that.

## Normal Desirable States are Different in Detail and are Influenced by Cultural Traditions

One of the findings of the study was that there were 'desirable states' of pupil activity by teachers and that these desirable states had common features. In general these concerned pupil involvement and assessment of pupil understanding. In this part is argued that in detail these desirable states were different and that they were influenced by the traditions of the country. Again, 'profiles' of classroom situations are given which were characteristic for teachers' pedagogies, before developing an understanding of the particular situations:

> In **English** mathematics classrooms the major aim was to convey a mathematical concept and let pupils get as much practice as possible. English teachers explained the concept and then let pupils work on their own, whilst teachers attended to individual pupils. Therefore, a desirable state associated with these practices was that pupils were attentive during teacher explanations and subsequently working on their own whilst teachers attended to individual pupils' needs . . .
>
> The major aim in **French** mathematics classrooms was to develop mathematical thinking by letting pupils discover a certain notion, either in whole-class conversation or pupils individually or in groups. Therefore, one of the desirable states associated with these practices was that pupils were discovering the notion with the help of selected cognitive activities. The teacher was acting as facilitator who initiated tasks and helped pupils to find out . . .
>
> The main objective in a **German** mathematics classroom was to discuss mathematical content. Teachers initiated tasks or took exercises from the homework, to be discussed by teachers and pupils in a conversational style, before giving pupils exercises to practise on their own. Therefore, a desirable state was that most pupils were involved in a teacher-led discussion about the mathematical content.
>
> (Pepin, 1997, p. 227)

In terms of desirable states, if teachers were interested in discussing a topic with the whole class (for example, in Germany), the desirable state was principally involvement and co-operation of everybody, and not a silent classroom. If teachers wanted pupils to work on their own with the teacher helping them individually (for example, in England), the desirable state was principally for pupils to get on with their work on their own and ask teachers for help if needed. If teachers wanted to set up a problem-solving situation and give pupils a cognitive activity (for example, in France), they expected involvement and discussions amongst groups of pupils. There-fore, although all teachers had desirable states and they always included pupil involvement and co-operation, these states were nevertheless dif-ferent in character and with respect to desired outcomes (learn to reason; learn a skill; learn to solve a problem).

The desirable states in Germany and England can be understood in the light of teaching traditions explained under whole-class teaching, but what was interesting about most of the French teachers was that they clearly tried to change (and had succeeded to a certain extent). They appeared to be trying to do what people, like the inspector, wanted them to do, in the 'right' sort of spirit. The question is why were they prepared to change? There are several possibilities. One could argue that they changed because the educational climate in France allowed them enough support (in terms of courses, for example) to be able to change. Another possibility is that the influence of the inspector was so strong that teachers felt obliged to change, or the influence of the textbooks pushed them into that direction. Perhaps they had enough time to think about their lesson during the lesson preparation, and the cultural traditions expected teachers to prepare their lessons thoroughly and to be up to date with current developments.

It is argued here that it was a mixture of reasons. First, the cognitive activity approach fitted comfortably within the cultural traditions in France of 'training the mind' (based on ideals of rationality). The perception in France of mathematics was that it should be 'training the mind' in order to educate pupils for rational and logical thinking. This went hand in hand with the notion of cognitive activities, where pupils trained their minds by (potentially) discovering a notion for themselves. Therefore, the aims of teaching mathematics were not undermined by using a problem-solving approach; on the contrary, they were supported.

Secondly, there was a climate in France where mathematics teachers were pushed and at the same time supported (by the inspector, for ex-ample) to change their teaching style towards 'letting pupils discover'. This, in turn, was manifested and supported in textbooks which were approved (by the ministry) and selected by schools.

## Teachers' Routines are Influenced by Cultural Traditions

It is argued that teachers in all three countries demonstrated that there were routines within their teaching. By routines the definition by Brown and McIntyre (1993) is adopted, who define routine as 'a standardised pattern of teacher action undertaken under certain recognised conditions in order to maintain a particular desired state of pupil activity or to promote a specific type of progress'. Some of those routines were common across the three countries, but others appeared to be influenced and could be understood to a large extent by the cultural and structural traditions of the countries.

As an example of routines which were common across countries, teachers in all three countries let pupils work on exercises, in order for pupils to practise what had been explained to them previously and, in turn, for teachers to assess whether understanding had taken place (in whatever way teachers regarded appropriate). These exercises had different forms (routine or thought-provoking), but all teachers nevertheless asked pupils during part of the lesson to work on exercises.

As an example of routines which were culturally determined, **English** teachers marked every pupil's book about once a week. This was a routine which could be understood by teachers' concern for analysing individual pupils' difficulties. They felt that it helped them to analyse diagnostically pupil understanding and, as a result, to identify any problem areas that individual pupils might have. Another reason was that it was traditionally expected from teachers by other people (for example, head of department, head of school or by parents).

**French** teachers traditionally asked pupils (and teachers are also expected by headteachers) to keep a *cahier de cours* (lesson book) and a *cahier d'exercices* (exercise book). This tradition involved certain routines. The *cahiers de cours* were used to write down the main concept of the lesson in a summarized form and possibly a worked example during or towards the end of the lesson. The origin of the *cahiers de cours* was to prepare a body of knowledge, well presented for pupils to learn and understand. A plausible explanation for teachers using the *cahier de cours* for a short summary of the essence of the lesson was that, if teachers during the lesson were involved in encouraging mathematical thinking and reasoning, they wanted to make sure not to lose sight of the essence of the lesson. At the end of the lesson, and whatever level pupils had reached, they made sure that the mathematical content was clearly stated.

This routine can be understood from traditions of whole-class teaching and efforts to keep 30 children together. Teachers commented that with the *cahier de cours* those pupils who did not understand during the lesson had the chance to learn at home with the help of the things recorded in the *cahier de cours*. French teachers were trying to teach pupils as a whole class and, although they were aware that not everybody might have understood at the end of the lesson, they knew that at least pupils recorded the main points of the lesson in their *cahier de cours*. Pupils might have got to different stages in the lesson, but at the end of it, everybody was writing the statement and an example in their *cahier de cours*, so that they could learn and revise the lesson at home if necessary.

In **Germany**, teachers started nearly every lesson with the correction of homework, with the whole class. It was a tradition in Germany to go over the homework, because it was considered to be the way in which teachers assessed in a diagnostic way (not explicitly) whether understanding (of what had been done previously) had taken place. This was done with the whole class and regarded by teachers as a manageable activity which helped them to assess pupil understanding as well as pupils to gain an understanding together. Therefore, this routine can be understood from traditions to keep the whole class together and that everybody understood. At the same time this routine was used for revision purposes, providing an introduction for what was to come.

## Conclusions

The findings from this study demonstrate that different cultural traditions were a large determinant and influence on teachers' pedagogies in the three countries. It was shown by examining the ways teachers employed whole-class teaching; the desirable states of pupil activity; and teachers' routines. This has implications for the potential transferral of teaching strategies across countries. The findings suggest that pedagogy needs to be understood in terms of national cultural traditions, and that national cultural traditions could impede the mobility of teachers across countries, which is the aim of many decision-makers in Europe.

## Acknowledgement

The research project was funded by the Economic and Social Research Council and the researcher is grateful for their financial support.

## References

Bierhoff, H. (1996) *Laying Foundations of Numeracy: A Comparison of Primary School Textbooks in Britain, Germany and Switzerland, Discussion Paper 90*, National Institute of Economic and Social Research.

Broadfoot, P. and Osborn, M. (1993) *Perceptions of Teaching – Primary School Teachers in England and France*, London and New York, Cassell.

Brown, S. and McIntyre, D. (1993) *Making Sense of Teaching*, Buckingham, Open University Press.

Hanks, P., McLeod, W. and Urdang, L. (eds) (1986) *Collins Dictionary of the English Language*, London and Glasgow, Collins.

Kassel Project (1996) *Year 3 – Progress Report* (http://www.ex.ac.uk/kassel/inter.htm), Exeter, Centre for Innovation in Mathematics Teaching, University of Exeter.

Lortie, D. C. (1975) *School-Teacher: A Sociological Study*, Chicago, IL, and London, University of Chicago Press.

Holmes, B. and McLean, M. (1989) *The Curriculum: a comparative perspective*, London, Unwin Hyman.

McLean, M. (1990) *Britain and a Single Market Europe*, London, Kogan Page in association with the Institute of Education, University of London.

Moon, B. (1986) *The 'New Maths' Curriculum Controversy*, London, New York and Philadelphia, Falmer Press.

NFER (1997) (by Sue Harris, Wendy Keys and Cres Fernandes) *Third International Mathematics and Science Study. Second National Report, Part 1*. Slough, NFER.

Pepin, B. (1997) Developing an understanding of mathematics teachers in England, France and Germany: an ethnographic study, PhD thesis, University of Reading.

Planel, C. (1997) National cultural values and their role in learning: a comparative ethnographic study of state primary schooling in England and France, *Comparative Education*, Vol. 33, no. 3, pp. 349–73.

Prais, S. (1995) Improving school mathematics in practice, in *Proceedings of a Seminar on Mathematics Education*, London, the Gatsby Charitable Foundation.

# SECTION 3
# PEDAGOGIC SETTINGS

# Introduction

## Jenny Leach and Bob Moon

This final section presents a range of examples of teaching and learning in practice. The chapters have been chosen to allow readers to consider critically some of the ways in which new developments in theory and research are being interpreted in educational contexts. The term 'pedagogic settings' (see Chapter 19) is used in part to underline that these chapters provide only brief glimpses, snapshots of ongoing interactions between particular teachers and learners across time. The term also serves to emphasise that pedagogy is more than the accumulation of teaching strategies: arranging a classroom, formulating questions, developing explanations, creating a curriculum. As the chapters which follow illustrate, pedagogy is informed by a view of mind, a view of learning and learners, a view of the kind of knowledge that is valuable and above all by the educational outcomes that are desired. The section as a whole enables readers to critically analyse the way in which different settings encourage different kinds of learning and knowing.

The Madagascan Giant Hissing Cockroach provides the starting point for this section. Caswell and Lamon's Grade 4 classroom (Chapter 10) was designed to mirror the scientific community at the University of Toronto's Zoological Department. The roach becomes the focus of a ten-week investigation carried out by the class, exploring concepts of adaptation, evolution, learning and perception. This chapter illustrates children working collaboratively on a range of learning tasks including initiating investigations and communicating findings. The role of the 'Knowledge Forum' technology in developing students' conceptual and metacognitive knowledge is explored in some detail. Caswell and Lamon's work raises some interesting questions about the creation of a 'scientific community of practice' in a school context.

Pirie and Martin (Chapter 11) focus on the teaching of linear equations, a statutory element of the secondary mathematics curriculum in the English education system. They are critical of what they call 'traditional pedagogic approaches' to this aspect of the maths curriculum which, they argue, adopt authentic tasks, supposedly real-life arithmetic associations, that are often outside the experience of many learners. Pedagogy can itself be an obstacle to understanding, they contend. This particular setting provides an interesting contrast to the previous chapter. The authors outline how the teacher, Alwyn, makes use of learning tasks such as 'guided image making', 'property noticing' and 'folding back' to develop students' understanding. This pedagogy is informed, however, by Alwyn's overarching view that mathematics is a way of thinking, a way of acting, about understanding ideas, not about achieving results: 'This was mathematics that was interesting for its own sake and all were capable of doing it.'

In Chapter 12 James Stredder analyses his own approach to the teaching of Shakespeare's narratives. He argues that his work is germane to any teaching and learning context, since narrative is a fundamental way of understanding and interpreting all subject disciplines. He gives detailed examples of what he terms active, structural, dynamic and investigative approaches to the teaching of Shakespearean texts, both with adult and younger learners. He also explores the nature of 'monumentalism' and the way in which representations of knowledge can exclude learners from the learning process. His own pedagogy emphasises a view of knowledge as identity.

May's focus in Chapter 13 is curriculum history with a class of graduate students. Her starting point, like Stredder's, is her learners' prior knowledge. She also leans on the importance of narrative, but in the sense of the graduate students' own biographies and experience. Whilst Stredder's focus is the interactions of himself as teacher-teller, his learners and the 'subject' (i.e. Shakespeare's narrative), May describes an approach to pedagogy which moves beyond the physical walls of her classroom, drawing on contemporary and historical resources such as art, photographs, scrapbooks and film; music; advertising; people; oral histories, diaries. Learners are encouraged to see their everyday experiences and communities as integral to their pedagogic setting, a connection to their own and others' history. Her pedagogic approach demands that they problematize historical interpretation and understand how history is a constructed and contested field of study.

Medical education provides the background for an exploration of the role of teacher as tutor in a problem-based approach to learning. Charles Engel (Chapter 14) outlines one such approach in some detail which, he advocates, supports the development of generalized professional competences such as the ability to: adapt to and participate in change; reason critically and creatively; and collaborate productively in teams. Teachers involved in introducing this kind of problem-based learning into a curriculum he suggests, would need the opportunity to practise the complex skills specific to planning, implementing and evaluating such learning, most especially the skills required for the tutorial process.

Anne-Mette Kruse (Chapter 15) outlines a distinctive pedagogic approach in single-sex settings: pedagogies for girls and boys in Danish schools. Her theory, which she terms the 'pedagogical method of polarization', describes a process which focuses on understanding how knowledge is created: using critical thinking to raise consciousness of stereotypes, gender inequalities, attitudes and behaviour; reflecting on the experience to develop new understandings and insight; communicating and acting on the new understandings. In this context it is the alternation between a boys-only, girls-only setting and reflecting on differences which seems to be the powerful factor in the learning process. Kruse provides some evidence to show transfer of understanding when students return to a mixed class, with girls less inclined to accept patriarchal values and patterns of work.

Peter Woods (Chapter 16) examines what he calls 'exceptional educational events'. The pedagogic settings he describes extend beyond the physical confines of classroom or workshop, including a whole-school drama production, the making of a film about a village and the planning and design of a heritage centre by pupils from neighbouring schools. He takes up themes explored in other chapters concerning learning activities that create motivation and self-esteem and emphasizes emotion as one crucial catalyst in the learning process.

In Chapter 17, Stone Wiske explores some of the dilemmas involved in articulating and developing a curriculum framework stemming from the work of Bruner and Gardner. For Wiske and her colleagues the key question for the teachers in the programme is, 'What do you want your students to understand by the end of the term or year in your class?' A view of the importance of assessment lies at the heart of this project, which is illustrated by the use of 'performances of understanding'. She identifies three progressive categories of perfomance: 'messing about', 'guided inquiry' and 'culminating performances'. The need to establish clear, overarching goals became apparent, when teachers in the project attempted to assess students' 'performances'. Wiske demonstrates the struggle involved in both articulating and using these goals.

Chapter 18 is written in the form of hypertext. Here Wendy Morgan attempts to recreate on the page both the challenges and possibilities for pedagogy – and literacy in particular – of the development of information and communications technologies. In creating a dialogue with her readers she invites us to explore critically a variety of electonic settings including project BushMOO. This chapter raises key questions about the future of pedagogy, the nature of knowledge and the roles of teachers and learners, as well as overarching questions about the purposes of education in an electronic age.

# 10

# Development of Scientific Literacy: The Evolution of Ideas in a Knowledge-building Classroom

## Beverly Caswell and Mary Lamon

## [Introduction]

This study describes cognitive and social aspects of children's development of scientific literacy in a Schools for Thought type classroom. Schools for Thought (SFT) is an education reform project designed to apply cognitive research about the active, reflective and social nature of learning into classroom practice. The idea is that learning environments in which children are given multiple opportunities to reflect on their ideas, compare perspectives and become aware that they are constructing knowledge as a group as well as individually can foster extraordinary learning for all students.

The subjects in this study are grade four students from the Institute of Child Study, a laboratory school affiliated with the University of Toronto. The study focusses mainly on the 1996–97 school year which was the school's (and teacher's) first introduction to CSILE (Computer Supported Intentional Learning Environments) and SFT and on the 1997–98 school year and the use of the new version of CSILE: Knowledge Forum. [ . . . ] During the SFT years, the classroom teacher (Caswell) worked collaboratively with researcher (Lamon) who had expertise in SFT implementation.

The school year science focus was biology, and the Giant Madagascan Hissing Roach was selected as an entry point because a unit had been created previously around this species, and children find the strangeness of this particular type of cockroach both interesting and awe inspiring. As well, the species is ancient in adaptation and evolution which are central concepts for understanding biology. Beginning with a sustained investigation of this cockroach (the children took care of and studied 11 cockroaches over a 10 week period) students progressively moved into an investigation of adaptation, evolution, learning and perception using aspects of a curriculum framework originally developed by Brown and Campione (1994). The development of students' scientific thinking became visible with the use of the CSILE/Knowledge Forum technology and their ideas progressed from simple and naive understandings to deeper understandings and quite complex experiments that were initiated, designed and carried out by the students.

Throughout the year, children were videotaped working with the teacher, working with peers, working with grade one students, and [the author] interviewed each student. In this [chapter], an analysis of the videotapes is used along with students' written work in CSILE/Knowledge Forum and in their research journals, to examine the changing nature of the social construction of knowledge across the SFT years and in comparison to the unit conducted in the previous year.

## Curriculum Outcomes

Canada's new Science Curriculum document (Common Framework of Science Learning Outcomes, 1997) outlines four skill areas required for scientific and technological inquiry. The four skill areas are as follows: initiating and planning, performing and recording, analyzing and interpreting, communication and teamwork.

Students in the grade four classroom were given an opportunity to become immersed in the culture of scientific inquiry, and to do it in such a way that would keep them motivated. We wanted our classroom to operate similarly to the way the scientific community operates at the University of Toronto's Zoological Department. Learning investigative skills became a by-product of students' in-depth research.

Our unit of study took place over an 8 to 10 week period. Students worked on science for approximately one to one and a half hours per day, three days per week. This extended amount of time enabled students to delve deeply into the subject area. It gave them time to think about questions, and to experiment with a variety of materials in order to test their theories.

## Method

### Introducing Cockroaches, CSILE and Personal Research Journals

The students were introduced to CSILE and to the cockroaches in the same session. We thought it was important to introduce specific activities such as writing in CSILE, reciprocal teaching, and taking research notes on a need-to-know basis. This in itself is a variation on a theme in SFT. Often, children are introduced to activities in their own right, practice those activities and then apply them. But if we want to keep focussed on ideas, it seems important to introduce activities *as ways to improve ideas*.

Students gathered in a circle on the carpet to meet the roaches and to hear a brief explanation of the insect's defence mechanisms: the two pronatal humps on the thorax which give the appearance of two fierce eyes, and the insect's ability to make a loud hissing noise. Then, in partners, students took turns either holding or sketching the insect. Half of the class drew on paper, while the other half drew on the CSILE, using computer graphics. Many of the students had never used graphics on the computer, and it was very surprising to see how rich and detailed the students' drawings were. The ability to add or change colours also kept the children very interested. After their drawings were complete, a hangman type game was played to help the children learn the scientific names in order to be able to label parts of the roach

We also gave each child their own research journal, which we told them was what scientists at the Zoological Department used. These would belong to the students, would not be checked for spelling, and would be used to jot down observations questions, research notes, and experiment designs.

Right away, a flurry of writing took place.

## Students' Observations

Children have a remarkable ability at this age for making acute observations. While the students were drawing, they talked excitedly about their observations: 'They've got little white suction cups on the bottom of their feet!', 'The antennae has about 20 sections in it!', 'They can sort of stretch, like an accordion', 'Its body looks all soft and white underneath, but it's got a hard shell on top.' Terms like 'exoskeleton' were introduced [ . . . ] by the teacher as the need arose. The scientific name for these roaches, *Gromphadorhina Portentosa*, was introduced at this point and a chant was created which included some roach facts:

Gromphadorhina Portentosa
Is a giant hissing roach
Gromphadorhina Portentosa
Slow and steady in its approach.

Gromphadorhina Portentosa
Something you will want to hold
Gromphadorhina Portentosa
Likes the warm and not the cold.

Gromphadorhina Portentosa
Prehistoric to modern time
Gromphadorhina Portentosa
With their sticky feet they climb.

Gromphadorhina Portentosa
You will see them in grade four
Gromphadorhina Portentosa
From the Madagascan shore.

These types of activities seemed to make the scientific language come easily to the students, and eventually, they constructed their own chants and songs.

## Question Generation and Research Groups

The group met for a **cross talk** session to discuss their observations, and this sparked further discussions and questions from other members of the class: 'I wonder what the antennae are used for?', 'If they've got suction cups, I wonder if they can walk on the ceiling?', 'What are those two pointy things at the back of the roach?' (cerci). Already, some students were offering theories. It seemed as though question asking within CSILE was the natural next step to support this scientific thinking. During the next days, students entered one or two pressing questions into the database. Questions ranged from, 'What kind of food do they prefer?' to 'What did cockroaches evolve from?' And because these questions were stored in the database, each child's question could be 'heard' and resources could be gathered to support a child's pursuit of knowledge in a particular interest area. The students also found it very exciting to be adding notes to build up the database. In the course of a week 100 new notes had been entered!

After the students entered their questions on the database, we could see that the questions were falling into specific categories. Here were the research groups, formed like they would in a scientific community – through the interest of the researchers. Each year, the categories [ . . . ] change[d]. For example, in 1996/97, the research groups were: external anatomy, internal anatomy, behaviour, reproduction, ecology and evolution. In 1997/98, the students were interested in: perception, learning, communication, evolution and anatomy.

## Research

Often, a benchmark lesson would be presented to the whole group. This might include an experiment that either responded to some of the questions on the database, or that had crowd appeal (such as the experiment which showed the male cockroach's aggressive behaviour). Students would then write on computer or in their lab books the things that surprised them or that they were puzzled about.

At this point, the classroom set up was such that students rotated in small groups during which time they had an opportunity to work on CSILE, conduct library/Internet research, conference with the teacher and so on.

Because there are few texts written about cockroaches for young students, we used primary sources written by and for zoologists. We introduced reciprocal teaching strategies (Brown & Campione) to the children at this time so that children could help each other understand these difficult texts. Again, the need drove the introduction of the activity. We did not pre-train children on RT before exposing them to texts.

After each research session, we would meet as a whole group to discuss what had been learned that day, or what surprises we found in the research materials. These cross-talk sessions acknowledged the importance and excitement of learning, and let the whole class feel as though they were valued members of a team working toward gaining knowledge and understanding about these insects.

## Language Arts

Sometimes we would work as a class to change the words of a song so that it became a song about cockroaches. The whole class would make up words for the chorus, then the research groups would spend 10 minutes coming up with new verses that reflected their new learning about the cockroaches:

*CUCARACHA COCKROACH* (by the Great Grade 4's at ICS)

I'm Cucaracha Cockroach from the Madagascan shores
I have an exoskeleton that protects me when it pours.
I was born in the lab of U of T
My brother and my sister nymphs were there with me.

We've been here for over 300 million years
We've hissed our way through all sorts of fears.
My hiss is horrible, but I'm not bad.
But when you touch my cerci I get really mad

I arch my back and ram, ram, ram.
I use my thorax to flip enemies on their backs.
Because I'm fighting for my territory
Is it instinct or hereditary?

I breathe through my trachea
My stomach's called a crop
My brain is called ganglion
And I've got a lot!
My fat body stores carbo's and stuff
Cut off my head and I'll still live because I'm tough!

When I feel air breathing down on my cerci
Then I know someone's after me!
So I head for my nearest log-house tree
Where me and my buddies are happy and free.

I'll eat everything that I can find.
My antennae will search until they die.
I'll go in your house and steal some food
To bring back to my little nymph dudes.

When we're in the wild, we eat rotten logs.
But when we're in the lab, we eat the food of dogs.
Our antennae sense lots of food
When we don't get food for a month we get in a bad mood.

This was another way that students could show their new learning and keep each group informed of other group's progress.

## Designing Experiments

One of the things that really sparked the design of experiments was our weekly visits from the grade one class, our Special Friends. When they came to visit the roaches, groups of children teamed up to build structures for the roaches to live and/or play in.

Soon they were creating mazes and one of the first experiments was a food preference test where the Ecology group set up a maze with three exits, each exit holding a different type of food. Another experiment was the one described below:

1 MT: Experiment . . .
1. make a long maze with walls
2. make a path of oranges through the maze.
3. put a roach at the start of the maze.
4. observe
5. after do the same experiment but without the oranges.
6. observe.

2 C: very interesting. I should try it (mg)

3 INTU: Do you think that the cockroach will learn the path through the maze after one try or will it take him several tries? (ML)

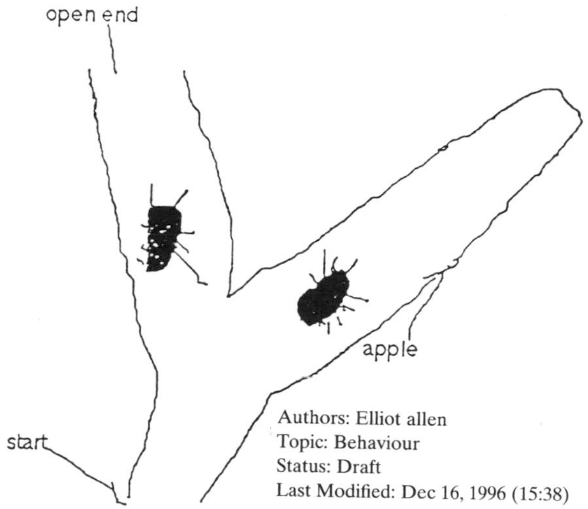

open end

start

apple

Authors: Elliot allen
Topic: Behaviour
Status: Draft
Last Modified: Dec 16, 1996 (15:38)

4 MT: Today Elliott Iona Amy and our little special friends were doing an experiment.
What we did is we made a path that went two different ways.
At one end there was food and at the other end there was no food at all.
The first time we only put one cockroach into the maze and they went to the end with no food.
We did that a few times.
Then we tried to put in two roaches.
What happened was the cockroach who had been in the maze before went the same way.
But the other cockroach went for the food.
So, the cockroach who went for the EXIT went 'hay' where are you going, so he followed the other cockroach to the food. If you want to see a diagram of this experiment called the 'Y maze exp't' then go to it under the behaviour notes. (ik)

5 WWHL: today (thursday, dec. 12) me (Amy) Iona and Elliott

Figure 10.1 *Elliott's y maze experiment*

It was important for the students to have building materials on hand, because through their play with these materials, they began to form design ideas for future experiments.

On the computer, students were planning or describing their experiments, building on each other's notes with new information or more questions, and the knowledge base was rapidly growing. Now we introduced the *jigsaw* approach to knowledge sharing [ . . . ], where one member of each research group formed a new group with individuals from each of the other research areas so that everyone was able to get a view of the 'bigger picture'. If any questions arose from this session, students did further research and if anything couldn't be answered, they now were able to write to an expert at the lab. Rather than just write a question, we had the students describe what their question had grown from and then the students wrote down their prediction or theory about an answer. In very many cases, the students' theories turned out to be correct.

## Lab Visit

Next we actually visited the lab where we watched a dissection and looked at the wide variety of roaches that are studied there. There was a persistence with which the students questioned the experts. They weren't satisfied with superficial answers. They didn't seem to want just the 'show and tell' approach, they wanted more of a 'let's discuss our findings and pursue our interests together' approach.

Each student had become somewhat of an expert in a specific area because enough time was given to think about that area of study and to experiment and develop her/his thinking and learning in that area. Now students talked to the scientists from a point of knowing and sharing information rather than merely being the recipients of someone else's knowledge.

## Sharing Knowledge: the Cockroach Documentary

A primary feature of most SFT implementations is the consequential task. The consequential task as originally defined by Bereiter and Scardamalia was meant to convey the idea that children's knowledge building should be of some consequence not only for the individual but for the community. As used in SFT, the term has acquired the meaning of creating a public display of knowledge – a research report, a play, etc. Often the nature of the consequential task is specified before children begin their investigation. The grade four children themselves came up with the idea of sharing their knowledge with a wider audience. The idea of doing a cockroach documentary came up because the students kept saying things like, 'We know a lot about cockroaches. How can we let other people know how much we know?' The urgency with which they asked made its importance realized.

How does a scientist like David Suzuki share his knowledge with the world? And the idea of the cockroach documentary was born. There was great excitement among the students about this idea, as each research group planned how they would present their work. The reproduction group decided they would ask the lab for a female roach and film an experiment 'live'. The internal anatomy group wanted to use the film of the cockroach dissection then add plasticine models for further descriptions. They wanted it to be exciting, 'like City TV'. The Ecology group would set up their food experiments to film them. The evolution group decided to write a script, dress up like scientists and have a combination of fact and humour. Motivation was high, and all they needed from us was help editing their scripts and showing them how to use the camera. Most of what they needed to write their scripts was easily accessible from our CSILE database. The documentary brought a nice closure to this unit of study.

## Discussion

### *Evolution of Ideas*

The following case studies of research groups show the progression of students' learning from their initial observations of the cockroaches to their final experimental designs.

### *Case 1: Can Cockroaches Learn? The Learning Group 1997/98*

This question was developed after the initial observations by a number of students:

Excerpt from student's lab book – see Figure 10.2.

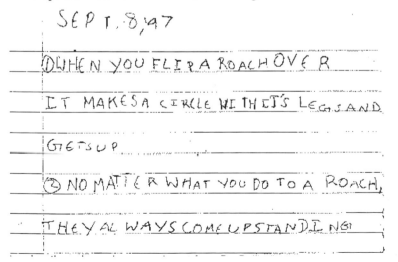

Figure 10.2 *Excerpt from student's lab book*

The teacher then showed an experiment from Dr. Bell's laboratory using stopwatches to see how quickly roaches were able to right themselves. Students tested each roach and recorded times.

About a week later, the same student writes in Knowledge Forum that he's noticed that the more the roaches are handled, the less quickly they right themselves. His theory is that they have learned to wait for students to flip them back over. He then poses the question: Can a roach learn? [Figure 10.3.]

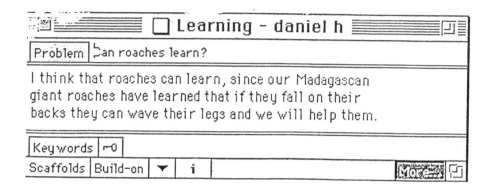

Figure 10.3  *Can roaches learn?*

He then teamed up with two other students who were also interested in the roaches' ability to learn. They did this teaming up initially through the use of Knowledge Forum. Then they met as a group and designed an experiment which involved building a structure with two chambers and two entrance ways [Figures 10.4–6].

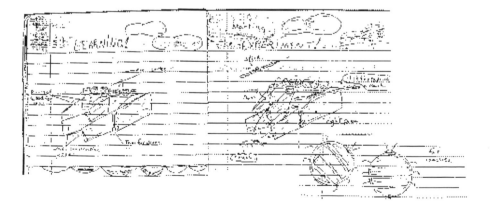

Figure 10.4  *Excerpt from student's lab book*

```
┌─────────────────────────────────────────────────────────────────┐
│ ▦      □ ARIS' learning of roaches - aris              ▤│
├─────────────────────────────────────────────────────────────────┤
│ │Problem│ Roaches learning of danger.                             │
├─────────────────────────────────────────────────────────────────┤
│ │My theory│ is that cockroaches can learn, but slowly. │New information│. I made an │
│ experiment with a roach, what I did was I made two rooms with wooden blocks and I taped two │
│ white peices of cardboard paper on the edges to make two doors. This experiment was │
│ supposed to prove that roaches can learn.It did prove that roaches can learn. │
│                                                                   │
│                                                                   │
├─────────────────────────────────────────────────────────────────┤
│ │Keywords│ ↻ │ learn                                              │
│ │Scaffolds│ Build-on │ ▼ │ i │                          │More...│ │
└─────────────────────────────────────────────────────────────────┘
```

Figure 10.5   *Aris's learning of roaches*

```
┌─────────────────────────────────────────────────────────────────┐
│ ▦      □ Roaches Can Learn - daniel b.               ▤│
├─────────────────────────────────────────────────────────────────┤
│ │Problem│ Roaches learning of danger.                             │
├─────────────────────────────────────────────────────────────────┤
│ │My theory│ is that you are right that roaches can learn. And I think you have a │
│ very good experiment. But how can your experiment proof tha roaches can │
│ learn?                                                            │
│                                                                   │
├─────────────────────────────────────────────────────────────────┤
│ │Keywords│ ↻ │ learn                                              │
│ │Scaffolds│ Build-on │ ▼ │ i │                         │More...│  │
└─────────────────────────────────────────────────────────────────┘
```

Figure 10.6   *Daniel's roaches can learn*

When the experiment began, one of the students wasn't comfortable with tapping the roach when it didn't enter the right door. Here is the conversation that followed:

> *Student #1:* OK, how about if we put something they like in door number one.
> *Student #2:* OK, let's try that. (*They ask around the classroom for pieces of grape or apple.*)
> *Student #1:* But how do we know the roach isn't just going in that door because he smells the apple?
> *Student #2:* Oh, yeah, you're right. Well, how about we just give it the apple if it goes in the right door?
> *Student #1:* OK, that might work.
>
> *They place roach outside the structure. Roach moves its antennae, but doesn't move.*
>
> *Student #1:* Why isn't it moving? Maybe we should tap it.
> *Student #2:* No, we can't touch it, remember?
>
> (*Roach makes move toward Door #1*)

*Student #2*: It's moving, it's moving! Oh no, it's going into door #2.
*Student #1*: Oh, well, let's just give it the apple if it goes in any door.
*Student #2*: Yeah, and then we can see if it goes back to that same door.
*Student #1*: OK.

*Roach goes in door #2. Students give it apple, then repeat experiment with same roach which goes back in door #2.*

*Students test three more roaches and conclude that roaches can learn.*

The following [Figure 10.7] is a copy of the Learning Group's script for the cockroach documentary, taken from one of the student's lab journals.

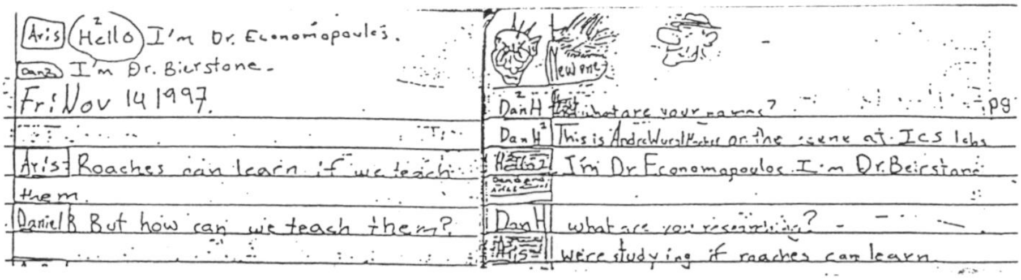

Figure 10.7    *Excerpt from student's lab book*

*Student 1*: We've made a structure with 2 rooms and 2 doors.
*Student 2*: We are trying to train the roach to go into door #1.
*Student 1*: Yes, you see, we give a reward to the roach if he goes into door #1. Then we test him again later to see if he remembers the reward and chooses door #1 again. Overtime, the roaches can learn to go into the right door.
*Student 3*: What is your opinion on whether roaches can learn?
*Students 1 & 2*: Yes, they can learn!

## Case 2: The Evolution Group asks, How did the Madagascan Roaches survive the Ice Age?

One student read somewhere that roaches survived the Ice Age. This made her curious. She writes [Figure 10.8].

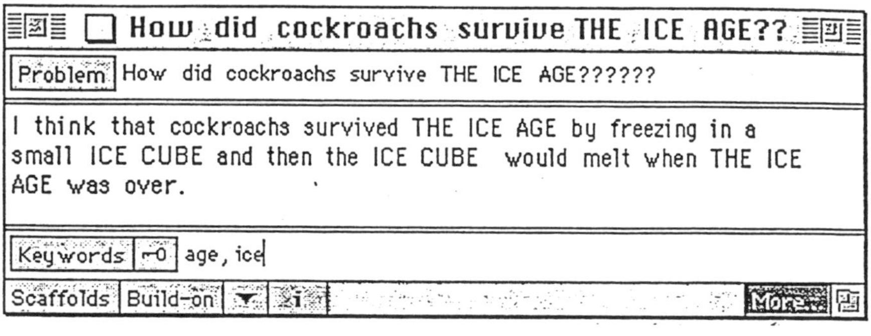

Figure 10.8    *How did cockroaches survive the Ice Age*

Next, she teams up with other interested students and plans an experiment to find out how roaches survived the Ice Age [Figure 10.9].

Friday Oct. 24 1997

Cockroach's likes the warm. Cockroach's can go in the cold but would rather go in the warm. So how I conducted this experiment is me Maddy, Cynthia and Mishki put one of the roach's on a ice pack it seemed that the roach was trying to get off. So we did it again it still tried to get off. Then we put the roach on a warm not hot but warm and it totally stood on it. So we think it likes the warm and not the cold.

Figure 10.9   *Excerpt from student's lab book*

She concludes, 'Cockroaches don't like hot areas, they like room temperature.'

Later, she and her group did some research on the Ice Age, then we invited a graduate student in to do a benchmark lesson on the Ice Age [Figures 10.10–15].

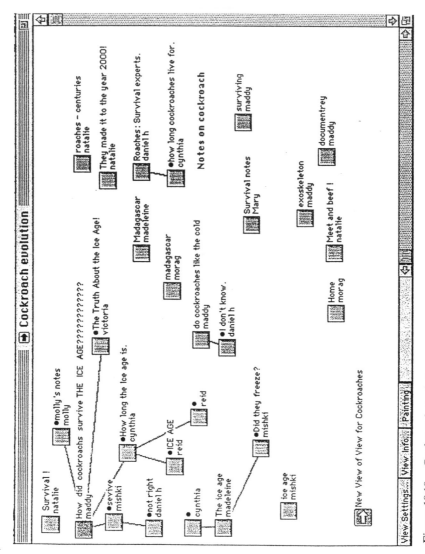

Figure 10.10 Cockroach evolution

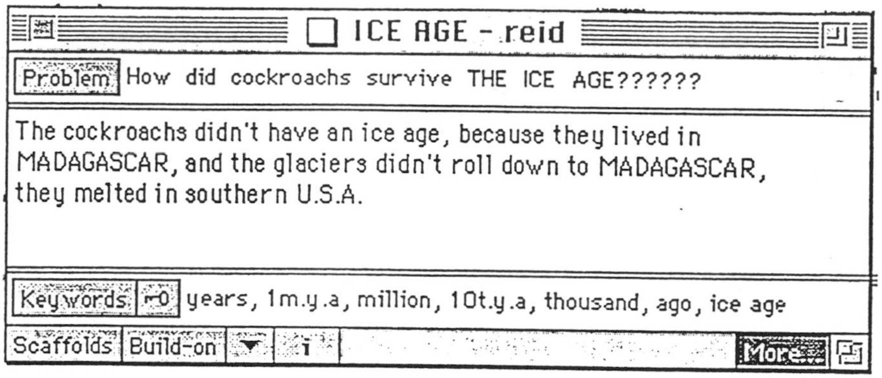
ICE AGE - reid
Problem
How did cockroachs survive THE ICE AGE??????
The cockroachs didn't have an ice age, because they lived in MADAGASCAR, and the glaciers didn't roll down to MADAGASCAR, they melted in southern U.S.A.
Keywords
years, 1m.y.a, million, 10t.y.a, thousand, ago, ice age
Scaffolds
Build-on
i
More...

Figure 10.11 *Reid Ice Age*

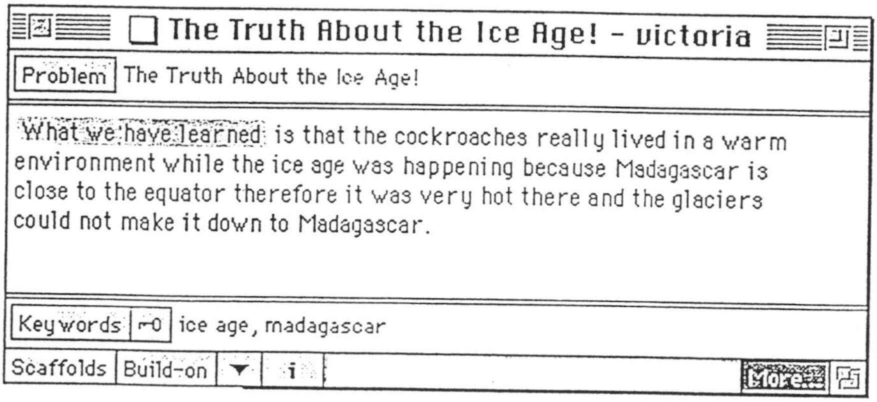
The Truth About the Ice Age! - victoria
Problem
The Truth About the Ice Age!
What we have learned is that the cockroaches really lived in a warm environment while the ice age was happening because Madagascar is close to the equator therefore it was very hot there and the glaciers could not make it down to Madagascar.
Keywords
ice age, madagascar
Scaffolds
Build-on
i
More...

Figure 10.12 *The truth about the Ice Age*

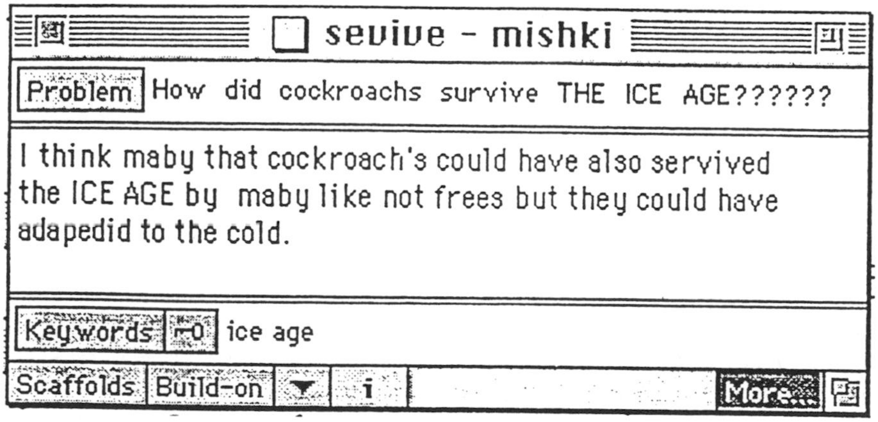
sevive - mishki
Problem
How did cockroachs survive THE ICE AGE??????
I think maby that cockroach's could have also servived the ICE AGE by maby like not frees but they could have adapedid to the cold.
Keywords
ice age
Scaffolds
Build-on
i
More...

Figure 10.13 *Survive – Mishki*

```
┌─────────────────────────────────────────────────────────────┐
│ ▤    □ not right – daniel h                              ▣   │
├─────────────────────────────────────────────────────────────┤
│ ┌────────┐                                                   │
│ │Problem │ How did cockroachs survive THE ICE AGE??????      │
│ └────────┘                                                   │
│                                                              │
│ ┌─────────────────────────────┐                              │
│  This theory cannot explain                                  │
│ Unfortunetly, roaches don't have much body fat, so your      │
│ theory isn't very                                            │
│ right                                                        │
│                                                              │
│                                                              │
│ ┌──────────┬───┐                                             │
│ │Keywords  │↵0 │                                             │
│ └──────────┴───┘                                             │
│ ┌─────────┬─────────┬───┬───┐                                │
│ │Scaffolds│Build-on │ ▼ │ i │              More  ⌐┘         │
│ └─────────┴─────────┴───┴───┘                                │
└─────────────────────────────────────────────────────────────┘
```

Figure 10.14  *Daniel – not right*

```
┌─────────────────────────────────────────────────────────────┐
│ ▤    □ How long the Ice age is. – cynthia               ▣   │
├─────────────────────────────────────────────────────────────┤
│ ┌────────┐                                                   │
│ │Problem │ How did cockroachs survive THE ICE AGE??????      │
│ └────────┘                                                   │
│ ┌─────────────────┐                                          │
│  New Information                                             │
│ There has been several Ice ages that humans know about but   │
│ the most                                                     │
│ resent Ice age was from 1m.y.a.(million years ago) to        │
│ 10t.y.a.(thousand years ago)                                 │
│ ┌──────────┬───┬──────────────────────────────────────────┐ │
│ │Keywords  │↵0 │ years, 1m.y.a, million, 10t.y.a, thousand,│ │
│ │          │   │ ago                                       │ │
│ └──────────┴───┴──────────────────────────────────────────┘ │
│ ┌─────────┬─────────┬───┬───┐                                │
│ │Scaffolds│Build-on │ ▼ │ i │              More  ⌐┘         │
│ └─────────┴─────────┴───┴───┘                                │
└─────────────────────────────────────────────────────────────┘
```

Figure 10.15  *Cynthia: how long the Ice Age is*

## Discussion

### *Differences between pre-SFT and SFT years*

During the pre-SFT year, there was a similar excitement with students about having the roaches in the classroom, but without the depth that we quickly began to see during the SFT years. In the pre-SFT year, the teacher recorded students' observations, questions and theories on large chart paper. The use of a technology such as CSILE/Knowledge Forum was like having someone in the class who heard all the interesting things kids were saying and organized them nicely for the teacher to view. It was then possible to see the direction students were heading, what areas of research they needed and what further resources were necessary for those students to support their studies.

Another difference was that a researcher with extensive experience in SFT implementation was in the classroom regularly which provided in-service training and learning for the classroom teacher. In pre-SFT year, the teacher designed all the experiments (from reading university level roach study texts), made nifty worksheets with roaches on them, experiment forms with charts that students could fill in and remembers being quite surprised at how the students weren't as excited as she was to fill these forms out. They enjoyed watching the experiments and calling out what was happening, but they didn't want to have to write about what happened during the experiment. Reflecting on that experience: 'Now I realize that I had unwittingly been trying to train my students into becoming mere observers. Maybe that was why they resisted. At the end of that year, the students' science binders were at varying degrees of disarray. Some were missing many of the roach pages, others were out of order and mixed in with our snow study and energy study pages. There was no evidence of the intentional learning that was so evident in the SFT years. With the use of CSILE/Knowledge Forum, ideas are saved and can be built upon, revised and have the potential of evolving into something quite complex.'

## Students' Writing

Perhaps the most visible difference is in the amount of writing that occurred with students during the SFT years. In a comparison of the actual number of words written per child between the years, the results are shocking. During the pre-SFT study of roaches, the actual number of words written by grade four students (gathered from their science binders) ranged from the lowest number of written words which was 30 to the highest which was 200. During the SFT years, in the students' lab books alone, the lowest number of words written was 70 and the highest 400. Add to this the amount of words written by the students in the CSILE database and the words comprising their documentary scripts and the results are at least 5 times higher.

## Summary

What factors contributed to the students' success in learning?

1) Having a researcher in the classroom – Mary has worked extensively with children in SFT settings. She knew the deep principles of the domain, saw the 'big picture' and recognized a child's thinking in that direction and could ask the right questions to keep the thinking moving.

Also, the researcher provided in-service training to the teacher (learning by doing). How can it be made possible to give more teachers the benefit of a researcher in the classroom?

2) The use of technology (CSILE and Knowledge Forum) provided support for students' thinking and learning as well as motivating the students to write. This public forum along with students' personal science lab books made a huge difference in the amount of writing that occurred compared to the year where the students had only a science binder to store their work. For one thing, students could go back into the database time and time again to read over their peer's work, revise their own work and make contributions that would move learning forward. This could not be achieved when students have only their own science binders tucked away in their desks.

3) Allowing students to become 'experts' in their interest areas provided them with the time to gain understanding of the subject area.

4) Teacher's in-service training allows for gaining experience in a SFT approach to the classroom: learning how to trust the child's ability to come up with important questions, to develop theories and to design experiments to test these theories.

5) Introducing activities opportunistically seemed a more meaningful and authentic way to use these learning strategies.

## Problems Encountered

1) Time needed to go through database/how to ensure each child is contributing.

2) How to deal with children unwilling/unable to express ideas on computer (or anywhere) – one solution we found useful for certain children was to actually type for them, let them tell us their ideas. For many of these students it was the fear of not spelling correctly. After entering three or four notes for these children, they were capable and willing to go on independently from then.

3) How to help certain children move from direct copying, to putting into own words, to building on to a theory or questioning an existing theory.

4) What to do about the child who gets a 'free ride' in group setting – hangs out with group, but doesn't make many contributions. Balance between support of students' ideas and providing enough structure for those who need it to keep their thinking and learning progressing.

## Conclusion

It has been interesting to see that the progression of students' thinking led many of them along paths that were similar to scientists working in the same areas of study. For example, many groups came up with experiments that were designed by Dr. Bell's laboratory in his roach study. Another example is the learning group designing their Skinner-like box.

The nature of a child's curiosity seems to give the child motivation, confidence and ability to solve difficult problems and questions that have occurred *in her/his own mind*. This ability to persist and pursue, to build and rebuild, to push for understanding, provides evidence of scientific thinking that seems to draw on an innate, exploratory and inquisitive nature. A question that requires further exploration: Is there a set sequence of developmental steps through which students progress to reach deep understanding?

In Canada, a new science curriculum has been launched which has as its vision the development of scientific literacy for all Canadian students.

> To achieve the vision of scientific literacy, students must increasingly become engaged in the planning, development, and evaluation of their own learning activities. In the process, they should have the opportunity to work collaboratively with other students, to initiate investigations, to communicate their findings, and to complete projects that demonstrate their learning. (p. 8)

It seems that the use of a technology such as Knowledge Forum in a SFT type classroom can provide the necessary framework to make this vision a reality.

# References

Brown, A. L. & Campione, J. C. (1994). Guided discovery in a community of learners. In K. McGilly (Ed.), *Classroom lessons: Integrating cognitive theory and classroom practice* (pp. 229–272). Cambridge, MA: MIT Press/Bradford Books.

Brown, A. L. & Palinscar, A. S. (1989). Guided, cooperative learning and individual knowledge acquisition. In L. B. Resnick (Ed.), *Knowing, learning and instruction: Essays in honor of Robert Glaser* (pp. 393–451). Hillsdale, NJ: Erlbaum.

Carey, S. (1985). *Conceptual change in childhood*. Cambridge, MA: The MIT Press.

Dauite C. & Dalton, B. (1993). Collaboration between children learning to write: Can novices be masters? *Cognition and instruction, 10(4), 281–333.*

Jones, I. & Pellegrini, A. D. (1996). The effects of social relationships, writing, media, and microgenetic development on first-grade students' written narratives. *American Educational Research Journal, 33(3), 691–718.*

Lamon M. (1996). Schools for thought: Schooling and cognitive development. In M. Scardamalia & C. Bereiter (Chairs) Operational Thought and the Democratization of Knowledge. Symposium presented at *The Growing Mind Conference*, Geneva, Switzerland, September.

Lamon, M., Lee, E. & Scardamalia, M. (1993). Cognitive Technologies and Peer Collaboration: The Growth of Reflection. Unpublished manuscript.

Lamon, M., Secules, T., Petrosino, A., Hackett, R., Bransford, J. D. & Goldman, S. (1996). Schools for thought: Overview of the project and lessons learned from one site. In L. Schauble & R. Glaser (Eds.), *Innovations in learning*. Hillsdale, NJ: Erlbaum.

Lamon, M. & Ward, C. (1996). Teacher beliefs and practice in establishing learning communities. In M. Lamon (Chair) *Developing Learning Communities: Implementer Perspectives on Schools for Thought* Symposium presented at the American Educational Research Association, New York, April.

Scardamalia, M., Bereiter, C., McLean, R. S., Swallow, J. & Woodruff, E. (1989). Computer supported intentional learning environments. *Journal of Educational Computing Research, 5, 51–68.*

# 11

# The Equation, the Whole Equation and Nothing but the Equation! One Approach to the Teaching of Linear Equations

## Susan E. B. Pirie and Lyndon Martin

[This chapter presents some of the results of a case study which looked at the mathematics classroom of one particular teacher, Alwyn. The authors' interest is those lessons which dealt specifically with the teaching of linear equations in which the teaching approach encouraged successful growth of understanding.]

## The Equation as Temporal Sequence of Actions or Static Entity

Learning related to linear equations is probably the first time that the images that students have built, from their arithmetic experiences, for the meaning of the equals sign, are challenged. Until this point, the fundamental image of '=' as 'indicating the result of an operation' has been sufficient to deal with all the symbolic expressions they have encountered (Matz, 1982; Mevarech and Yitschak, 1983; Booth, 1984). Failure to acknowledge this potential problem, and deal with it at this point, can lead to pupils *ostensibly* demonstrating an ability to solve linear equations, but masking a deeper lack of understanding. This *apparent* comprehension arises because equations presented in the familiar form of $2x - 3 = 5$ can be interpreted as 'twice something take away three makes five' – a coherent verbalisation that is compatible with a variety of solution methods. The introduction of equations of the form $5 = 2x - 3$, however, leads to a verbalisation of 'five makes two times something take away three', which is seen to be as meaningless as the arithmetic statement 'five makes eight take away three' (Wolters, 1991). 'Five' is the result of an action, not the instigator. Since most school text books introduce algebra by linking it to arithmetic (Herscovics and Kieran, 1980) it is not unnatural that pupils should seek to transfer the

---

This chapter has been edited

associated linguistic understanding also. Equations are read from left to right in real time. 'Twice something take away three gives five' is understood as: 'I have something (the first state); after that (in actual time) three is taken from me; after that (again in time) I realise I have five left (a second state occurring after the first.' This situation has a logical, temporal order and the action can be envisaged as performed and the possibility of a solution is evident. In the second situation, 'five makes eight take away three', the verbalisations lack meaning because the temporal notion of action (take away) *leading to* result (makes five) is violated. Verbally, the temporal sequence has the result preceding the action. The crux of this problem lies in this conception of an equation as a temporal event, corresponding to a verbal left–right reading, rather than a static state. We will return to this later in this [chapter], but offer here a personal interpretation of a striking analogy from the writings of Oliver Sacks (1995). Virgil, a fifty-year old man, had his sight restored after many years of blindness. He owned a cat and a dog, both of which were coloured black and white and which, to his embarrassment and their annoyance, he had difficulty in distinguishing until he could touch them too. He would examine the cat carefully, 'looking at its head, its ears, its paws, its tail, and touching each part gently as he did so' (p. 139). We suggest that he was used in the past to identify objects, through touch, *in real time*. To distinguish a cat he would have had to feel *first* the ears, *then* the paws, *then* the tail, etc. With sight, however, we see the cat as a whole, at one instant, not as an accumulation of details built over time into a recognisable object. It is just this need to see an equation as a whole, in one instant, rather than as an accumulation of items and operations processed over time, that is crucial for the complete understanding of linear equations.

## The Mythical 'Didactic Cut'?

According to Lins (1992), 'the arithmetical operations are a fundamental model for our understanding of algebraic operations; the elements in non-numerical algebras are in fact treated as if they were numbers of a different kind'. Filloy and Rojano (1984), however, suggest that there exists a clear delineation between arithmetic and algebra at the point when students encounter linear equations with the unknown quantity on both sides of the equals sign and they term this the 'didactic cut'. Although agreeing that such a demarcation exists, Herscovics and Linchevski (1991) dispute its precise location in the student's cognitive development. Linear equations, in their variety of forms ranging from $ax = b$ to $ax + b = cx + d$, nonetheless seem to be located somewhere around this ill-defined boundary between arithmetic and algebra. We would contend that this 'cut', this implied specific cognitive difficulty, is, in reality a notion imposed by the observer, with hind sight, to explain an artefact of particular methods of teaching. We believe it to be a perceived, rather than actual, phenomenon. It results from the method of approaching the solution of equations through appeal to arithmetic parallel thinking, coupled with the introduction of expressions of supposedly increasing difficulty. Rather than an inherent difficulty in the solution of linear equations, the cognitive obstacle is created by the very method which purports to provide a logical introduction to equation solution. We take this argument further, later in this [chapter], when we show that this supposed stumbling block does not exist for the pupils – and it must be constantly remembered that they have been judged mathematically less able pupils – in Alwyn's class. One might at this point wish to question why linear equations are taught at all to lower ability pupils, but given that their study is written into the curriculum, we will not pursue this question here.

## Standard Teaching Approaches

In brief, general terms there are two different approaches to the teaching of the solution of linear equations that predominate across classrooms. One method is to repeatedly change the equation, by 'doing the same to both sides' until one has an equation that directly gives the answer. Understanding is assumed to come through the notion of 'undoing' a series of operations to get back to the original value. In other words, $ax + b = cx + d$ becomes, $ax + b - b = cx + d - b$, becomes $ax = cx + d - b$, becomes $ax - cx = cx - cx + d - b$, becomes $x(a - c) \div (a - c) = (d - b) \div (a - c)$, becomes $x = (d - b) \div (a - c)$. The alternative approach is that of 'change sides, change signs', based on the concept of inverse operations. Here, understanding is built on the assumption that the integrity of the original equation is preserved. In other words, $ax + b = cx + d$ becomes $ax = cx + d - b$ becomes $ax - cx = d - b$ becomes $x \times (a - c) = d - b$ becomes $x = (d - c) \div (a - c)$.

In reality, of course, whichever approach is taken, the students do not start with the most difficult generalised form, they progress from simple equations of the form $x + b = d$ to $ax = d$ to $ax + b = d$ to $x - b = d$ to $ax - b = d$ before finally encountering $ax + b = cx + d$.

The commonality between these methods is that they both involve transforming the original equation, and lead to the pupils 'solving' an equation that is not the original given one, but is some altered, in some sense simplified, equation. One consequence of this is that, if pupils have really been convinced by the notion that their manipulations leave the equations 'the same', many either see no reason to check their solution since it came directly from an equation that is the 'same' as the original, or see no problem, when told to check their answers, with simply substituting their calculated value in the line above, rather than going back to the early, harder version of the equation. The approach that we shall describe, from Alwyn's classroom, relies upon the solving of an equation *in the form in which it is given*, with none of these attendant checking problems.

# The Equation as 'Balance'

Given the difficulty of the topic, what are some of the ways in which teachers introduce the solution of linear equations? Standard methods for dealing with the complexity of any mathematical concept are *either*

to relate it to a real life situation – most often by starting with a life situation and drawing the mathematics out of it, *or*

to introduce materials to model the problem – in other words to start with the mathematics and illustrate it in some way through objects or pictures, *or*

to teach alogorithms by which mathematically formulated problems may be solved – that is to say, staying with the mathematical notions as such and finding generalisable methods of solution.

The most common method of introduction for linear equations is an example of the first alternative, that of 'the equation as a balance'. Typically, pictures of a weighing machine with two balancing scale pans are presented with objects and weights in the scale pans. The problem is to find the weight of a single object. Initially students solve the early simple problems intuitively; they can 'see' the answers. More difficult examples are offered with objects and weights mixed together in the scale pans and the suggestion is made that they take things off (pseudo-physically) each scale pan until they have an answer. An immediate difficulty arises: unless the students are to keep drawing pictures of scale pans, objects and weights, they must invent, or be taught, a symbolic representation of the problem. The 'equals sign' (=) is taken to represent the pivot of the balance and the solution of the problem is achieved by 'taking the same things away from both sides, to preserve the balance'. The clear link is being made between physical removal and subtraction. This does, however, add to the complexity of coming to understand the concept of linear equations, the need for the ability to symbolise from a verbal problem. A similar burden arises from the use of materials in the second method given above.

There is, in fact, a major problem attached to the whole idea of 'real life' associations in mathematics. The mathematics is presented as a way of representing a real life situation with the intention of giving meaning for the mathematics to the students. The expectation is that the call to existing understanding outside the classroom will ground the new mathematics in 'reality'. We use inverted commas here because this begs two questions: Whose reality? and How real is the reality? In answer to the first question, we would have to say that it is usually an adult's world that is taken as the grounding image, for example bank balances and overdrafts for negative numbers, rates of interest and buying on credit for percentages. The alternative to this tends to be to insult the intelligence of secondary pupils with cute little animals and cartoon figures, more appropriate to the development of primary children. The intention, in either case, is for the situation to present the mathematics and for common sense to be brought into play to inform the mathematical processes. This approach has developed as a direct challenge to the traditional idea of simply developing (possibly meaningless) algorithms. The attendant difficulty, however, as we shall illustrate, is that not too much common sense should be applied!

Returning to the specific topic of linear equations we would ask: How strongly do the pupils actually have the image of such a balance? How 'real' is this image? What images does the language call to mind? The vocabulary of 'balancing' is more likely to conjure up images of attempting to stand on one leg, and the physical principle of centre of gravity used here depends on moments of inertia and not directly on the idea of equal weight on either side. For adults the most common use of the word is probably in the context of the money available for spending, namely their bank 'balance'. While accountants may think in terms of two columns of figures adding up to the same thing, most adults are looking for a single, positive number, the result of total expenditure subtracted from total income, as the 'balance'. Indeed they are probably hoping that the two totals will *not* be the same, resulting in the figure zero! In monetary terms it is quite possible to have a 'negative balance', a phrase with no meaning in terms of weight. We would further suggest that the type of balance scales used here are in fact not understood by today's children. Weighing is simply not done in this way any more. Most students have never seen such an apparatus and do not understand the physical activity of weighing in this way. For them, in reality weighing is done on single scale pans with weight given by digital or pointer-indicated numerical read-outs. Pirie (forthcoming) discusses a particular pupil, who, having no understanding of the notion of two-scale-pan balances actually re-draws the diagrams to show a scale with a moving pointer. The upshot of this situation is that it is likely that the intuition expected of the pupils may not readily come to hand, even though the concept has been 'made easier' by replacing the notion of 'unknowns' with 'real things' such as rabbits, and the numbers have been assigned 'meaning' as actual weights.

[. . .]

## Alwyn's Approach: Making the Necessary Primitive Knowing Overt

Let us now move on to the method of teaching linear equations used by Alwyn. In the lessons prior to starting linear equations the class had been working on arithmagons and in that context Alwyn had introduced the word 'fence' to describe the equals sign. He opened the lesson on the new topic by referring them back to this and saying:

> This idea of a fence is going to be important. The equals sign represents the splitting up of one side and another side.

It is important to note the distinction here between real-life modelling and the use of a realistic metaphor to aid image formation. He was setting the scene for the visualisation of an equation as a static whole, rather than an instruction to act.

> The equals sign is more than just a fence. It actually is a fence that says something like 'this side must have exactly the same number as this side'. Now you have been dealing with that. When you were checking your equations and statements [for arithmagons] you were doing that. You were saying like 'a add b must equal six. Four add two is six, yes that's correct'. Or you might have said 'five and three is eight, oh, that's not six so it can't be right.

The purpose of arithmagons as an introductory activity for equations was fivefold:

(i)    to introduce them to finding numbers that fit certain rules;
(ii)   to have them practise their general arithmetic skills as these were going to be vital in the equations approach he would adopt. Alwyn was very deliberate in his intention to pull to the forefront of the pupils' minds the Primitive Knowing that was going to be the basis for their learning. The need to do this is supported by Richens (1994), who indicates that it can be the very lack of facility with the general skills of addition and subtraction that can, in fact, mitigate against pupils grasping the concept of equations. This is a serious consideration if, as some of the literature indicates, algebra is built upon arithmetic;
(iii)  to put them in situations where they can 'see' that the numbers they want can be got by addition or subtraction of known numbers, even though they cannot 'see' the actual solution number;
(iv)   to introduce the use of a drawn square (subsequently called a 'box' by the pupils) simply as a place that needs a number writing into it;
(v)    to undertake activities which involved inserting numbers in expressions to check whether they had solved the arithmagons.

Having spent just a couple of minutes reminding the pupils of their previous activities, Alwyn put up the following on the chalk-board:

$$\Box + \Box + 18 = \Box + 53$$

He did not read it out. He simply presented them with a bald symbolic statement. It was not a symbolic *representation of anything*, and the boxes did not have 'values', they were just places for physically writing numbers. He did not intend to tie it to a pseudo-real scenario in any way. He presented the equation as quite simply a static entity. Even for these less able pupils, he was presenting mathematics as mathematics, not trying to disguise it. He made no pretence that at some future moment in their out-of-school lives they would need to do this kind of mathematics. This was mathematics that was *interesting for its own sake* and *they were all capable of doing it*.

The word 'fence' contains no implicit notions of motion or action. On the board was simply a mathematical expression. The boxes could contain any numbers, except that the fence represented a special relationship between the expressions on either side of it. The numbers that go in the boxes have to be such as to make the two sides of the fence the same. This approach to the symbol '=' representing but one of many possible relationships is suggested by Wolters (1991) as a strategy to use when first introducing the symbol at primary level. She suggests a teaching sequence that emphasises the distinction between relationships and mathematical operations and it is certainly this distinction that Alwyn had in mind. The unknown is not seen as 'the answer' – that is, a result of performing operations. The equality symbol is seen as simply that, a relationship-defining symbol, not an operation. Following his definition for the equals sign as 'fence', Alwyn then explicitly added a further restriction on the expression on the board: it has to be the same number in all of the boxes.

## 1. Guided Image Making

Two notions had governed his choice of what equation to offer as the introductory task. It had to have the unknown on both sides and the numbers had to be such that it was highly unlikely that anyone in the class could 'see' the answer. In this respect he was working totally counter to the traditional method of starting with easy numbers and forms, and was ignoring the possible problematic existence of the didactic cut. His rationale was that if they could not 'see' the answer, they would have to think about *how* to find it out, and thus to think about a strategy for solving any such equation.

Having put up the equation Alwyn asked for some member of the class to suggest a number. He made it clear that he did not expect the suggestion to be correct, but to:

> nudge or push us towards a solution. You might want to say, to get us warmed up, a value that does not work.

One pupil suggested '13'. Alwyn wrote the '13' into each of the boxes and asked:

> Is that a correct statement or not?

He asked the class to calculate each side and took numbers from the pupils.

> This side of the fence is 44. What's on that side of the fence? 66. OK so that isn't a correct answer. That's fine.

He asked for another offer and received '15'. This time the sides came to 48 and 68. Before asking them to suggest a further number to try, he made the statement:

> Maybe now, as good mathematicians, we'll be using the two answers we've got to maybe suggest roughly what the correct answer is. Were you too small on this side when we did it?

It is this early statement (less than eight minutes into the lesson) which distinguishes Alwyn's approach from random 'guess and test' and from simply seeing mathematics as solving number puzzles. From almost the beginning they were strategy hunting and deliberately using their existing mathematical knowledge. Alwyn gave them a minute to all try their own numbers. Pencils and a few calculators were out and every one of the pupils was engaged in working their way towards a number that worked. The important feature of this method that distinguishes it from the solution by balance method is they were finding a solution to the original problem, not a reduced version of it. The motivation of the class was palpable. At the end of the minute Alwyn said:

> Now whilst we're doing this, I don't mind taking time like this, but one of the reasons for doing this then is we're actually going to try and find a method by the end of this period to get to that answer a lot quicker than trial and error that we're doing now.

He then asked a particular pupil for his number – even if it did not work. The response was 25 and Alwyn repeated the procedure for checking its validity as a solution, getting the sides as 68 and 78.

> So that doesn't work. That's fine. Maybe that's still nudging us towards an answer. Are we getting closer? What does that tell you about the box number?

Even while he was talking the majority of the class returned to trying higher numbers, although he did not make that explicit connection for them. Within two minutes one pupil had the answer, 35 and the class checked it gave 88 on each side of the equation.

> That took a while. I'm going to give you lots of those to do. It could take us two weeks to do 30 like that – that one has taken us about 15 minutes [*since the beginning of the lesson*] – there's nothing wrong with that. But I do want you as mathematicians to try maybe to come up with a method which gets us there a lot quicker.

He handed out question sheets which were quite simply a list of 30 similarly presented equations.

> As you go through the questions I've given you, is there a short cut? Is there a quick way? Is there a mathematical way? Can we use the work we've done over the last two or three lessons to help us? Start off maybe by doing it the way we've done and then, as you go through, you get a bit fed up with that slower method, then go for maybe a quicker method.

They had been given a hint of where they were going but an emphasis that there was no hurry. They knew they were expected to be on the lookout for patterns emerging as they solved successive equations.

## Image Having and Property Noticing

The class now had a new form of challenge that all of them could, *and did*, rise to. The obvious problem with this method of solution, if pupils are left at this point, is its inefficiency in terms of time to achieve that solution (Kieran, 1991). Alwyn was confident, however, that they would not remain at the level of guess and test for very long, but he knew that it was important for these students to understand what they were doing and where any future strategies came from and why they worked.

Very rapidly, two students wanted to offer what they suggested were short cuts. They felt that they had some image of how to solve linear equations and each of them had noticed a 'short cut', a property which they predicted (not necessarily correctly) would hold across the solution of other equations.

| | |
|---|---|
| Paul: | I think I've thought of a method. |
| Alwyn: | Do you want to tell us about that then? |
| P: | You . . . say it was this one you add fifty three to thirty five and that's eighty eight then you half it to forty four and then take away eighteen. |
| A: | I think because the thirty five is missing at that first stage you can't use the thirty five to add up because it's not there. All right Paul? (*pause till Paul nods*) Marie? |
| Marie: | If you add . . . on erm . . . this side (*points to left hand side of equation on the board*) it says thirty five add thirty five add eighteen. If you must add the last two numbers, thirty five and eighteen, it should make fifty three and then the last . . . if you erm, so if you've got eighteen you add something, you try and add something with it to make the last number (*points at end of right hand side of equation*) . . . it's confusing but . . . |
| A: | No its not confusing, its good. |

Notice that Marie was suggesting an efficient way to guess the correct number to go in the box. She was not suggesting that the original equation be altered in any way, she was not 'taking things away', nor was she trying to solve an altered version of the original symbolic expression. Although the rest of the class were called to listen to these suggestions, no attempt was made to get them to use the idea. It was too soon for many of them to have the motivation or understanding to take on board short cuts. One needs to have an image before one can begin to understand its generalisable qualities. Marie's suggestion was just left hanging, as a suggestion, and the class carried on working and talking. It was clear from eavesdropping, however, that several of the pupils did, in fact, try to relate their working to what became known as 'Marie's method'.

| | |
|---|---|
| Joan: | (*having done the first two questions of the sheet by adding on to the left hand number to get the right hand number, as suggested by 'Marie's method' and then checking by substitution in the given equation*) Sir we know how to do it now. It worked, Marie's thing, Marie's . . . |
| Marie: | (*Shyly*) . . . method |
| J: | Method, that's the one. |

Other methods were publicly offered throughout the time the pupils worked on the exercise sheet, as different pupils tried to articulate their search for efficient strategies:

| | |
|---|---|
| Liam: | Sir I've found a rule. You just take that one (*points to left hand number*) away from that one (*points to right hand number*). |

Simon:   Erm, you got two boxes then you got erm the unbox number and at the
         other end you also got another unbox number so what you do is add
         those two together and the number, if that gives you twenty eight then
         that's the number you put in the box.

Joan:    (*Working with* □ + □ + □ + □ + □ − 10 = □ + □ + □ + 4) These three
         boxes (*on the right hand side*), cover up these three boxes (*three of the
         five on the left hand side*) like that (*putting her fingers over the two sets
         of three drawn boxes*) and then that will leave you two (*boxes*). So it'll
         be two boxes take away ten and four, and then it'll be two boxes equals
         fourteen. (*This covering up action was used by several of the pupils*).

Kevin:   Well say when you've got the pluses you take the umm . . . it gives you
         the number on the sheet . . . erm on [*question*] A(i) it gives you fifteen
         and thirty three, take fifteen from thirty three . . . and that gives you
         eighteen, and then that's what the missing answers are. And that's the
         way for plus sign but when it's take away, when it's got take away in it
         you, you erm . . . add the two numbers together instead of taking them
         away

Gary:    It's the same as Kevin's but divide by 2.

Tom:     I've found an algebra rule . . . (*Pause*) *C* equals *B* minus *A* divided by
         open bracket *L* minus *R* close bracket. (*Pause*) Okay, *C* is the answer.
         Oh erm, . . . *C* is the answer, *A* is the first number, the first proper given
         number, *B* is the last given number, *L* is the left hand's number of
         boxes you've got to begin with and *R* is the right.

Alwyn:   Brilliant!

As the lessons progressed, Alwyn started to question why the strategies
worked and gently pushed the pupils into trying to explain their own
methods. It was clear that they had all understood the idea of the fence as a
separator between two equalities, and most could articulate why 'Marie's
method', in its various personalised guises, was a legitimate 'short cut'. By
the end of the second lesson, none of them was still solving the equations
by random trial and error and at the end of two weeks all the pupils were
confidently solving generalised equations of the form $ax + b = cx + d$ – not
totally without errors, of course, but many of these were caused by mis-
reading not lack of understanding. Sometimes they were using their own
rules, such as those of Tom and Kevin above, and sometimes folding back
to earlier methods if they needed to check their own thinking for a particular question.

## 2. Alwyn's Approach, Grounded in His Own Personal Philosophy of Teaching

The key elements of Alwyn's approach to the teaching of linear equations
can be summarised as follows:

(i)   He was teaching the mathematics as mathematics, unrelated to any
      'real life' situations.

(ii)  From the start he presented the class with an equation in almost the
      most complicated form possible, namely $ax + b = cx + d$, although

initially with $c = a - 1$ and the unknown represented by a place to write its value, namely a drawn box, rather than a letter.

(iii) The class worked together for a comparatively short time on the guess and test approach, but already with the understanding that they should be taking account of the erroneous solutions to guide their further guessing.

(iv) They were given a sheet of examples to work on and they had an obligation to spot patterns, to look for strategies that made the solution quicker. There was no suggestion that this would be *easier*. No reduction of the equation to a simpler form was called for.

(v) Throughout the subsequent lessons, as the pupils worked through the examples sheets, there was a firm understanding that they must *all* be able to talk about what they were doing and why. Alwyn frequently pulled the class together to share the strategies they were developing, continually getting them all to verbalise what they were doing.

One may be tempted, by the language used by pupils and teachers, to argue for a similarity between the 'boxes' in Alwyn's parlance and the 'tins' of the balance method (e.g., SMP). The connection, however, is merely a superficial, linguistic one. The mathematical notions in the two approaches are in fact different. For the pupils working with balances the 'tins' are actual objects with physical weight, with the attendant snags mentioned earlier. For Alwyn's pupils the boxes are merely place holders, somewhere to write the number when you have found it. For pupils working in other scenarios they have a weight or value, they are containers for a number of objects, not merely for a written number. Alwyn's boxes have no physical meaning other than the drawn square in the symbolic equation. They do *not* represent three dimensional cartons or 'boxes' in the common language sense.

[. . .]

## Accounting for the Method's Success

Judged against those difficulties enumerated earlier in this [chapter], which are frequently encountered in the learning of linear equations, Alwyn's method appears to have been a success. How can we account for this? What are the features that can be theoretically justified, enabling the success to be attributed to more than fluke or charisma?

Alwyn's intention was that all his pupils should build a sound and secure basic image for the solution of linear equations from which they could work with confidence. This in turn depended on a clear understanding of what an equation is. It might perhaps seem rash to risk all, on the creation of one image, in the hope that it works for everyone in the class, but the chosen image has roots deep in what it means to do mathematics. Mathematics for Alwyn is a way of thinking, a way of acting, that requires making errors, reflection on success as well as failure and an ability to look for and build